CW00470427

The Guards Brigade in the Crimea

The Guards Brigade in the Crimea

Michael Springman

Pen & Sword
MILITARY

First published in Great Britain in 2008 by
Pen & Sword Military
An imprint of
Pen & Sword Books Ltd
47 Church Street
Barnsley
South Yorkshire
S70 2AS

ISBN 978 1 84415 6788

A CIP catalogue record for this book is
available from the British Library

Typeset in 10pt Plantin by Mac Style, Beverley, East Yorkshire
Printed and bound in the UK by Biddles

Pen & Sword Books Ltd incorporates the Imprints of Pen & Sword
Aviation, Pen & Sword Maritime, Pen & Sword Military, Wharncliffe
Local History, Pen & Sword Select, Pen & Sword Military Classics, Leo
Cooper, Remember When, Seaforth Publishing and Frontline Publishing

For a complete list of Pen & Sword titles please contact
PEN & SWORD BOOKS LIMITED
47 Church Street, Barnsley, South Yorkshire, S70 2AS, England
E-mail: enquiries@pen-and-sword.co.uk
Website: www.pen-and-sword.co.uk

Contents

Maps

Preface and Acknowledgements

I am very grateful to Major J.W.S. Lawrie, the Regimental Adjutant Scots Guards, for permission to use the painting by Lady Butler, *Saving the Colours at the Alma*, on the cover of the book. I am indebted to Lieutenant Colonel Conway Seymour, the former Regimental Adjutant Grenadier Guards, who is now in charge of Regimental Archives, for his help, and to Major Edward Crofton, the Regimental Adjutant Coldstream Guards, for his assistance. Lance Sergeant Gorman, the Archivist of the Scots Guards, has been unstinting in his help, for which I am most grateful.

I have used extensively extracts from the letters of Captain Alfred Tipping, Grenadier Guards, and I am most grateful to Egerton Skipwith, his great-great-grandson, for his permission to do so. Similarly John Drummond has allowed me to quote from the letters of his forebear, Brevet Major Hugh Drummond, the Adjutant of 1 Scots Guards, for which I am also very grateful. Colonel Patrick Mercer has allowed me to quote an extract from his book, *Give Them a Volley and Charge*, for which I thank him.

I must also thank the owner, who wishes to remain anonymous, of four pictures of the War from his collection, which he has allowed me to reproduce in the book.

I am very grateful to Dr Alastair Massie for his permission to quote two letters written by the Duke of Cambridge to Lord Raglan from his book, *The Crimean War – The Untold Stories*.

Many of my fellow members of the Crimean War Research Society have given me valuable help. Major Colin Robins, late Royal Artillery, the former Editor of the Society's journal, *The War Correspondent*, has acted as my mentor and guide throughout the writing of this book. He has read the proofs and made valuable suggestions.

I am greatly indebted to him for his help and advice, which I asked for and obtained on a regular basis throughout the writing of the book.

Other members who have given me help include David Paine, late Grenadier Guards, who has given me information from his records on the Regiment, including information on those who fought in the war. Keith

Smith has, with Colin Robins, helped to identify the content of pictures of various battle scenes.

Brian Oldham has consulted his Great Crimean War Index to help me to verify my list of officers of the Scots Fusilier Guards. Anthony James has also consulted his records of officers who fought in the war to help me to verify the entries on my list.

Ron McGuigan has extensive knowledge of the command structure of the British Army in the Crimean War. The chapter on the command structure of the 1st Division, the Guards Brigade and the three Battalions in the war could not have been written without his help.

Brian Cantwell has advised me on solving the computer problems I have come across in writing the book. He has also helped me by enhancing images for the book and in assembling them on CDs for the publisher.

I would finally like to thank my wife for her help in checking the corrected pages, and Bobby Gainher for his help and for his highly efficient editing of the book.

Every effort has been made to locate and contact the holders of copyright material reproduced in this book and apologies are extended to anyone who has been inadvertently overlooked.

Michael Springman
Bembridge

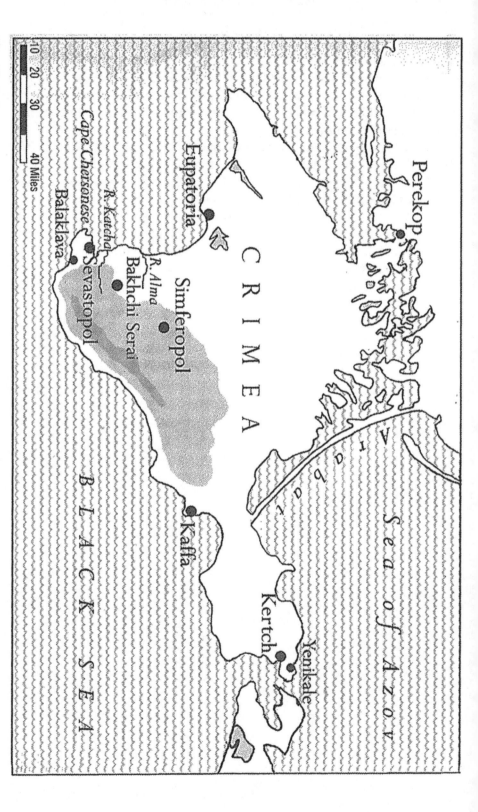

The Black Sea.

The Crimea and the Chersonese Peninsular

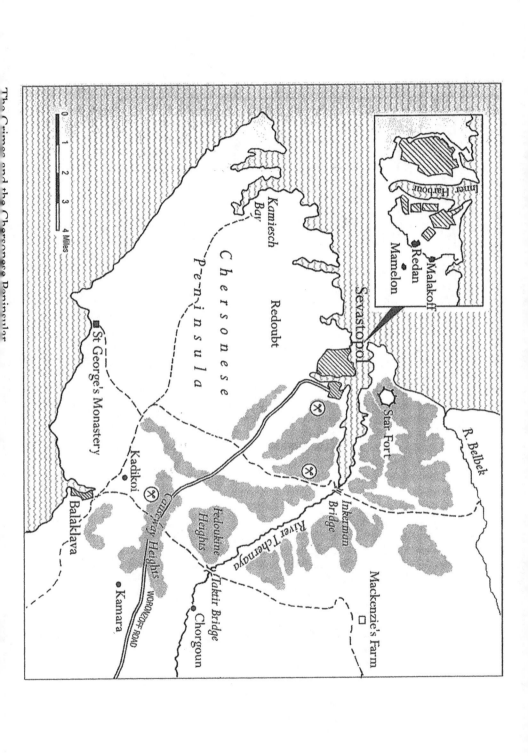

OPERATIONS AROUND SEVASTOPOL

© C.D.Robins 1999

Operations around Sevastopol. C.D. Robins.

CHAPTER 1

British Foreign Policy and the Origins and Reasons for the Crimean War

Trafalgar gave Great Britain control of the sea; Waterloo secured her against the domination of the continent of Europe by one nation. The maintenance of naval supremacy and of a European balance of power were the governing principles of British foreign policy, throughout the nineteenth century. The safeguarding of British naval supremacy was primarily a domestic affair, a matter of men and ships and money. The preservation of the balance of power implied diplomatic action, and, at times, the threat or the use of force. The balance of power was not a fact, but an ideal towards which all reasonable men worked.[1]

In nineteenth-century terms maintaining the balance of power was establishing an equilibrium between states or group of states, based upon an assessment of their material and moral strength. This equilibrium was always changing, as the powers of states waxed and waned, and these changes required continual adjustment. In fact, Europe never attained this equilibrium. Britain could not dictate to the powers of Europe the policy they should adopt, but she could use her wealth and influence to persuade any power or combination of powers, which wished to disturb the existing balance, to desist. No single continental power was capable of challenging the Royal Navy, and British naval supremacy was accepted as a fact by its allies. Britain's principal aim was to maintain the peace and the stability of the European state system, so that its merchants could buy and sell in European markets.[2]

Britain was concerned about Russia's aims to control the Bosphorus, including Constantinople, and its interest in taking over Mesopotamia, which would give Russia control over the overland route to India, where Britain had substantial commercial interests.[3]

In 1853 the Russian Empire stretched from Germany to the Pacific and its territory bordered the Black Sea, the Ottoman Empire, Persia and China. The

Tsar, who ruled over this immense land, was an absolute despot, whose rule was imposed by his secret police. With limited access to the sea, Russia had little foreign trade and thus was not able to develop her considerable resources. Furthermore, her road and rail links were very primitive. She lacked a warm-weather port to enable her to develop foreign trade. To further her expansionist policies, her objective was to conquer Constantinople and the Dardanelles, and thus gain entry to the Mediterranean Sea. In addition, Russia had aims to expand its empire into Turkey, Mesopotamia, Persia and India. The influence of her agents with the rulers of Afghanistan had caused the British Government considerable problems in eliminating Russian influence in this country, which threatened India's security.

In 1844 Tsar Nicholas I had made it clear to the British Government that Russia regarded the Ottoman Empire as the 'sick man of Europe' and offered Britain dominion over Egypt and Crete, provided Russia could have a free hand elsewhere. The British Government refused his offer as it had no wish for Russia to extend its borders further into Europe and Central Asia and thus to threaten the route to India.

Russia used as the occasion for their dispute with the Ottoman Empire the Tsar's desire to obtain protection over the Christian subjects in these territories, for which there were some historical precedents. Russia asked for this right in the spring of 1853, but the Sultan refused, as this would give Russia sovereignty over these lands.

The hesitation of Lord Aberdeen's divided cabinet, which faced opposition from Cobden, Bright and the radicals to any policy which risked war with Russia, encouraged Russia to take the decisive step of invading the Danubian Principalities, if Turkey did not accept their demands.[4]

In July 1853 Russia invaded Moldavia and Wallachia (modern-day Rumania). The British Government then ordered Admiral Dundas's squadron of six warships to proceed to Besika Bay, at the entrance of the Dardanelles, to join the French Navy there and, if necessary, to protect Constantinople from attack. The Austrian Government meanwhile attempted to use its influence to settle the differences between both parties. The Tsar's military might had enabled Austria to put down the recent revolt by Magyar nationalists in Hungary and he was therefore sure that Austria was his ally. The Austrian Government was disturbed by the Tsar's expansionist aims in the Balkans, which could also upset its trade in Europe, as the Danube was a major trade route. They feared Russia, which controlled the German-speaking nations and had intervened in the dispute between the German Confederation and Denmark over the ownership of Schleswig Holstein. It had succeeded in obtaining the annexation of this territory by the German Confederation. With Turkey refusing to agree to Russia's demands, Turkish resistance was stiffened by the belief that Britain and France would not allow Russia to take Constantinople.[5]

In France Louis Napoleon became President in December 1848. He was elected President for ten years in 1851 and in 1852, after a coup d'etat appointed himself Emperor Napoleon III. He was keen to demonstrate France's power on the world stage and furthermore wanted to redeem France's reputation after its defeat at Waterloo.

The Sultan was pleased that Britain and France were supporting him against Russia and put his defences in order. In October 1853 he issued an ultimatum to Russia to withdraw their troops from the Turkish territories in a fortnight, but in November 1853 the Russian Fleet surprised and sank a Turkish squadron at Sinope on the Black Sea.

The effect on British public opinion was dramatic. The action was called a massacre, as there was antipathy towards Nicholas, who the public felt was an enemy of liberty abroad and an upholder of serfdom at home. Furthermore it was felt that Russian designs on Turkey threatened Britain's political and economic interests. Lord Aberdeen was accused of cowardice and of betraying his country to Russia. Lord Palmerston, the Home Secretary, resigned over the proposed Reform Bill, but it was generally interpreted as a result of disagreement on the policy of handling the disagreement with Russia.[6]

In January 1854 the British, French and Turkish fleets sailed into the Black Sea, as Russia needed to control this sea to be able to invade the Ottoman Empire. The British and French navies were sufficiently powerful and numerous to give the Allies undoubted command of the sea. The Russian Navy, whose warships were inferior to those of the Royal Navy, returned to Sevastopol, where Nicholas had constructed new forts and new docks. He had turned it into a strong naval base, from which he could dominate the Black Sea and plan an attack on Constantinople.[7]

In February 1854 Russia broke off diplomatic relations with Britain, but the two nations did not then declare war on one another. The Tsar was sent an ultimatum by the allies to evacuate his armies from Rumania. He failed to do so and the British Government declared war on Russia on 28 March 1854.

[**Author's Note:** Woodward, E.L., *The Age of Reform*, pages 243 to 254 explains the background to the British Government's disagreements with Russia. Royle, Trevor, *The Great Crimean War 1854–1856* gives a full account of the development of Britain's disagreements with Russia, which preceded the declaration of war by the British Government.]

Notes
1. Woodward, E.L., *The Age of Reform 1815–1870*, Clarendon Press, Oxford, 1938, p. 186.
2. *Ibid.*, p. 186.
3. *Ibid.*, p. 202.
4. *Ibid.*, p. 248.
5. *Ibid.*, p. 249.
6. *Ibid.*, pp. 251 & 253.
7. *Ibid.*, p. 229.

CHAPTER 2

The Royal Navy and the Army in the 1850s – Their Development and Relative Efficiencies

From the earliest part of its existence as a nation, England, as an island, has faced the danger of invasion by its enemies. Although invasion of parts of the country by the Norsemen took place in the first millennium, the first invasion of the whole country was by the Normans in 1066. The next major invasion was by the Spanish Armada in 1588, repulsed by Sir Francis Drake.

The Navy has always been the most important service to the English Government, with the Army being of importance only when the sovereign wanted to invade a European country, to repulse an invasion or put down a rising in a part of the country.

What is of great interest to students of the Army is how far behind the Navy the Army was in the efficient direction of its operations, manning and administration, and especially in its strategic planning for the future. The Navy built its ships so that they were capable of achieving its strategic objectives and beating its enemies' ships; it researched new materials and equipment for ships to improve their handling ability and to reduce their manning; it constantly improved its methods of preserving fleet supplies to avoid wastage and to maximize ships' ability to stay at sea. On the medical side, it almost stamped out the outbreak of scurvy and was aware of what caused typhus. The Army seemed to struggle from one disaster to another without learning from its mistakes and certainly never planned for the future.

Professor N.A.M. Rodger in his book, The Command of the Ocean, discusses in great detail, the operations, staffing and administration of the Royal Navy during the seventeenth, eighteenth and the early part of the nineteenth centuries. He divides British eighteenth-century government into two parts: the Crown's and Parliament's. The Crown's government, which included the Army and foreign affairs, was based on a balance of central and local forces, as the powers of the Crown were checked by those of the nobility and gentry. It was traditional, dispersed and inefficient. On the other hand, Parliament's government was highly centralized and precociously professional. It included the Treasury and the revenue-collecting departments, especially Customs and Excise, and of course the Navy.

Parliament had taken control of the Navy during the Commonwealth and it was able to make British sea power the ideal expression of the nation in arms, which was founded on the folk-memory of the Elizabethan age. It made the Navy an expression of the liberty of the people, while the Army was an expression of the power of the crown.[1]

The Royal Navy

The Royal Navy was originally commanded by the Lord High Admiral, appointed by the Crown, but from 1673 onwards, the post was, more often than not, put into commission. From 1709 it was permanently in commission. Its powers were then exercised by a committee of Lord Commissioners, the Board of Admiralty, headed by the First Lord of the Admiralty, who was the political head of the Navy and a member of the Cabinet. The Navy had four separate organizations. The main strategic objectives of the Royal Navy were agreed in Cabinet. The First Lord made these objectives known to the Board of Admiralty, which was responsible for carrying out these tasks. It decided policy and controlled operations, it allocated ships to tasks, it appointed the captains and officers of naval vessels, and formulated naval strategy and tactics.

The second organization was the Navy Board, which was established by Henry VIII in 1546, to oversee the administrative affairs of the Navy. It operated as a separate entity to the Board of Admiralty, put into effect the ship building plans required, repaired and refurbished ships, purchased guns, through the Ordnance Board,[2] and also warlike stores. Some ships were built in naval yards and others in private yards to the Board's specifications.

The third organization was the Victualling Board, which bought all the foodstuffs required by the fleets, preserved them and shipped them out to the fleets. It was responsible for making it possible for fleets to remain on station much longer through developing higher standards for preserving food.

In 1693 the Allied fleet was barely able to remain at sea a fortnight and returned with its crews very sickly, leaving a convoy to its fate. Sixty-five years later Admiral Hawke was able to stay continually at sea for six months, keeping his men healthy and well fed far into the winter. No professional skill or strategic vision would have been of any avail, if means had not been developed to keep squadrons at sea for long periods in home waters, and on long overseas voyages. Moreover it was precisely in these matters of administration that the British opened a decisive superiority over their enemies, above all France.[3]

British naval victualling is a remarkable story of rising standards making ever more extended operations possible. It cost approximately the same to provide excellent victualling for 70–85,000 men during the Seven Years' War, as it did to provide inadequate victualling for 40–50,000 men during the War of the Spanish Succession half a century before.

The Board was the largest single purchaser on the London market for agricultural products. It managed the markets to encourage the growth of large firms, while at the same time promoting competition. The suppliers were paid by bills, which they could discount locally in the City.[4]

During the American War the Victualling Office coped efficiently with the victualling of troops overseas, which was transferred to it from the Treasury. There was a marked improvement in efficiency and economy.[5]

The fourth organization was the Sick and Hurt Board, which was in charge of taking care of all sick and wounded sailors. It also initiated new measures to reduce disease on board ships. Medical matters were managed in the Navy by the Board. The general issue of lemon juice virtually eliminated scurvy from the Channel Fleet by 1800.[6] Scurvy was only a problem on long sea voyages and by the end of the Seven Years' War, in 1763 scurvy was no longer a problem in British warships. Typhus was a serious problem on board a ship where men lived in close quarters, carried as it is by lice in dirty clothing. Throughout the eighteenth century British naval officers' fanatical attention to the cleanliness of their ships and men resulted in typhus occurring mainly among new recruits.[7]

The Navy avoided depending on the Treasury for providing the finance it required to run its operations. The Earl of Egmont became First Lord of the Admiralty in 1755. He bypassed the Treasury by dealing with the King direct over financing a plan of improvements for the dockyards.[8] Finance for the Navy and Victualling Boards was provided through perpetual annuities, which were first issued in 1715. The holder had no right to repayment, but was able to sell his annuity on the Stock Exchange. The Treasury could redeem these annuities at will if interest rates changed. Few of Britain's overseas trades balanced by themselves, but the system overall was balanced by bills exchanged in London. This international credit system, combined with banking, brokerage and insurance, made London the centre of a financial empire which earned large sums in invisible trade. The capital market in government stock drew capital to London from all over the British Isles, and indeed from over the Western World. The Navy was normally the largest single consumer of British public revenue, and the Army was its only rival.

Britain was a great power before she was an industrial power. By 1815, France had destroyed herself and much of Europe with her. Britain, at this time, was incontestably the dominant world trading power, but the Industrial Revolution was still in its infancy. Naval warfare was Britain's apprenticeship for commercial and industrial supremacy. There were three significant economic activities in Britain: agriculture, foreign trade and war. Foreign trade, especially the rich colonial and East India trades, generated the liquid capital which paid for wars. The effect of raising and simultaneous spending vast sums of capital acted like a bellows, fanning the development of Western capitalism and of the nation state itself. What was spent on the Navy was nearly all spent in Britain, or spent overseas in buying from British merchants, who remitted their profits home. The economic burden of war was therefore remarkably low, except when our large armies, campaigning overseas, had to pay for what they purchased locally in cash. The Navy protected trade and protected the country. Trade generated the seamen to man the Navy and the money to pay for it.[9] This system of administration was very logical and extremely effective.

The Army

The Army suffered from two disadvantages: a divided responsibility and from the distrust of the House of Commons. The distrust arose through Charles I's and James II's attempts to use the Army to coerce the House of Commons, and through Cromwell's actions, first in excluding Members of Parliament in Pride's Purge.[10] Then in 1655 he dismissed the Parliament and closed it down. From 1655 to 1656, he ruled the country through major generals, installed in every district to enforce local order, but after two years the system collapsed. His action has left an abiding hatred of military rule in Britain. Furthermore the Putney Debates of the New Model Army in 1647 showed very clearly that the Army wished to exercise political control over the House of Commons and to have a veto over the exercise of its powers. This influence was exercised by the Leveller Movement, which wished Parliament to support its revolutionary policies.[11]

The first act of the Cavalier Parliament, after the restoration of the monarchy in 1660, was to disband the New Model Army and to pay off its arrears of pay. The only exception was General Monck's Regiment of Foot, which later became the Coldstream Guards. This was the beginning of the establishment of a standing army in England, which James II used to coerce Parliament. The Commons then decided that the powers of the King to use a standing army had to be restricted.

In the Bill of Rights of 1689, it was made illegal for the Crown to raise or keep a standing army in time of peace without the consent of Parliament. By passing the Mutiny Act in 1689,[12] the Commons obtained political control over the Army. This Act authorized the annual Army budget, as well as the maintenance of Military Law by Courts Martial. The Act had to be passed every year to maintain the existence of Military Law, unless the country was at war. This situation obtained until 1955, when a new Army Act was passed, which required the Act to be renewed every five years.

The Commons were determined that the Army would never be able to dominate Parliament again. They decided that the type of officer they required in the Army would be the opposite to those in the New Model Army, who were highly religious, very political and very professional. They made sure of this by ensuring that entry to the cavalry and infantry would only be by purchasing a commission, so that only men of substance could become officers. Therefore, British Army officers tended to behave like amateurs in peacetime. Consequently, the British Army was not capable of operating in the field at the same high professional standards which the German Army was trained to achieve.

In wartime the British Army usually starts unprepared and ends a war as a highly professional army. Wellington transformed his army during the Peninsular War into a highly professional fighting force at battalion level. His army had an efficient command structure and a highly effective staff organization, handling operations, intelligence and also an efficient commissariat organization.

The Military Train, which Wellington had built up to be an efficient and effective organization for supplying the Army in wartime with arms, ammunition, food and materials, was finally disbanded in 1833 to save money. It was clear therefore that there was no adequate supply system in existence which would be able to provision an army in the Crimea.

This also happened in the First World War, but by the end of the war, the British Army was judged to be the most professional in the world. In an article on the letters of an artillery officer in Flanders 1918–19, it was said:

> Frederick Turner's war had been mercifully short. He had survived the great carnage unscathed. When he came to the front in 1918 the British Army, and at least the heavy artillery, had learned all that there was to know about trench warfare and spent the last phase of the war rigorously and victoriously applying the lessons of the three previous years, lessons which Turner, to his great good fortune, had not had to learn.[13]

Army Organization & the General Staff

The organization of the Army in 1854 was difficult to understand, as a number of autonomous bodies, each pursuing their own objectives, shared in managing and controlling its operations, and because there was no overall authority. These persons were the Secretary of State for War, the Commander-in-Chief, in charge of the cavalry and infantry, but only in this country, and the Master General of the Ordnance, in charge of the artillery and engineers, and also responsible for procuring weapons, munitions and warlike stores. The Master General was responsible as well for building and repairing forts and barracks. The Secretary at War, a different minister from the Secretary of State for War, was responsible for finance and for medical services. The Treasury managed the Commissariat, which supplied food and clothing.

All these bodies, including the Treasury, attempted to control and manage the Army. However, this confused and illogical organization made it nearly impossible to produce a coordinated plan and to give it unity of direction. This situation, as Prince Albert said, reduced the Army to a mere 'aggregate of battalions'.[14]

When peace came, there was great public pressure to reduce expenditure and these organizations had been disbanded in order to save money. The lesson that armies, to be effective, need command, operational, logistical and intelligence structures had been forgotten.

Because there was no proper staff training in the British Army, as there was in the German Army, the Army as a body, as distinct from individual regiments, was largely untrained. Out of more than a hundred officers on the staff, only nine had attended the staff course at the Senior Department of the Royal Military College, Sandhurst. The officers that made up the efficient general staff, built up by Wellington during the Peninsular War, had all retired or died. In the interests of economy, the Government did not feel it necessary to keep an embryo general staff in existence in peacetime.

General officers were able to influence the appointment of the staff officers they wanted, especially their ADCs, which in Lord Raglan's case were all his relations. However, the Secretary of State for War could appoint a senior officer as Chief of Staff, as happened when General Simpson was appointed Lord Raglan's Chief of Staff.

Without divisional organizations or manoeuvres, the generals had no experience of handling large numbers of troops. The first Camp of Exercise took place at Chobham in 1853, at the suggestion of the Prince Consort, where 8,000 men were in camp.

The men were splendidly clothed but they were led by officers who had no conception of military tactics. Units frequently got lost, were found by distracted staff officers advancing with smart determination and affected grimness on men of their own side, or were taken off the field altogether by commanding officers who thought the 'whole damned thing' was 'a waste of time'.[15] 'This Army,' remarked an officer in the Royal Artillery, with angry exasperation, 'is a shambles.' A few months later, with hope and confidence and the cheers of an admiring people, it was sent to war.[16]

The Army's uniforms were completely unsuitable for a campaign in the Crimea, let alone a winter one. The officers of the Brigade of Guards wore cut-away scarlet long-tailed coats, with large gold-braid epaulettes. The men fought wearing scarlet coats. All ranks of the Foot Guards wore bearskins for the first and last time on active service. Prince Albert had designed a side cap for the Brigade, which was worn by the sharpshooters and in the trenches. All ranks in the Brigade of Guards wore grey greatcoats, as did many soldiers in the Russian Army.

There were no reserves available either to replace casualties or to increase the size of the Army in the Crimea, except by depleting other regiments at home. The Government had to resort to raising various foreign legions to solve this problem temporarily.

No consideration had been given to the logistical problems that the Crimean Army would face, how much and what type of transport would be needed to move the troops, what systems should be set up to supply them and to keep them supplied in the field in all seasons, and how they would be provided with a regular supply of munitions and suitable food, clothing etc. The Treasury assumed, without any basis for their decision, that the Army would be able to purchase transport and find sufficient drivers for its requirements locally, which proved to be incorrect.

All of these problems arose and were not considered properly because there was not an efficient staff organization in existence. This organization, had it existed, would have proved conclusively to the Cabinet that it was impossible to send the Army to war in its present condition.

Army Promotion and the Purchase of Commissions

During the seventeenth and eighteenth centuries the Crown and its ministers wanted to prevent the appointment of officers, like those in Cromwell's New Model Army. These men had wanted to exercise political power and wished to challenge and limit the power and authority of the Commons.

Governments wished the officer corps to consist of people with a stake in the country, who were thus unlikely to act like mercenaries, revolutionaries or political firebrands. They did not want professional soldiers, but gentlemen who would regard the Army as an occupation for an amateur with private means, before he inherited his estate.

> The Army had never been a profession for which an officer need prepare himself nor once commissioned to take seriously. It had consequently persisted throughout these years of peace, without a hard core of experts, without even an organization. It remained as it had been in the eighteenth century a collection of regiments, each a self-contained unit, efficient or no, depending upon the qualities of its commanding officer, adjutant and its non-commissioned officers.[17]

The exceptions to this rule were those wishing to become officers in the Artillery and Engineers, where entry to the Royal Military Academy at Woolwich was by examination.

Those wishing to join a regiment in the cavalry, foot guards or infantry, had to purchase their commissions from officers who were retiring or were being promoted. It was not necessary for a candidate for a commission in the cavalry, foot guards or the infantry to attend and pass out from Sandhurst, until the Purchase of Commissions was abolished by Royal Warrant on 1 November 1871.

The most senior officer of any rank in a regiment, up to the rank of colonel, had the first choice to be promoted, regardless of merit, provided he paid the Regulation Fee. There was frequently an unofficial fee on top of this, which would be very low if the battalion or regiment was ordered for active service, or for service in India, which was very unpopular. It was much higher if the unit was on home service. The reason for the lower unofficial fee was that if an officer died or was killed his commission reverted to the Crown, whereas if he survived and retired, the sum raised from selling his commission would finance his retirement. This system was very unfair to the widows of officers who were killed or who had died, as it left them without any means of support.

No fee was paid for promotions to fill vacancies caused by death on active service by the officers appointed to these posts. In the same way, appointments made because of an augmentation, an increase in the officer establishment, were normally made without a fee being charged to those appointed.

Officers who could not pay the Regulation Fee would have more junior officers, who could afford to pay, promoted over their heads. This was both unfair and inefficient as experienced officers often had incompetent or inexperienced officers promoted over them. Finding or procuring the necessary funds was required to finance promotion up to the rank of colonel.

Promotion to the rank of major general resulted in the colonel losing the right to sell his position to the officer taking over from him. It should be noted that all general officers of the same seniority were promoted at the same time, regardless of their merit, to fill vacancies which had arisen up to and including Field Marshal.

Double Rank in the Brigade of Guards

Officers in the Brigade of Guards had the advantage of holding a dual rank, their rank in their regiment and a higher rank in the Army, either captain and lieutenant colonel, lieutenant and captain, or ensign and lieutenant. The double-rank privilege had been awarded to the Brigade of Guards by King James II, King William III and the Prince Regent. This had been done partly to reinforce their loyalty to the Crown and also for their bravery on the field of battle. The double rank gave officers in the Brigade of Guards great advantages in seniority in the Army, which was reflected in the purchase price of commissions. In 1856 a lieutenant colonelcy in the Foot Guards cost a regulation price of £9,000 plus an extra 'over regulation fee' of £4,200, making a total of £13,200, whereas a lieutenant colonelcy in a line regiment cost a regulation fee of £4,500, plus an extra £2,500, total £7,000.[18] The double rank was abolished in 1871 for officers commissioned after that date, but officers still serving retained their double rank for life.

Sir Colin Campbell's position in the Crimean War provides an interesting example of the advantage of the dual rank to officers in the Brigade of Guards. Sir Colin had started the war commanding the Highland Brigade and, as he had no private wealth, he had only obtained his lieutenant colonelcy by augmentation.[19]

Captain and Lieutenant Colonel William Codrington, who had been promoted in 1846 to Colonel in the Army without any change in his regimental rank, started the war as a company commander in 1 Coldstream. In June 1854, Codrington was promoted to Major General and on 1 September 1854 became Commander of 1 Brigade of the Light Division, in the place of Brigadier General Airey, who became Quartermaster General. In June 1855, Codrington was promoted to Lieutenant General as Commander of the Light Division, when Sir George

Brown went home sick. When General Simpson resigned as Commander-in-Chief, Codrington succeeded him and not Sir Colin Campbell, who had distinguished himself in India, as well as at Alma and at Balaklava. However, Sir Colin ended his military career as a Field Marshal and was created Baron Clyde.[20] Codrington turned down the offer of promotion to Field Marshal, as he had had experience of only one campaign.

Medical

The Medical Department was a staff department, which purchased medicines, bandages etc. for the Army, but it had no doctors or medical staff under its control. Each regiment had a Surgeon and two Assistant Surgeons, who established a battalion hospital.

Badly wounded casualties were sent to one of the general hospitals. Although the surgeons wore uniforms, they were not officers and were treated by the Army as civilians. However, as civilians they were subject to the Mutiny Act (The Army Act of that period) and could be court-martialled.

No one had considered how soldiers would cook their food, as the Army provided no unit cooking facilities. No studies had been made to ensure that the soldiers' diet was suitable for the heavy tasks they had to carry out or for the hardships they had to endure.

The experience learned in past campaigns had been forgotten. No one was made responsible for the general hygiene of the Army, as Army and Navy doctors, not being officers, lacked executive power and could only recommend measures, which their superiors could and did ignore. In these times, cholera epidemics from contaminated water supplies occurred regularly in London in summer, as the Thames was used both as a source of drinking water and as a sewer since it was not then known that this disease was caused by drinking contaminated water. By 1894 effective main drainage systems had eliminated this disease in the main cities in England.

In the Crimea lack of knowledge of this fact caused some regiments to be careless in preventing their water supplies from becoming contaminated by their latrines. This caused cholera epidemics to break out both in Bulgaria and in the Crimea.

Ordnance

In 1847 the Duke of Wellington pointed out that the country was defenceless, as the Government had cut the purchase of armaments drastically after Waterloo. The Army had only seventy field guns, which had last been used at Waterloo. In 1852 Lord Hardinge, the Commander-in-Chief, and Sidney Herbert, the Secretary at War, organized the purchase of three hundred 9-pounder guns, which became the Army's moveable armament in the Crimean War.[21]

The Iron Duke had reluctantly agreed to the introduction of a new rifle, the Pattern '51 Rifle/Musket, based on the principles of the French Minie, which had been proved to be greatly superior in trials against the standard infantry musket, the Brown Bess, and the Prussian breech-loader.[22] The Duke died in 1852 and his replacement Lord Hardinge had carried on with the gradual introduction of the Minie when he had funds to do so.

The School of Musketry at Hythe, which was established in 1852, studied the increased range and accuracy of the Minie. Soldiers, firing the Minie had to learn how to judge distances accurately and to set the sights correctly, in order to use effectively the increased range and accuracy of the Pattern '51, the Minie. This skill was not required when they fired the short-range Brown Bess.

During the war the record of inefficient and bungled supply chains, inept planning, the lack of a proper command system and an effective medical service showed that the Army organization was both incompetent and ineffective. These inadequacies and the horrific casualty lists made it clear to the public that reform of the Army was mandatory, if it was to survive as a fighting force.

The process of reform took place during the nineteenth and twentieth centuries, ending in the reorganization of the Ministry of Defence as a tri-services ministry. This process started in 1964 and ended in 1998 with the formation of the Joint Services Command and Staff College.

Notes

1. Rodger, Prof. N.A.M. *The Command of the Ocean*, Allen Lane, 2004, pp. 48–9.
2. The Master General of the Ordnance was in charge of the Ordnance Board, founded in 1414. He was appointed by the Prime Minister and frequently was a member of the Cabinet, providing military advice. The Board provided both services with arms, munitions and warlike stores. It also handled the building and maintenance of forts and barracks. It was not subject to Treasury control. Gordon, Hampden, *The War Office*, Putnam, 1935, pp. 14–15.
3. Rodger, p. 291.
4. *Ibid.*, p. 307.
5. *Ibid.*, p. 306.
6. *Ibid.*, p. 485.
7. *Ibid.*, p. 308.
8. *Ibid.*, p. 369.
9. *Ibid.*, p. 577–81.
10. In 1648, Colonel Pride and his musketeers excluded all Members of Parliament from entering the Commons, who had voted to reach an agreement with Charles I, which would have allowed him to continue to rule.
11. The Levellers' aims were equality for all by adopting republicanism, universal suffrage and religious toleration. John Lilliburne was their leader. Trevelyan, G.M., *England under the Stuarts*, Methuen, 1904, pp. 282–3 & 310.
12. In 1689 a regiment in Ipswich mutinied and declared their loyalty to the deposed James II. William III found he was unable to prosecute the mutineers,

as military courts had unintentionally been abolished by the Petition of Right of 1628. This Act ensured that all taxation was approved by Parliament and it also prevented the King from using Privy Council, Military or other Prerogative Courts, which had been used to try civilians. Unfortunately it did not retain the right to use Military Courts to try soldiers and sailors. Gordon, p. 25 and Trevelyan, pp. 144–5.

13. Spain, Jonathan, 'Frederick Turner: An Artillery Officer in Flanders ', *The Society for Army Historical Research Journal*, Spring 2006, p. 40.
14. Hibbert, Christopher, *The Destruction of Lord Raglan*, Viking, 1984, p. 7.
15. Pemberton, W. Baring, *Battles of the Crimean War*, B.T. Batsford, 1962, p. 18.
16. *Ibid.*
17. *Ibid.*, p. 19.
18. Robins, Colin, 'Double Rank in the Guards', *War Correspondent*, April 1996.
19. An increase of the number of officers in a battalion or regiment.
20. Robins, 1996.
21. Gordon, p. 179.
22. Hamilton, Lt Gen Sir W.F., *The Origins & History of the First or Grenadier Guards*, vol. 3, John Murray, 1871, pp. 153–4 and Addenda, p. XX,.

CHAPTER 3

The Journey to the Crimea, February–August 1854

Gren Gds = Grenadier Guards Cold Gds = Coldstream Guards
SFG = Scots Fusilier Guards

Guards Brigade-Movements & Events
1854

22 February	Embarked at Southampton.

Gren Gds   6 Coys – *Ripon*
                       2 Coys – *Manilla*
Cold Gds – *Orinoco*

28 February   Embarked at Southampton.
                       SFG – *Simoon*

MALTA
5 March   Landed at Malta and quartered at Lazaretto.
                       Gren Gds – *Ripon*
                       Cold Gds – *Orinoco*

12 March   Landed at Malta and quartered at Lazaretto.
                       Gren Gds – *Manilla*

14 March   Landed in Malta and quartered at Lazaretto.
                       SFG – *Simoon*

24 April   Embark at Malta.
                       Gren Gds – *Golden Fleece*
                       Cold Gds – *Vulcan*
                       SFG – *Kangaroo*

25 April	Anchor in Dardanelles.
	SCUTARI
29 April	The Guards Brigade landed at Scutari and encamped near Kadikoi. Lord Raglan, the Commander-in-Chief, lands at Scutari.
13 June	Embarked at Scutari. Gren Gds – *Golden Fleece* Cold Gds – *Andes* SFG – *Simoon*
	BULGARIA
14 June	Landed at Varna and encamped outside the gates.
5 July	Marched to Aladyn and encamped at head of Lake Devna.
27 July	Marched to Gevreclek and encamped.
7 August	Varna town burnt down.
16 August	Marched to Hadjimmeh Village [Dschaseli] and encamped.
17 August	Marched to Varna Plain and encamped.
18 August	Marched to Galata Serai on the Adrianople Road and encamped.
29 August	Marched to Varna and embarked. Gren Gds – *Simoom* Cold Gds – *Tonning & Simoom* SFG – *Kangaroo*

The Journey to Bulgaria and Invasion Plans

As the likelihood of war increased it was decided to move troops to the East. On 10 February 1854 a Brigade Order was issued, warning the 3rd Battalion Grenadier Guards, the 1st Battalion Coldstream Guards and the 1st Battalion Scots Fusilier Guards to be prepared to embark at Southampton for foreign service by the 18th of the month. Each battalion was to be made up of forty sergeants, besides the usual staff sergeants, and 850 rank and file. The Grenadiers and the Coldstream embarked on 22 February and sailed to Malta, to join the Army of the East. The Scots Fusilier Guards did not embark until 28 February.

Captain C.T. Wilson, Coldstream Guards, describes the scene as the Guards leave London:

The Guards quitted London, huzzaed by tens of thousands: patrician Belgravia sorrowfully lisped its farewell; the city burghers shouted, as only the Anglo-

Saxon can shout; the 'dangerous classes' of Bermondsey and the Borough whistled, yelled, and screeched bellicose enthusiasm. 'Keep yer pecker up, my boys,' was counsel unceasingly tendered by the roughs; 'bring us back the big bear in a cage,' was a solution of the Turkish difficulty exceedingly in favour with the practical have-at-em masses.

Four years have passed away, so has the mighty Czar, so have three-quarters of the flushed soldiery that then strode along the Strand: pride of England's aristocracy, flower of her sturdy peasantry.[1]

At Southampton, another ovation cheered the 'brigade', as it embarked on board the mail-steamers *Orinoco*, *Ripon*, and *Manilla*.[2]

Captain A. Tipping, Grenadier Guards, records the Battalion's departure in his letter home. He sailed to Malta in the *Manilla*.

We paraded at 3:45 a.m. on the following morning. It was pitch dark and slightly drizzling and a good many of our men, not being forthcoming, having adieus to make to departing friends, we remained on the barrack square, waiting till all were ready. We did not march till past five all the way up the Strand to the station, the windows of all the upper stories were filled with females waving their handkerchiefs, men in demi-costume cheering, and during the distance of all our March there were heads innumerable of undefined genders, making demonstrations and waving adieux to us. At the station, the crowd was so immense, it was utterly impossible to make our way through it. I, like many others, was lifted completely off my legs and went into the station on the shoulders of the rabble, whom the police treated most roughly for all their pains. They bore all the kicks and cuffs, which they received with the utmost good humour. They seemed to consider themselves well repaid by having taken a last look at the British Grenadier. I could not help at the time speculating upon what the chances were against at least one half of us seeing that station again.[3]

On 21 February Lord Raglan was appointed Field Commander of the Eastern Army. The Brigade was commanded by Colonel Bentinck, Coldstream Guards, who was appointed Brigadier General on 21 February. The Brigade remained in Malta for seven weeks.

Captain Wilson describes the journey by sea to Malta:

But a few days of fine Mediterranean weather, assisted by the exertions of some bustling regimental officers, and the vessel's worthy Commander, restored health and happiness, set ensigns, who had studied under Jack Hannan, to pummel one another with the 'gloves', sergeants to glee-singing, drums to rattle, fifes to squeak, and turned the saloon, but lately almost deserted, into a symposium, where eating and drinking, perpetual and prodigious, testified to a copper-fastened strength of digestion seldom enjoyed in the precincts of St James's.

For all things immediately concerning the soldiers, the military officer 'on watch' is responsible; at night, he occasionally inspects the ship above and below, and, in the course of his explorations sees many strange sights. Guided by a Sergeant carrying a lantern, the punctilious Subaltern clambers up and stumbles down sea-going, and therefore, breakneck ladders; groping in every frouzy hole, and every greasy corner of decks and forecastle, that he may be sure that no lights burn, except as glimmer under the guardianship of sentinels.[4]

Captain Tipping remembers the rough voyage:

The wind blew hard against us, with a heavy sea, of course everyone was now more or less sick. Not a soul, apart from myself and the officers on the ship, came to dinner the first day. I always find myself nearly the only one on board, who does not suffer, when it is at all rough, but with seeing so many ill all around, I must say I was nearly being upset myself.[5]

The Brigade arrived in Malta over a period of ten days. The first to arrive were six companies of the Grenadiers in the *Ripon* and 1 Coldstream in the *Orinoco*, both of which landed on 5 March. The *Manilla*, which carried the remaining two companies of the Grenadiers, had engine trouble and did not arrive till 12 March. The Scots Fusilier Guards in the *Simoon* did not land in Malta till 14 March.

The barracks provided for the Brigade meets with Captain Wilson's approval:

The Lazzaretto, and forts adjacent, were the quarters assigned to the Guards. Scarcely an agreeable appellation in Lazzaretto, being in a manner suggestive of plague spots and cholera; nevertheless, in reality, his station is pleasure enough, the galleries overhanging the quarantine harbour being cool lounging places, whence you get a charming view of the churches, convents, batteries, and palaces of which the Maltese metropolis is made up.[6]

Captain Wilson comments upon the British Army's preparedness for war:

The ill-organized medical department was unequal to [such] a strain. As for the baggage-train, I will quote the opinion of Sir De Lacy Evans [GOC 2nd Division], a first-rate authority. 'As I happened to pass through Malta immediately after the commissary-general sent out by direction of Sir Charles Trevelyan [Treasury official responsible for the Commissariat], I asked by accident what means of transport had been provided, and I found that in order to provide for the army (then about 10,000 men) he had bought thirty mules and thirty carts – it may have been thirty-five, but I think I am correct in saying thirty was about the number.' (Speech in Parliament, July 19, 1855.)

Furthermore, no Commander-in-Chief, no staff, no division leaders, but one brigadier (Col. Bentinck) had appeared as yet. In a word, every essential of an army was either absent or imperfect, except a splendid body of infantry, under active regimental officers. For want of Adjutants-General and Quarter-Masters General, this noble foot could not be shaped into brigades and divisions. Infantry was shoveled out to Malta, but no artillery accompanied it; cavalry was apparently deemed superfluous in the *veni, vidi, vici* campaign, dreamt of at Whitehall. The commissariat consisted of a few zealous, intelligent clerks, shackled with the 'wise saws and modern instances' of those highly connected bureaucrats, Routine and Red-tape.[7]

In *The Times* of Feb. 22, 1856, a well-informed writer made the following statement: – 'Why did it happen that out of 291 officers serving on the staff of the British army in May, 1854, two months after we had declared war against Russia, only fifteen had been trained at the senior department of Sandhurst? Although 216 officers obtained certificates of qualification at the senior school of Sandhurst in the period from 1836 to 1854, only twenty have been employed during the whole of that time. In 1852, there were but seven officers on the whole staff of the British army who had passed through the senior school.'[8]

The Pattern '54 Rifle/Musket

From 1722 till 1852, through the Seven Years' War and from Waterloo to the Crimean War, the Land Service muzzle-loading musket was the weapon used by the British infantry. It was smooth-bored. Over the years it was developed into the 1842 pattern.

The infantry tactic was to use it to provide rolling volleys, fired by formations in close order, either in companies, platoons or files (file-firing). This tactic was designed to break the enemy's formation. This was then followed by a bayonet charge to rout the enemy and to put them to flight. The only exception was when the company was skirmishing, either covering the defensive position over else working in front of an attacking force. They were, however, under the close control of officers and NCOs.

The range of this weapon was up to 200 yards but the effective range was between 50 to 100 yards. It was not accurate for ranges of over 80 yards, so for that reason it was used for firing volleys Experienced soldiers could fire three to four rounds a minute and keep up this rate for a short time, without having to clean the weapon.[9] Unlike the Minie, which had adjustable sights, the 1842 Pattern Musket, called the Brown Bess by the soldiers, had only one fixed sight.

The adoption of the Minie rifle/musket was one of the reasons that the British Army was able to defeat the Russian Army in the Crimean War.

In 1852 the Regimental Adjutant of the Grenadier Guards was appointed president of a committee to carry out a series of experiments at Woolwich with a view to testing the relative merits, at various ranges from 100 to 900 yards, and in all weathers, of the Pattern 1842, the French version of the proposed Pattern 1854 rifle and the Prussian breech-loading gun. After the experiments had been completed, the committee presented their report to the Adjutant General, which led to the adoption of the Minie rifle.

Captain Augustus Lane Fox, Grenadier Guards, who was a member of the committee, played a major part in developing the system of musketry instruction of the troops, using the Minie in the Crimean War. He was first appointed musketry instructor to 2nd Battalion Grenadier Guards. After spending some months on the Continent in studying the systems of instruction in France, Belgium and Piedmont, Captain Fox revised these drills. Lord Hardinge, the Commander-in-Chief, then sent for Captain Fox and instructed him to redesign these regulations to make them applicable for the whole Army.[10]

To exploit to the full the potential of the Minie, a complete change in infantry tactics was required, as its increased range enabled its sights to be set from 100 to 900 yards. At short ranges, volleys could be devastating, as the bullet could go through several men in a column of Russian troops, as our troops found out during the Battle of the Alma, and at Inkerman. Although the Minie's loading process was different to that of the Brown Bess, properly trained and experienced troops could fire about three to four rounds a minute. However, the greatest advantage of the Minie was that, in the hands of competent shots it could be used for effective firing at ranges of 200 to 400 yards, by marksmen and sharpshooters for sniping at ranges up to 800 yards, and at individual targets, such as any officers and artillerymen.[11] To fire the Minie effectively, troops had to learn how to judge distances in order to set the sights accurately.

The time in Malta, *en route* to the East, was well spent firing the new Minie rifle/musket on the ranges. Each battalion was issued with 200 Minies before sailing and more were issued in Malta and Varna, so that by then the Brigade was fully equipped with the new weapon.

Captain Wilson comments upon the adoption of the new weapon:

When the Household Brigade was ordered abroad, the military Court of Chancery had come to no decision relative to the suitableness of the Minie rifle for the general use of infantry. As yet, that amazing tool was in the possession of only a few select men in every regiment. Hence, Lord Hardinge, who, it must be confessed, did much for the improvement of English small arms, judged it expedient that the Guards should take 'Brown Bess' to Malta; but, at the same time, he despatched thither cases of Minies, under the charge of a competent instructor of musketry, Captain Lane Fox. Thus, his lordship provided us with two strings to our bow; we had old and new weapons ready to our hands; if we took the inferior article, we had only ourselves to blame. Thanks to Captain Fox's exertions in favour of modern betterment, and a few experiments, a right verdict was at length delivered. At Scutari, old Brown Bess was marched off ignominiously to the Ordnance stores, and the Minie maiden became the faithful consort of every foot soldier. How completely have subsequent events substantiated the truth of Fox's arguments.[12]

The British Government still hoped that the naval demonstration would persuade the Tsar to sue for peace. However, as Russia did not reply to the British and French governments' ultimatum demanding the withdrawal of Russian forces from the principalities, the two governments formally declared war on Russia on 28 March 1854. After war was declared on Russia, Lord Raglan left England for Varna on 10 April and arrived there on 27 April 1854.

Scutari

Meanwhile from 14 April, the Turkish Army in Silistria, on the Danube in Bulgaria, had been besieged by the Russians. On 22 April the Guards Brigade left Malta bound for Scutari, so that the Army was on hand to defend Constantinople and to support the Turks in case they needed help.

Silistria and Shumla were fortified towns in Bulgaria, located south-west of the Dobrudja, the marshy area between the mountains and the east coast of the Black Sea. These towns were defended by experienced Egyptian and Albanian troops, which Marshal Pashevich, the Russian commander, attacked. Meanwhile, the Brigade arrived in Scutari on 29 April.

Captain Wilson describes the Army's unfamiliarity with using pack animals, as the Army had not been to war for nearly fifty years, and therefore all ranks were ignorant on how to handle and how to use them:

The baggage parade, at which I assisted – a sample of all the rest, I believe – was a most provoking affair to principals, whatever it might have been to unconcerned spectators. Everything went amiss. Steeds marked out, by fiery mettle or Arabian ancestry, for more honourable vassalage than the porterage of camp-properties, positively refused to budge an inch, and concentrating their frisky energies on an unbroken series of kickings and plungings, quickly rid themselves of their vile loads, to the rage and despair of masters and grooms. For no sooner did the poor creatures feel how sorely the new pack-saddles galled, how lop-sided and ill-balanced rode the clumsy bullock-trunks, than they meekly assumed the recumbent position, which the more energetic did their best to vary with a roll. Flesh and blood could not stand these aggravations, the *bat-men* began to curse and to swear, and to rain showers of blows upon the piteous beasts, instead of remedying the mischief, which ignorance of 'common things' had perhaps mainly brought about.

Presently, however, some Turks, who had been amused spectators of our troubles, interfered between us and the refractory beasts, with such happy effect, that an armistice was speedily concluded. The animals were led peaceably to their tethers, and we set about gathering together our household goods, now scattered over the field of strife. We were wiser and more humble after this trial, for it taught us that the muleteer's cunning, and no end of useful dodges beside (which in our unwarlike blindness we had despised) are not learnt in a day.[13]

Captain Tipping has similar memories of such parades:

You have no idea there of the difficulty of putting on your beasts back all that you require, and to pack it in such a manner as to be able to go up and down hills, cross rivers, or go through trees or other obstacles. It is quite marvellous how one has to curtail what have hitherto been considered essential to one's existence. We are obliged to carry three days provision with us, this amounts to 100 lbs.

The tent we have to carry weighs 60lbs; but I have bought a little portable one and waterproof, which weighs 6 pounds, but when you consider that these articles when your bedding, independently of your canteen for cooking your dinner, are almost enough for a mule, before your personal luggage begins, you may fancy how few things we can take. Our dinners are precisely the same as those of the soldiers, consisting of one pound of bread and one pound of meat, cooked over sticks in the open air; of course there is not such a thing as a cooking stove in the Brigade, as it could not be carried.[14]

The Army's health in Scutari was good. Captain Wilson comments:

Throughout our stay at Scutari, the health of the troops was remarkably good, the percentage of sick being generally below the home average; the rations, too, were all that soldiers could desire. *Apropos* of the creature comforts, I overheard the following conversation in a company's tent, within ear-shot of mine own. First private *loquitur*, 'Well, Bill, these ere rations ain't bad; give me my wittals sweet and juicy, and I'm not the chap to *hargify* about the weight of the mess; little and good, says I.' Second private, 'I don't agree with ye, Tom, I always puts quantity in the front rank and quality in the rear. After my dinner, d'ye see, I likes to have all my buttons standing "at attention", because I knows then as how I've got a belly-full.'[15]

He also comments upon the unpredictable weather in the area of the Black Sea:

There burst forth a thunder-storm, which for flash, roar, rain, I have not seen equalled, even in the tropics. Of course we all, more or less, got a share of the deluge; for the tents were of every sort, good, bad, and indifferent; some, being new, resisted the wet pretty well – others, said to have served the Egyptian campaign, were downright sieves.

However, generally speaking, officers and men, who had been wise enough to dig a trench round about their habitations, had little to complain of, beyond, perhaps, the obstinacy of a streamlet, which would persist in trickling between the sheets, or purling capriciously among portmanteaux, saddle-bags, and the like; but the thoughtless 'Johns', whom the sunny aspect of Kadi-Koi had deluded into neglect of drainage, were enabled to form an idea how very inconvenient a flood is, when it invades the domestic privacy. The books, boots, epaulettes, under-raiment, and the thousand cherished knick-knacks of neglectful subalternism, floated recklessly about, plastered o'er with a slimy and deteriorating compound of dust and rain. However, the rage of the tempest soon died out, the sun again struggled into gorgeous being, and ill hands went so heartily to work to repair damage, that our humid, sticky economies were quickly as well as could be expected. Would to God clammy blankets and damp linen had been our sole griefs![16]

HM Queen Victoria's birthday – 24 May – was marked by a parade and the troops celebrated in the evening. Captain Goodlake reports in a letter that he and Astley (J.D. Astley, Captain and Lieutenant, Scots Fusilier Guards) were seized by the inebriated men and carried round the illuminations. Goodlake had his only suit of mufti (plain or civilian clothes) torn to shreds off his back.[17]
Captain Wilson describes the celebrations:

Thanks to the liberality of the officers, the men amused themselves on this royal afternoon (and prodigiously surprised the Moslem) with the rustic games dear to our West Country peasantry. The Cornish hug, climbing the greased pole, jumping in sacks, the wheel-barrow race, were all satisfactory achievements; but what most tickled the fancy of the spectators was the grinning through a horse-collar, a capital bit of tom-foolery, a *chef-d'oeuvre* of village farce! I have seldom heard more genuine applause than that which rewarded the final grimace of the successful competitor, a curiously ugly, but withal waggish, Coldstreamer, who certainly had it all his own way in the art of making mouths with comical effect.[18]

Varna, Bulgaria

As it was clear that Constantinople was unlikely to be captured by the Russians, the Brigade embarked for Varna in Bulgaria on 13 June, arriving there the following day.

At ten am on the 14th of June, we let go our anchor in the Bay of Varna, usually deserted, but now teeming with line-of-battle ships, steam frigates and transports. In the midst of it all, our regiment seemed to have been completely forgotten for it was three pm before the Quarter-Master General's people had made up their minds what to do with us.
    In consequence of this tardy determination, the left wing of the battalion (the last to leave the ship) fared ill, inasmuch as it was quite dark before the

rear companies gained their camping ground, and then, just as the tent-bags were being distributed, down poured the rain; thus, we had to stretch our canvas blindly, in the midst of the black storm, without a chance of choosing a pleasant bit of moss, or a soft-looking stone for our pillows – but there was no help for it. One must adapt oneself to circumstances in this world, take things as they come. So, that night we slept (aye! and well slept) amongst a damp medley of saddle-bags, trunks, and bedding, with a soaking hurley-burley above, and rather glutinous mire below. While the circum-ambient air was charged with smells exceedingly nauseous and subtle, the natural consequences of a previous occupation of the ground by a squadron of Turkish cavalry, whose domestic habits, when in the field, are never peculiarly refined; not that the traduced Mohammedan trooper is an unclean beast, far from it, for his religion forces him to wash whenever water is plenteously available; and to dry rub, when that commodity (as often happens in the East) is very scarce. Nevertheless, these are respects in which he is unquestionably not nice; in other words, his olfactory sensibilities must be singularly blunt and soldier-like.

At day-break next morning (he that leads a nomadic life is an early riser), I popped my head out into the open, for the purpose of obtaining a sniff of fresh air and of forming an idea of the country we inhabited at present. The prospect was by no means inviting, for a regular London fog, greasy, fetid (you might almost have cut it with a knife) enveloped the camp in its noisome shroud. A walk of a hundred yards explained the cause of this ominous murkiness, and awakened forebodings. We had located ourselves close to a lake, the edges of which were cropped with rank herbage, smacking of ague, dysentery and rheumatics, making it an undesirable location. Omar Pacha had warned us against this place, but this warning had been been ignored.[19]

Captain Tipping describes the incompetence of the Commissariat in their handling of bullock-wagon drivers, the making of gabions and the training operations conducted by the Duke of Cambridge:

About 140 bullock wagons of the country were hired, each vehicle being drawn by two bullocks. These were to have accompanied the expedition for the various purposes of conveying ammunition, carrying the sick and wounded etc. so they were to have started on Monday, but on the previous Saturday every driver disappeared and nothing could be seen or heard of them afterwards.

We found that the commissariat had promised the Arabs rations and a certain amount of daily pay and hay. Four days had elapsed without a mouthful of one or a farthing of the other having been supplied to them. But like all Easterners, being suspicious of foul play, they thought they were going to be cajoled, and no power can now get them back. We are literally prevented from moving on this account, as well as from them not having made any provision for giving us food in any way; in short the whole business seems to have no director. The Commissary General Filder was the person, whom poor Picton[20] threatened to hang, in the Peninsular [War]. Most of their subs got their appointments from interest, without being in a way qualified for their work.

We have just received orders to make 3000 Gabions in 10 days, and we have been two days hard at work. This looks like an intention on the part of the authorities to proceed against some fort or other. Of course you are aware that Gabions are, as you know, hollow baskets, 4 feet deep, and 16 inches in diameter, and when filled with soil, make a good protection against musketry, which the sappers use in making the trenches and approaches, etc.

Duke George [The Duke of Cambridge] gives us four to five hours manoeuvring on the plane, two to three times a week. It is killing work in this burning heat, and we don't get back to our tents till between nine and 10 o'clock. He being on horseback totally forgets the difference between carrying oneself and being carried; however the medics remonstrated, on account of many of the men suffering from the intense heat, and an order has now been sent out from the Commander-in-Chief, that the men should not be kept out after eight o'clock. It is very tiresome work, and we are all anxious to accomplish the objectives for which we came out here, instead of transforming the old Phoenix Park work to this climate. The disadvantages of the latter, without the advantages of the former. The thermometer is every day from 92 to 97° in our tents.[21]

The British Army campsite at Varna was on wet ground and near to a stagnant lake, which caused sickness amongst the soldiers. The French occupied higher ground and suffered fewer casualties.

On 1 July the Brigade moved 10 miles inland to Aladyn, on the edge of Lake Devna, which proved to be a very unhealthy place. The men suffered from typhus and dysentery and about a fifth of the men were admitted to hospital. On 27 July, the Brigade marched to the village of Gevreklek, 3 miles away, where cholera broke out.

[**Author's Note:** cholera is an acute, infectious, water-borne disease, characterized by watery diarrhoea, vomiting, cramps, suppression of urine, collapse and death. The disease is carried by water or clothing and is infected by sewage etc., a fact that was unknown at the time. In 1866, deaths from cholera in London were 5,596, 18.4 per cent per 1,000 living, but by 1894 the installation of a sewage system for London, which treated the sewage and discharged it in the Thames Estuary, reduced the deaths in that year to zero for London. Similar operations installing sewage systems took place elsewhere in the country, so that deaths from cholera in 1866 in the rest of England and Wales were also zero.][22]

On 16 August the Battalion moved to a seaside camp in Varna, which improved the Brigade's health. Captain Wilson describes the situation:

> While the Battalion was at Varna, fifty-seven men of 1 Coldstream died in the camp hospital, nearly all from cholera and typhus.
>
> There was a general feeling among both officers and men, that Lord Raglan did not visit the troops in their camps as frequently as he should have done, and certainly not as frequently as Marshal St Arnaud did. Unfortunately he made little impact, when he did, unlike the French who made the visit very memorable.
>
> Marshal St Arnaud frequently visited our lines. On such occasions, the English soldiers always turned out of their tents, and cheered the French Generals, who, evidently pleased and flattered, responded to the hearty hurrahs with gracious smiles and doffing of laced hats. Seeing the excellent effect of this noble cordiality, one could not avoid wishing some of our own chiefs had been less chary of their presence, and not quite so stiff in their bearing, when they did appear among the troops. 'Oh,' but it's sometimes said, 'our privates don't care for that sort of thing.' Really! Why, then, are Sir De Lacy Evans [GOC 2nd Division] and Sir Colin Campbell [Highland Brigade] so cherished by their men? May it not be, because, apart from their undeniable professional value, they have ever as kind a word, and as beaming a countenance for the Pats and Sandies on sentry, as for a Royal Duke.[23]

There was no question in the mind of the British troops that the French Army was better equipped than the British. Furthermore its generals and its government cared more about the welfare of their soldiers than did the British Government. Captain Wilson gives an excellent example of more up-to-date thinking by the French:

> During their frequent visits to our camp, I had many opportunities of asking the French soldiers what they thought of our knapsacks, accoutrements, and so forth, but one always got the same answer – '0 mon Dieu, tres lourd.' One day a keen-witted young corporal of Chasseurs de Vincennes told me, he believed the troops of his nation were formerly half-smothered in harness somewhat similar to what the English wore at present, but Napoleon had swept away tous les restes militaires du moyen age.[24]

Aladyn
Captain Wilson continues:

> At three a.m., Saturday, July 1st, a note of preparation sounds through the camp, down come the tents, and the loading of baggage-animals is begun. In the meanwhile, the bagpipes shriek the advance, and away marches the Royal

Duke's division, with the old Black Watch (forty-twa's) in front, leaving the luggage train to follow, whenever its arrangements were completed. It soon became manifest that the rear-guard was anything but a sinecure.

Here we stand, a handful of crude campaigners, attempting to get really upon our legs for the first time. In front of us is chaos—the field strewed with tent bags and black boxes, cases of Cognac, and hampers of 'Bass', a mountain of pack saddles, and, last but not least, a herd of beasts of burden, generally evincing very perverse dispositions. No ways daunted, our excellent fellows set to work with a zeal and good will, which ought to have smoothed away every obstacle. Saddles were girthed and re-girthed; loads all shapes and sizes were packed and repacked with untiring assiduity; nevertheless, miscarriages seemed endless. We were almost led to fear our painstaking efforts might prove as ineffectual as the labours of the unprincipled daughters of Danaus.[25] But as time, temper, and perseverance will see man through most earthly troubles, the train by slow, very slow, degrees, assumed a trim which promised a start. The train moves on, and in rear follows the guard, which is ordered to repair every disaster, and on no account to allow 'luggage to be left behind'.

We had barely journeyed half a mile, before it was proved to us how know-nothing we were in the muleteer's art, what infants we were in the science of packing for active service! Most humiliating confession!—the road was getting cumbered with various domestic constituents of the defunct camp. Here, we have an Irish batman full of oaths, choler, and paternosters, calling on the saints for aid, while his master's property lies neglected in the mud, and the quondam porter trots off in the distance. There, in the very middle of the way, a mule is determinately rolling amongst a heap of trunks, baskets, and bedding; in another place, a poor galled brute has irretrievably broken down, and it is a chance whether his lading of sherry and pale ale ever reach the proprietor. Nevertheless, by dint of a judicious admixture of coaxing and cudgeling, un-intermitting vigilance, and continual picking up of pieces, on the part of the soldiers, the wire-drawn caravan (it was now about five miles in length) was kept slowly going.[26]

But how was it that that cheery, light company guard marched along in such high spirits? – how was it that broiling heat and suffocating dust made no impression, seemingly, on the stockless, unbuttoned sharp-shooters? Because, (according to a report prevalent in the ranks) we were now actually *en route* for the Danube, 'to take a turn at the Rooshians', and thereby qualify ourselves for a medal. Fighting and clasps were the sole topics of conversation. Yet, there are people who would insinuate that military honour is not understood by the private soldier – that it is a caste monopoly, forsooth, the prerogative of titles and broad acres, of purple and fine linen. Out upon it![27]

Captain Wilson describes the daily routine and the establishment of Colonel Drummond's bazaar:

Distant about half a mile from this scene of pestilential beauty was a deserted village. Not a living thing stirred in that once peaceful hamlet; an entire community had been driven forth by the ruffianism of a few blackguards, belonging to the division which had preceded us; for example, when you entered a village, women and children fled from before your face, responding to your beseeching for *yoormootah* (eggs) with the inhospitable screech yok, yok, (no, no,) despite the insidious chink of your sixpenny pieces.

At length, political economy re-asserted its sway; love of gain and assurances of protection induced a few enterprising rustics to bring fowls, milk, and vegetables to our lines. This desultory huckstering, Colonel Gordon Drummond, of the Coldstream Guards, took in hand; he fostered it, he guided its first tottering steps, and, in the fullness of time, he had the gratification of seeing it expand into the semblance of a regular bazaar. As the gallant Coldstreamer's persevering tact mainly set the rickety bantling on its legs, so did his solicitude sustain the progress of the nervous adult. Had it been left to itself, this commercial institution would have been as an exhalation of the morning; it could not have survived a week. Never was Stock Exchange more sensitive than that rude poultry-market, a few casual 'god-damns', delivered with the force and unction characteristic of the English soldier, being enough to scare half the farmers for days to come. Albeit, Bulgarian susceptibility had its uses, it taught the necessity of toning down the asperities of our John Bull manner, and the advantage of having recourse, in all transactions with the awe-stricken boors, to that almost omnipotent spell – soft sawder. Moral lessons which, being wound up in the great dinner question, were not altogether thrown away.[28]

Our day may be said to have been divided into three portions; the first, being devoted to drill and exhaustion and the second to torpor and tobacco; the third-and most agreeable – to foraging and feeding. Towards six p.m. – the dinner hour in most companies – the foragers begin to drop in, some, pretty heavily laden with good things; others, with haversacks altogether empty. One man will live, where another starves, so would Ensign Jones pick up 'grub', where unobservant Lieutenant Robinson saw naught but dust and ashes: a pleasant voice, a good eye for country, and a knowing way of rattling piastres rarely failed of success, after the establishment of the Drummond Bazaar.[29]

In order to increase our confined accommodation, we set about building arbors; in a few days officers and soldiers had constructed a number of cool retreats, in which they fed, smoked and slumbered, during the mid-day heats. The most famous architect of these abodes was Colonel Cadogan, of the Grenadier Guards, under whose ingenious superintendence arose a spacious vegetable pavilion, containing several spacious rooms. Under the title of the 'Guards' Club' this chef d'oeuvre of artistic booth-building became the resort of the jeunesse doree, lately conspicuous in the bay windows of Pall Mall.[30]

Gewlecker

On 27 July the Brigade left Aladyn, after cholera broke out in the camp, to march to Gewlecker, but only stayed at this place until 16 August, as it was found to be as unhealthy as Aladyn. Captain Wilson describes the situation:

> From head-quarters arrived orders, directing all the soldiers to be employed in the manufacture of gabions;[31] thereon, the poor fellows, recorded 'fit for duty' in the 'morning states', marched every day to the woods, (distant about three miles from the camp) where they spent several hours; first, in cutting long limber twigs; and then, in twisting them, according to the teaching of intelligent sappers, into those queer bottomless baskets which figure so conspicuously in the interminable catalogue of siege stores. The knives and bill-hooks requisite for the work were issued to the 'fatigue parties' by the engineers. Pretty articles were those knives and bill-hooks – 'made', as the soldiers bitterly expressed it, 'for sale to government, not for our use!' No manufacturer who makes good articles has any chance of ever obtaining a. government contract for cutlery, as the goods required are so common and so low in price, that it is impossible to make an article worthy to receive any maker's name, who has any thought for his future standing in trade.
>
> In that sorrowful encampment of Gewleckler ministered not a few 'good Samaritans'. The watchfulness, the skill, the unwearying patience with which the regimental surgeons performed their important duties, were themes of almost universal recommendation. So it came to pass, that Mackenzie, Skelton, Bostock, Wyatt, Trotter, with many another, acquired the confidence and earned the gratitude and confidence of all ranks, which time, disease, and misery served only to widen and to strengthen. Albeit, the merits of these admirable surgeons waited a long time for official recognition. Assuredly, the doctors may comfort themselves with the reflection, that 'To some honours are given; to others, honour.'[32]

Captain Tipping describes the terrible fire at Varna, which destroyed half the town and a great deal of the stores of both armies. The French, who believed this arson was carried out by the Greeks, who were pro Russian, captured several Greeks behaving very suspiciously. They were summarily executed by order of the French higher command.

> A most fearful conflagration took place a few nights ago in Varna and there were scenes of the extraordinary kind going forward, during the fire, which burned down more than half the town. The soldiers broke into the spirit stores, and some of them died at the casks, vowing eternal fidelity and that nothing but death should part them. One fellow was burned to death from the barrel igniting, while he was tapping it. The powder magazine was surrounded with flames and our 50th Regiment climbed to the top of the roof of the building then spread blankets, over which they poured water, and thus saved our powder stores from destruction.[33]

Varna

It was decided that Varna was a more healthy place for the Brigade to camp, prior to embarking for the Crimea.

Captain Wilson describes the dismal march of the very dispirited and downcast troops back to Varna:

August 16. – The Brigade of Guards turned their backs on Gewleckler abhorred graveyard of their goodly kind. Seldom has there been a more dismal march. The men were very ghosts of the rosy giants, who, but six short months before had stepped so cheerily across Waterloo Bridge, now plodded along in gloomy silence. Not the most tremulous version of a song, not the feeblest effort at a. joke proceeded from the haggard ranks; and, worst sign of all, even tobacco had fallen to a discount. When the British Grenadier loses his voice, 'chaffs' not, and is careless about blowing a cloud, be sure there must be something very wrong; and yet, 'twas the flesh alone that ailed, the spirit was willing as ever; ay, that it was!

In a few days, the whole British force had fallen back upon Varna, and was scattered about the high ground to the South, wherever clear spaces and potable water could be discovered. Presently, the health of the troops began to improve; the change of air and scene, the hope of going at something soon, had evidently given the rare fellows a salutary fillip, for there was more bustle, more coming and going among them, conversation was carried on in louder tones, laughter, even, made itself heard sometimes; nevertheless cholera still lurked in our neighbourhood, creeping into our tents the moment we began to congratulate ourselves on freedom from the curse. Russell is, as usual, close upon the mark, in estimating them as follows: The Duke's Division (first) has lost 160 men, of these 100 belonged to the Guards. In the Brigade of Guards there were, before the march to Varna, upwards of 600 men sick.[34]

Captain Tipping describes camp conditions at Galata, near Varna:

The tents are all dripping wet, everything inside ditto, and your clothes sticking to the skin, as if glued on. Such a tremendous hurry skurry. Mules are all to be packed to the sound of bugles. The tents thrown down at the same moment, at a signal from the instrument, whatever the state of its interior may be, the men let go the ropes, and in a second, everything is suddenly transformed, from, as it were the midst of the town, to that of the field, where you are sometimes caught with one stocking on and one stocking off, or trying to get your arm through a damp sleeve in your shirt, as the first had penetrated, and then sticking half way. However here we stay, I believe till we embark, soon that these measures will not take place again, for, at any rate, a week or 10 days.[35]

Embarkation

Captain Wilson describes the embarkation:

On August 28, at ten p.m., the companies' orderlies bawl, amongst the tents of the Guards Brigade, 'Be ready to go on board ship at six am tomorrow.' Early on Tuesday, the 29th, the Guards and Highlanders marched for the beach; the soldiery in highest spirits, and looking all the better for the bustle of the past night.

After standing for a couple of hours in thawing columns on the hot sandy beach, we found ourselves on board ship, sitting down to a plenteous lunch of cold mutton, Cheshire cheese, and 'Bass'; ample justice was naturally done to the hospitable cheer, and right merry and content we were; the die being cast, speculative arguments as to the future ceased, and every man braced himself to a determination to do his duty – come weal, come woe.

Sea air and wholesome ship rations are certainly magical restoratives, for our men, lately pale and languid, are growing quite ruddy and playful; notwithstanding, there's no casting loose the foul fiend cholera.[36]

Captain Tipping expresses his happiness that they are embarking for the Crimea:

We came on board at a few hours notice, and have been lying in the Bay for four or five days. We are all glad of the change, and hope to sail tomorrow or the next day for Baltchek Bay, where we all rendezvous, and then make our descent upon the Crimea. It'll be a splendid thing to see, and to have seen, and a capital thing to have had a part in, if Providence brings one out of it. If it depends upon British pluck, and military zeal, I'm sure we'd all succeed and then I hope we may see some prospect of a termination of the war.

The expedition is certainly on a magnificent scale; as far as the eye can see masses of vessels of all sorts and sizes. Such a fleet is a most formidable armament, when you add to those on the plan the fleet of vessels of war, which are three three-deckers and several others, carrying 90 and 91 guns each. Then the French line of steamers and transports, numbering about the same as our own, in addition to several Turkish men of war, and their force of about 10,000. We are about 50 miles from the Crimea now, so I expect we shall soon see our enemy.[37]

The Invasion Plan

The written orders from the Secretary of State for War, the Duke of Newcastle, instructed Lord Raglan that his first duty was to defend Constantinople. He was also informed by the Duke that the war aims of the Government were to check and repel the unjust aggression of Russia, and that there was no prospect of a safe and honourable peace until Sevastopol was taken, and the Russian fleet destroyed.

Lord Raglan was told by the Duke to find out as much as he could about Russian troop strengths in the Crimea and about the defences of Sevastopol. The maps available were unreliable and there was no clear idea of Russian troop strengths.

In the opinion of Lieutenant Colonel Ross-of-Bladensburg, the Coldstream Guards historian,[38] the Government suddenly decided on a change of policy to make Russia submit, as Russia had ignored both our diplomatic and our naval demonstrations. The country was losing its patience and wanted action. As the Army was not required to help the Turks, and since the Russians had raised the siege of Silistria, some other task had to be found for it to perform. The Government then accepted the first plausible scheme put forward, without considering the risks involved. It decided to take Sevastopol by a coup de main, although they were in ignorance of the strength, defences, armament and capacity of the fortress and had little idea of its layout.

The highly optimistic opinion of the Government assumed that the problem could be resolved in a few months and that the Army would not have to winter in the Crimea. The government knew that both the transport system for supplies and the medical services were defective, and that we had no reserves of troops to replace casualties and to reinforce the Army. It also had been informed by our diplomats that winter in the Crimea came in November, leaving only six weeks of good weather to carry out this task.

Furthermore, if this operation could not be successfully completed within the six weeks, it would be necessary to besiege this fortress. To complete such an operation successfully, sufficient troops would be required to construct and defend a trench system, and also to contain the enemy's field army. This would take time and no estimate had been made of the number of troops required to carry this out. However, the decision was taken to go ahead, despite the fact that our fleet had control of the Black Sea and that the Russian fleet was blockaded in Sevastopol.

Hence the descent on Sevastopol was in the nature of an afterthought; a crude design, hastily proposed and rashly adopted, without reflection or calculation, and concerted without reference to the commanders at the seat of war, who nevertheless were forced to accept it and were held responsible for its execution.[39]

On 29 June Lord Raglan received a despatch from the Duke of Newcastle, instructing him to prepare an expedition to take Sevastopol. Lord Raglan had little option than to comply, which he did against his better judgment.

Crimea

On 29 August the Brigade embarked at Varna and sailed to the Crimea. On 25 August 1854, Captain Goodlake, Coldstream Guards, writes that 'next Friday the Army sails for the Crimea'. He says that it will be an impressive sight to see the combined fleets of England, France and Turkey, 100,000 living souls going to attack Sevastopol, just like a review of the fleet at Spithead. 'The fleet will cover our landing,' but he says shrewdly that 'it will be a rougher job than the people of England expect.'[40]

Changes in Command

There were many changes in the command of the 1st Division, the Guards Brigade and its three battalions, the 3rd Grenadiers, the 1st Coldstream and the 1st Scots Fusilier Guards, during the Crimean War, as their commanders changed throughout the war, owing to death, disease, promotion or for other reasons.

The 3rd Division was formed by General Order, issued in May 1854, when the Division was in the Turkish Dominions. When it landed in the Crimea, it was commanded by HRH Major General the Duke of Cambridge, with Brigadier General Bentinck commanding the Guards Brigade. Colonel Thomas Wood commanded 3rd Grenadiers, Colonel C. Hay the 1st Coldstream and Colonel G. Dixon the 1st Scots Fusilier Guards.

Over this period of twenty-one months, there had been ten changes in the command of the 1st Division, involving six people, and in the Guards Brigade, nine changes, involving eight people. The figures for the three battalions were as follows: Grenadiers, eight changes and six people; Coldstream, nine changes and seven people; Scots Fusiliers, six changes and five people.

[**Author's Note:** Appendix C contains a description and a list of changes in command in date order for the 1st Division, the Guards Brigade and the three Battalions.]

Notes

1. Wilson, Capt C.T., *A Regimental Officer, Our Veterans of 1854*, Street, 1859, p.2.
2. *Ibid.*, p. 2.
3. Tipping, Capt A., 'Letters from the East during the Campaign of 1854', MS, pp. 1–2.
4. Wilson, pp. 3–4.
5. Tipping, vol. 1, pp. 9–10.
6. Wilson, p. 7.
7. *Ibid.*, p. 14.
8. *Ibid.*, pp. 20–2.
9. Springman, M., *Sharpshooter in the Crimea*, Pen & Sword, 2005, pp. 49–50.
10. Hamilton, Lt Gen Sir J.F., *The Origins & History of the First or Grenadier Guards*, vol. III, pp. 153–4 & Addenda, pp. xix-xx, John Murray, 1871.
11. Springman, p. 50.
12. Wilson, p. 15.
13. *Ibid.* pp. 25–6.

14. Tipping, vol. 1, p. 49.
15. Wilson, p. 26.
16. *Ibid.*, p. 32.
17. Springman, p. 31.
18. Wilson, p. 35. Omar Pacha was the Commander of the Turkish Army.
19. *Ibid*, pp. 44–6.
20. Lieutenant General Sir Thomas Picton. He commanded the 3rd Division in the Peninsular War. After a brilliant military career, he commanded the 5th Division at Quatre Bras and Waterloo, where he was shot leading one of his brigades in a charge against the French.
21. Tipping, vol. 1, pp. 93–4, 123 & 133.
22. *Encyclopaedia Britannica 1910–1911*, Cholera, p. 266.
23. Wilson, p. 49.
24. *Ibid.*, pp. 50–1.
25. Aegyptus, King of Aegyptus, demanded that his brother Danaus' fifty daughters marry his fifty sons. Danaus agreed but to each daughter he gave a dagger, so that they could murder their husbands on their wedding night. All were murdered except for one, who was spared by his wife.
26. Wilson, pp. 61–3.
27. *Ibid.*, pp. 63–4.
28. *Ibid.*, pp. 65–6.
29. *Ibid.*, pp. 67–8.
30. *Ibid.*, p. 75.
31. Gabions are cylindrical wicker baskets, filled with earth and stones and used to build fortifications.
32. Wilson, pp. 87–9.
33. Tipping, vol. 2, p. 6.
34. Wilson, pp. 91 & 93.
35. Tipping, vol. 2, pp. 7–8.
36. Wilson, pp. 97–8 & 101.
37. Tipping, vol. 2, p. 18.
38. Ross-of-Bladensburg, Lt Col M., *The Coldstream Guards in the Crimea*, Innes, 1896, pp. 52–6.
39. *Ibid.*, p. 54.
40. Springman, p. 23.

CHAPTER 4

The Landing at Old Fort and the Battle of the Alma, September–October 1854

Guards Brigade – Movements and Events

29 August	Embarked at Varna.
6 September	Having received orders, left Varna Bay and anchored in Balchik Bay.
7 September	Left Balchik Bay.
12 September	Off Eupatoria at noon.
14 September	Left Eupatoria at 1.00 pm.
	CRIMEA
14 September	Landed (without knapsacks) at Old Fort, Kalamita Bay, marched 3 miles inland and bivouacked.
16 September	Encamped.
19 September	Marched to a location between the Rivers Bulganak and Alma, and bivouacked.
20 September	The Battle of the Alma; at 7.30 am the British Army marched to the Alma and fought the Battle of the Alma, which started at 1.20 pm and ended at 5.45 pm. Bivouacked about 2 miles from the Alma in the old Russian Camp.
23 September	Marched over the steppe to the River Katcha and bivouacked.
24 September	Marched to the River Belbek and bivouacked 2 miles beyond.
25 September	Marshal St Arnaud resigns as C-in-C of the French Army and dies on 29 Sept. Marshal Canrobert becomes C-in-C.
25 September	Flank March, marched by Mackenzie's Farm to the Traktir Bridge over the River Tchernaya, and bivouacked on the Fediukine Heights at 9.00 pm.
26 September	Flank March, marched to Balaklava and bivouacked near Kadikoi.

2 October	The 1st Division marches to the Heights before Sevastopol and bivouacked near a windmill.
5 October	Tents issued.
15 October	General Liprandi arrives at Sevastopol with 25,000 Russian troops.
16 October	Divisional order issued on setting up a sharpshooting unit consisting of ten privates from each of the three Guards Battalions.
17–19 October	First Bombardment of Sevastopol.
24 October	Soldiers at work for four out of five nights.
25 October	The Battle of Balaklava, from 10.00 am to 4.30 pm.
26 October	Little Inkerman, defence of the British position on its being attacked by the Russian reconnaissance in force.
2 November	Knapsacks, left on board ship, are received by the Grenadiers and Scots Fusilier Guards.
5 November	The Battle of Inkerman, from 6.30 am to 5.00 pm.

The Invasion of the Crimea

Without accurate maps it had been necessary to reconnoitre the coastline to find a suitable landing site. Lieutenant General Sir George Brown and Marshal Canrobert had made the first reconnaissance and had chosen the Katcha River as a landing site. On 8 September 1854, Lord Raglan, together with these two officers and others, had made a second reconnaissance. Lord Raglan had decided on Eupatoria as a landing site for the Army.

On 29 August, 1 Grenadiers, 1,000 strong had embarked at Varna in the *Simoon*;[1] 1 Coldstream, consisting of twenty-six officers and 737 men, had embarked at Varna for the Crimea. The Battalion was divided into two wings: the left wing and headquarters sailed in the *Simoom* with the Grenadiers, and the right wing were on board the *Tonning*.[2] The strength of 1 Scots Fusilier Guards was thirty-one officers and 701 other ranks. They had sailed in the *Kangaroo*.[3]

The British Army numbered 26,000 infantry, 2,000 cavalry and sixty guns. The five divisions – the 1st Division, made up of the Guards Brigade and the Highland Brigade, the 2nd, 3rd, 4th and Light Divisions – were each about 5,000 strong. The Cavalry Division, which consisted of the Light Brigade and the Heavy Brigade, was around 2,000 strong. The French had four infantry divisions, each about 7,000 in all, no cavalry and sixty-eight guns, making a total force of around 28,000, the same size as the British Army. There were also 5,000 Turks attached to the French Army.

This impressive armada sailed towards the coast of the Crimea. On 14 September 1854 the troops disembarked, without any opposition from the enemy, at Old Fort, Kalamita Bay, marched 3 miles inland and bivouacked.

Baggage and Tents

The Treasury had assumed that the Army would be able to acquire transport locally. Therefore no capacity was reserved by the British Army to carry baggage horses in their transports, but they were wrong and the British Army was unable to provide horses to carry tents and baggage for its troops. The French and the Turkish Armies were properly provided with transport and their men had tents, while the British Army's troops slept in the open air.

Each division was only allowed nine arabas or carts, of which four were allowed for entrenching tools, two for general officers, two for tents and medical stores, and one for the sick and casualties on the line of march. Owing to the shortage of carts, the soldiers' packs were left on board ship, as the Medical Department advised Lord Raglan that the soldiers were too weak to carry their packs. The battalion commanding officers were not consulted over this. The officers and other ranks had to roll up what they needed in a blanket roll, which was carried across their shoulder and chest. For three and a half months they had no changes of clothing and all ranks were covered in lice by the time the packs were delivered to the men. When the packs were recovered many items of kit had been stolen and some never saw their packs again.

Lieutenant Colonel Lord Frederick Paulet's two companies of the Coldstream Guards retained their packs. In his letter of 1 January 1855, Goodlake reports that on that day 1 Coldstream had at last received its baggage. The Grenadiers and the Scots Fusilier Guards received their baggage on 2 November.

Goodlake had to reduce the kit he took with him to the Crimea, as all officers were restricted to having one pack animal, which can carry 20 stone (280 lb). This load had to include a pack saddle, bed, bedding, canteen, riding saddle, rope trunks, covers, etc., so there was little room for luxuries. He discarded his waterproof bed, 28 lb, for a wooden stretcher, 15 lb.[4]

The March to the Alma

The armies marched towards the River Alma, with the French on the right, with their right flank next to the sea and protected by the Fleet. The British were on the left, with their open flank being patrolled by their cavalry. The troops marched in column, with the Light Division leading on the left flank, with the 2nd Division marching parallel to it and the 1st Division marching behind the Light Division. Many men fell out through the effect of cholera or thirst.

Captain Tipping complained that after sleeping in the open air, he awoke feeling just like a dead rabbit – as stiff as a poker and soaking in dew. He describes some of the incidents which occurred on the march:

There has been no provision made for transporting either tents or baggage. We have to carry on our own shoulders, whatever they have, unless, as some have contrived to do, one can find a strong pony of the country to carry our provisions, which consist of hard sea biscuit. On the first day of landing we procured some fowls from the country people; however the French have been before us, and ransacked every cottage for food, so we shall get no more here, but perhaps we may do so as we go on further. I firmly believe this to be the first instance on record, in which officers were required to carry their baggage and provisions, without the smallest assistance from man or beast.

That night we were all well asleep, when a cry roused us 'Guards turn out and stand to your arms'. The night was pitch dark, and the clanking of the firearms suddenly snatched up by the men, who rushed to the point marked out as the rendezvous in case of alarm, which sounded exactly like what we were led to expect, viz, a troop of Cossacks galloping into the bivouac.

The darkness prevented our finding anything we wanted, but by groping about, I at last secured something to cover my head, and a weapon to repel an invader, and without waiting to ascertain what pistol or cap I had appropriated, made off as fast as I could to the rendezvous. I soon found however that the last was not made for me, as before had gone twenty yards, it had dropped down to my nose, I had not long joined my company when I heard a man swearing in either his bearskin had run in, or his head had swelled out for it would not fit for any price. So the truth flashing on me, I rushed up and found my unfortunate cap, going through a variety of operations in order to increase its natural dimensions. I suggested an exchange and we both happily found that the caps fitted.[5]

The Battle of the Alma

Prince Menshikov, the commander of the Russian Army, had drawn up his troops on the slopes of a line of hills, along the south bank of the Alma River.

Lieutenant Colonel Ross-of-Bladensburg in his book, *The Coldstream Guards in the Crimea*, describes the field of battle as follows:

It is a sloping plain from the north to the river, which is fordable in summer. From the south bank the land rises to a height of 300 to 400 feet. This commanding range of hills overlooks the plain, and runs from the sea, for a distance of five miles, to a bluff, called Kourgane Hill. The river makes a trifling bend, forming a slightly re-entering angle towards these heights, on the western side of Kourgane; and here the post-road crosses the stream, close to the village of Bourliuk, by a wooden bridge, which had not been destroyed. This point marks the junction of the British right and the French left. The Russian Army, numerically weaker than the Allies, being 33,000 infantry, 3,400 cavalry and 120 guns, occupied the plateau. The main portion, 21,000 infantry, 3,000 cavalry, and 84 guns, was placed on Kourgane and on the post-road, opposite the British section; the remainder, 12,000 infantry, 400 cavalry and 36 guns, near the post-road and on Telegraph Hill, were opposed to the French. The cavalry took post on the enemy's right and rear, supported by horse artillery; but no troops were further to the west, where

Map of the Battle of the Alma, 2nd Period opposite p. 189, *History of the Grenadier Guards, Hamilton.*

SHEWING 2ND PERIOD OF THE BATTLE OF THE ALMA.

Pl. LXI.

Highland Brigade crossing the river

Coldstreams crossing river, and reforming

Vineyards

HIGHLANDERS RELIEVING BULLER'S BRIGADE

Buller's Brigade

Lord R. 95

Lord R. 95

1ST DIVISION AFTER ACTION

1ST DIVISION

S.F.G. reforming

S.F.G. reforming

1st BRIG: Lt. DIV: reforming

Grenadiers

Grenadiers

Former position of Grenadier Brigade

THIRD DIVISION AFTER ACTION

Adams's Brigade crossing the river

Bourljouk

Advance of Campbell's Brig: 3rd Division

Advance of Campbell's Brig:

ADAMS'S BRIGADE crossing the river AFTER THE ACTION

the ground was under fire from the warships. Menshikov, however, forgot, although he had time at his disposal, to block the roads which ascend the cliffs and the precipitous hillsides opposite the French position. Nor did he construct fieldworks on his front and right flank, contenting himself with only two gun-epaulments on Kourgane, one of which, about 300 yards from the river, was armed with 14 heavy guns of position.[6]

The Greater Redoubt, which was opposite the British attack, was constructed on rising ground about 700 yards south of the river. It commanded the road to Sevastopol, which ran from the north through the village of Bourliuk and past the British left, over a bridge over the river, only suitable for foot traffic. Prince Menshikov assured the Tsar that he could hold this position for three weeks against all the efforts of the allies.

The plan of attack, which Lord Raglan and Marshal St Arnaud agreed upon, was for the French Army to march to the mouth of the Alma, cross the river and climb the heights, and then move to attack the main force of the Russians, which faced the British assault. Their assault would be supported by the fire of the combined fleets on the enemy's positions.[7] A direct frontal attack by the British was decided upon. A left-flanking attack was rejected, as it would lay the troops open to attack by the Russian cavalry, which greatly outnumbered the British cavalry.

Shortly after 1.00 pm on 20 September, the attack began. The Light Division, on the left wing of the British Army, led the attack, with Brigadier General Codrington, Coldstream Guards, commanding 2 Brigade of the Light Division, with the Guards Brigade directly behind. On the right of the line, in line with the Light Division, Brigadier Pennefather commanded 1 Brigade of the 2nd Division. The British line was much confused by the Russians firing the village of Bourliuk, which upset its alignment.

The first line of attack went through the vineyard and crossed the river, which in most places was only waist deep; in some places the depth was breast high, and in others it was only ankle deep. The attacking troops had lost some of the regularity of their original formation in passing through the vineyard and the several fords of the river. They therefore continued their attack in somewhat loose order, but achieved their objective of storming the Greater Battery. However it became clear that the attack would fail without further support, and in the face of the arrival of large Russian reinforcements on the battlefield.

Before this happened, Lord Raglan and his staff rode through the skirmishing lines, where one ADC was wounded, and on to a hill, overlooking the British attack, from which the Russians had only recently retired. Lord Raglan ordered up a troop of guns, which successfully enfiladed the Russian position and caused their artillery to withdraw to avoid being captured. But as he was not in a position that enabled him to issue orders to the Army as the battle developed, command of the army was now in the hands of the Quartermaster-General, Brigadier General Airey, who ordered the 1st Division to advance and support the attack.

The Guards Brigade passed through the vineyard and crossed the river. The Scots Fusilier Guards were the first over, while Colonel Hood ordered his Grenadiers to lie under the river bank, until they were all over and together in one line. When Brigadier General Bentinck ordered the Scots Fusilier Guards to support the attack without delay, they had not had time to dress their ranks in line. They charged in a mass and some soldiers had to ask their officers if they should fix bayonets. When they met the retiring troops of the Brigade, commanded by Brigadier General Codrington, they were not in a position to open their ranks and let them through, and as a result some were carried back. Meanwhile, the Grenadiers and Coldstream crossed the river, dressed their lines and advanced towards the enemy. The Scots Fusilier Guards quickly reformed and caught up with the other two battalions. The Brigade advanced on the battery, with the Grenadiers and the Scots Fusilier Guards firing directly at it, while the Coldstream, being on the left of the line, fired obliquely at the Battery. At the same time, the Highland Brigade was carrying out a left-flanking movement. This action further confused the enemy and, faced by the strength of the attack and the continuous fire of the Brigade of Guards, the enemy retreated in disorder.

Scots Fusilier Guards

Summarized below is the account of the Battle of the Alma, given by Major General Sir F. Maurice in his *History of the Scots Guards*.

The numbers of the Battalion engaged were 26 officers, 53 sergeants, 18 drummers, and 694 rank and file.

The officers commanding companies were:

Right Flank, Lieutenant Colonel Dalrymple.	No. 4, Lieutenant Colonel Berkeley.
No. 1, Captain Hon. S. Jocelyn.	No. 5 Lieutenant Colonel Hepburn.
No. 2, Lieutenant Colonel Haygarth.	No. 6 Lieutenant Colonel Seymour.
No. 3, Captain Viscount Chewton.	Left Flank Lieutenant Colonel Stephenson.

The Russian force, which had come out from Sevastopol to dispute the passage of the Alma, comprised about 3,400 sabres, 33,000 infantry and 120 guns, under the command of Menshikov. Against this, Lord Raglan had 1,000 sabres, 33,000 infantry and sixty guns, and St Arnaud about 35,000 French and Turks. Believing that the cliffs close to the sea were too steep to attack, he posted none of his troops there and had the bulk of his force on the ridge east of the main road, with his reserve near that road and behind the left centre; apart from the works for the protection of his guns, he had made no entrenchments.

Lord Raglan and St Arnaud reconnoitred the position and made their plan of attack. It was then agreed that the French move first and climb up to the plateau under the covering fire of the fleet, and that when they were well on their way, the British should attack the Russian position in front.

The British advanced with the 2nd Division on the right and the Light Division on the left of the first line. In the second line the 3rd Division followed the 2nd, and the 1st Division followed the Light Division. The portion of the valley of the Alma, to which our troops were advancing, was a distance of about 2 miles. Almost all these 2 miles on the north bank of the river were occupied by gardens and vineyards, enclosed with stone walls. As our skirmishers advanced they were met in the village and in the vineyards by Russian skirmishers, who were driven back, but not before the village of Bourliuk had been set on fire. The 2nd and Light Divisions were deployed with some difficulty owing to the fire and to the enclosures in the valley.

Lord Raglan then gave the order to attack and galloped off with a few of his staff round the burning village, across the Alma to a knoll north of Telegraph Hill, where he was in considerable personal danger and, as we have seen, could exercise no control whatever over the battle. The 1st Battalion of the Regiment was to suffer heavily because of this wild action of the Commander-in-Chief.

The 2nd Division was delayed by the burning village, and Brown's Light Division was the first to attack. Codrington went on with his two battalions, with two battalions, the 95th and the 55th, of the 2nd Division advancing on his right. These men swarmed up the slope towards the Great Redoubt and to their amazement the Russians made no attempt to defend it. Had Codrington been properly supported the battle might well have been won sooner and with much less loss. But there was no one keeping a watchful and directing eye on the battle such as Wellington had kept at Waterloo.

The 1st and 3rd Divisions, without orders, lay in the valley under the long-range fire of the Russian guns. When the enemy saw the British were in the Great Redoubt they turned their guns upon them and soon forced them to take cover on its north side, where they were attacked on either side by Russian columns. Just then a British bugler blew the 'Cease-Fire' followed by 'Retreat', the Brigade fell back slowly, harried by heavy fire from the Russian batteries, and tumbled back in a confused mass right into the advancing line of the Scots Fusilier Guards.

In the Guards Brigade, the Grenadiers were on the right, near the road to Sevastopol, the Scots Fusilier Guards were in the centre and the Coldstream on the left.

When the Guards Brigade came down into the valley and reached the walled enclosures of the gardens and vineyards, General Bentinck ordered the battalions to get through the vineyards and across the river in any way they could do so, and to reform on the far side. On the right, part of the Grenadiers crossed by the bridge and part waded the river; on the left, the Coldstream crossed the river at an S-bend and had to wade the river three times. In the centre, the Scots Fusilier Guards moved through the vineyards, got across the river in a rough line, being the first of the Brigade across it. It was in the process of forming up in the shelter of the dead

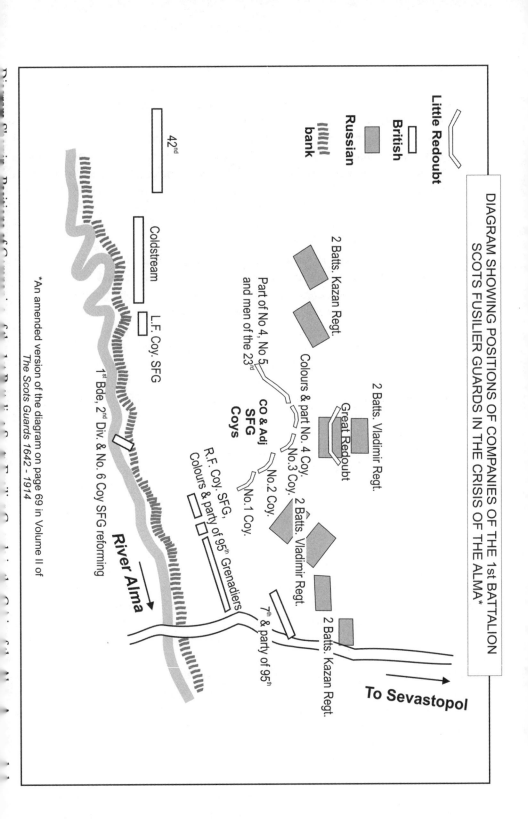

DIAGRAM SHOWING POSITIONS OF COMPANIES OF THE 1st BATTALION
SCOTS FUSILIER GUARDS IN THE CRISIS OF THE ALMA*

Little Redoubt

British

Russian
bank

42nd

Coldstream

L.F. Coy. SFG

2 Batts. Kazan Regt.

Part of No 4, No 5
and men of the 23rd

Colours & part No. 4 Coy.

CO & Adj
SFG
Coys

2 Batts. Vladimir Regt.

Great Redoubt

No.3 Coy.

No.2 Coy.

No.1 Coy.

2 Batts. Vladimir Regt.

R.F. Coy. SFG,
Colours & party of 95th Grenadiers

River Alma

1st Bde, 2nd Div. & No. 6 Coy SFG reforming

7th & party of 95th

2 Batts. Kazan Regt.

To Sevastopol

*An amended version of the diagram on page 69 in Volume II of
The Scots Guards 1642 - 1914

ground on the south bank, when General Bentinck ordered it to advance at once. The Left-flank Company had then not come up, being delayed crossing the river.

On receiving Bentinck's order the Battalion advanced without waiting to complete its formation. The remaining seven companies moved up the slope and were about halfway between the river and the Great Redoubt when they were met by the retreating mass of Codrington's Brigade, which swept back the 6th and a part of the 5th companies on the left, and caused some confusion in the others. A number of men of the Light Division rallied to the Battalion and advanced with it. The Scots Fusilier Guards got within about 30 yards of the Great Redoubt, where they found themselves unsupported with two strong bodies of Russians from the Kazan Regiment, on either flank, while its right and centre were swept with canister at point-blank range by a Russian battery on its right front. Sir Charles Hamilton ordered the Battalion to halt and to open fire. Just then someone rode up to Sir Charles Hamilton and shouted 'Fusiliers Retire'. Captain Gipps (later General Sir Reginald Gipps) was near Hamilton at the time and was positive as to the receipt of the order. It was probably meant for the 7th or 23rd Fusiliers, which were to the right of Codrington's brigade, but the order came by mistake to the Scots Fusilier Guards. Fortunately the officers of the right companies, seeing the Grenadiers coming up, stopped the retreat and proceeded to rally their men to the colours.

At this time the five and a half companies with Sir Charles Hamilton were formed in a rough triangle with the colour party at its apex, some 50 yards from the Great Redoubt. The 4th and part of the 5th Company, with some men of Codrington's brigade who rallied to them, formed the left side of the triangle. The 3rd, 2nd and 1st Companies in a ragged line formed the right side [see diagram on page 43].

The colour party consisted of Lieutenant R.J. Lindsay, afterwards Lord Wantage, who carried the Queen's Colour, and Lieutenant Thistlethwayte, who had the Regimental Colour. For a time it was almost isolated and surrounded by the enemy, for by now a column of the Vladimir Regiment had come over the Great Redoubt. The little party, inspired by Lindsay's gallant bearing, and aided by part of No. 4 Company, stood fast long enough to enable the right of the Battalion to rally on it. Captain Viscount Chewton, commanding the 3rd Company, was wounded and badly mauled by the men of the Vladimir Regiment. Captain Haygarth, commanding No. 2 Company, was also wounded and was also bayoneted by a Russian. Lieutenant Colonel Dalrymple, who commanded the Right-flank Company, formed it on the left of the Grenadiers as soon as they came in line.

On the left of the Battalion, the 5th and half of the 6th Company were engaged with two battalions of the Kazan Regiment, and were hard-pressed when they were in turn relieved by the Coldstream. This Battalion had been delayed in crossing the river and had formed up on its markers in dead ground on the south bank. It now came forward in splendid line with the Left-flank Company of the Scots Fusilier Guards on its right. The Coldstream drove back the Kazan Regiment in its stately progress. The remainder of the 5th and 6th Companies rallied to the Left-flank Company of the Battalion, which had been born back in the retreat of Codrington's brigade. Then the whole line of the Guards was reformed.

The Highland Brigade, in echelon of battalions from the right, forced the Russians to withdraw their guns from the Lesser Redoubt, and bringing forward with them the right of Buller's brigade of the Light Division, bore back Menshikov's right. In the centre were the left column of the Kazan Regiment's two battalions, shattered by the gallant stand of the 7th Fusiliers and the left-wing of the 95th, the Vladimir Regiment of four battalions, which had advanced over and on the other side of the Great Redoubt against the Scots Fusilier Guards, and the right column of the Kazan Regiment of two battalions, which had been held in check by the 5th Company of the Scots Fusilier Guards and the right of Buller's brigade.

Now with the Grenadiers and Coldstream up and the Scots Fusilier Guards reformed, the fire of the line of the Guards, supported on the right by the 7th and 95th, and on the left by the Highlanders, broke the resistance of these eight battalions. The Russians were soon in retreat and the British lines swept forward, gaining touch with Canrobert's division, which was occupying Telegraph Hill. The stand of the Scots Fusilier Guards checked the advance of the Vladimir Regiment just long enough to prevent this and to enable the Guards Brigade to form a complete line.

After the battle the Duke of Cambridge thanked Lieutenant Lindsay before the Guards Brigade for his gallant stand. He later received the Victoria Cross.

Captain Lord Chewton was mortally wounded. The other wounded officers were: Lieutenant Colonels Berkeley, Dalrymple, Hepburn and Haygarth; Captains Astley, Bulwer, Buckley and Gipps; and Lieutenants Viscount Ennismore and the Hon. H. Annesley.

The casualties were 11 officers wounded, 43 rank and file killed, and 121 wounded, making a total of 175.[8]

Grenadier Guards

The strength of the Battalion on 20 September was 33 officers, 41 sergeants, 18 drummers and 781 rank and file, making a total of 873.[9]

Colonel Hamilton, the author of the history of the Regiment, was present throughout the battle, as Mounted Officer in charge of the Left Wing of the Battalion. Colonel Reynardson, the other Mounted Officer and the Adjutant, Captain Higginson, superintended the Right Wing; the officers commanding companies were as follows:

RIGHT WING	**LEFT WING**
No. 1, Lt Col A. Cox	No. 5, Lt Col S. Brownrigg
No. 2, Lt Col Prince Edward of	
Saxe Weimar	No. 6, Lt Col R. Bradford
No. 3, Lt Col Hon. G. Cadogan	No. 7, Lt Col Robert Pakenham
No. 4, Lt Col J. Reeve	No. 8. Lt Col Hon. H. Percy

Queen's Colour, Lt Viscount Balgonie; Regimental Colour, Lt Burgoyne, Lt Hamilton.

Colonel Hamilton's account of the battle is summarized below:

When the order was given to advance, the Battalion moved forward. The left wing advanced over stone walls and through vineyards, in which the companies could only advance by fours or in loose line formation; the right wing advanced over ground equally enclosed and cultivated, until the commanders of Nos 2 and 3 Companies found themselves opposite the half-ruined bridge. Forming fours inwards, they rushed over the bridge, while the rest of the Battalion dashed through the river, above and below the bridge. In many places the river was easily fordable, and did not reach above the middle; in others it was breast high.

Colonel Hood, seeing that his line was irregular, after passing through these obstacles, halted the leading files under the river bank, while the rear files moved up and the officers got their men into their correct places. With his Battalion now well in hand, he gave the order to advance. On mounting the river bank, the Battalion became exposed to the enemy's fire, but was unable to reply, as confused masses of our troops were in front and were mixed up with the enemy. After proceeding a few yards, the Regimental Colour was seen to fall, as Lieutenant Burgoyne, the bearer, having been hit in the ankle, went down; Lieutenant Hamilton immediately seized the Colour and carried it through the rest of the attack.

The Russians, who had been supported by numerous reinforcements, drove the British from the battery. The Brigade of Guards was at this moment approaching, the left of the Grenadiers and the right of the Fusiliers[10] being more immediately in front of the Great Battery. These two regiments, as they advanced, were met by the mass of the first line who, having done their duty and having been overwhelmed by superior numbers, were retiring to reform behind the oncoming supports.

The Grenadiers, being in line, were able to open their ranks to allow the detached parties to pass through, and then immediately reformed. The Fusilier Guards, being in a looser formation, were met by even larger bodies from the first line; these troops became mixed up with the Fusiliers, who, except for their Right-Flank Company, were carried back a short distance with them until they could extricate themselves and again form line [see diagram on page 43].

Colonel Hood, seeing that the Light Division had cleared his Battalion's front, opened fire on the opposing columns of Russians whilst still advancing. The Grenadiers had advanced to within a short distance of the battery, when two battalions of Russians, the 31st and 33rd Regiments, rushed over the parapets to pursue the first line. One column was advancing round the Battalion's left flank, and thus was threatening their rear. The Battalion was then halted and poured its fire onto the battery, while part of the Left-Flank Company was dressed back on the right, and began to pour a flanking fire on the Russians who were attempting to turn its flank. The Battalion was unsupported on both flanks, as the Scots Fusiliers had not yet come up level to them, and as the 2nd Division, delayed by the burning village, had not yet come up on the Grenadiers' right flank.

As gaps were made in the ranks of the Grenadiers, there were many eager volunteers from the line to fill the vacant places. Major Home, carrying one of his Regiment's (the 95th) Colours, with ten men, asked leave to fight with the Guards. They were directed to fall in on the left wing, as were the Right-Flank Company of the Fusiliers, commanded by Lieutenant Colonel Dalrymple, which had been reformed in the rear. By this time, the Fusiliers had advanced up to their former position and the Coldstream had come level with the Fusiliers' left flank. The Highland Brigade had executed their left-flanking movement and was pouring a heavy flanking fire into the Russian columns. The whole Guards Brigade, being in an unbroken line, poured its fire into the enemy, which finally gave way, and the Brigade advanced with a cheer, driving the Russians before them. The Grenadiers entered the battery, cleared it of the enemy and captured the remaining gun left there. The Guards Brigade continued its advance beyond the battery and bivouaced on the heights.

The Grenadier casualties were 4 officers wounded, 13 sergeants wounded, 11 men killed and 110 wounded. The officers wounded were Lieutenant Colonel Percy, Captain Rowley, Lieutenant J.M. Burgoyne and Lieutenant R.W. Hamilton.

After the battle, the Duke rode up to the Grenadiers and, calling Colonel Hood out to the front, publicly thanked him for the skill, judgement and coolness with which he had directed his Battalion, and the Grenadiers for the manner in which they had executed their advance that day.[11]

Coldstream Guards
Summarized below is the account of the battle given by Lieutenant Colonel Ross-of-Bladensburg in his book, *The Coldstream Guards in the Crimea*.[12]

There was a pause when the allies approached the position they were about to assail. In the interval, all eyes were turned to the Heights which frowned in front, and saw in the distance the hostile sharpshooters extended along the river, in the vineyards and gardens, through which the advance was about to be made. Nor were we unconscious that the whole of our force was easily to be discerned, and our intentions to be divined by our antagonist; for we halted boldly on the sloping plain, in full view of the enemy, who, perched on the higher ground, was enabled to make his observations and to conceal much of his own order of battle from our anxious gaze.[13]

The whole of the British Army, 23,000 infantry, 1,000 cavalry and 60 guns, [for part of the 4th Division was still on the road from Old Fort] covered by the Rifles, now moved straight for the enemy's strong position on Kourgane, the right being directed upon Bourliuk. The Russians skirmishers retired, setting fire to that village as the first line approached it; while the latter, coming nearly within range of the hostile artillery, deployed. But too little ground been taken up, and, in spite of every effort to rectify the mistake, the battalions overlapped and were dangerously crowded. Lord Raglan now delayed the attack, but Marshal St Arnaud urged his colleague to wait no longer. In response to this strong request, Lord Raglan ordered his first line to advance. The 2nd Division was delayed by the smoke from the conflagration, but the Light Division broke through the vineyards and forded the river. General Codrington, heading his Brigade, led them boldly up the slope under the fire of the battery behind the epaulment; on his right were three of Evans' battalions [2nd Division]. The other two crossed the river and pushed into the space to the west of the post-road.

The Russians, seriously alarmed by Codrington's impetuous onslaught, withdrew their heavy guns, except for two which were captured. The British gained the breastwork and took possession of it; but they now found themselves face to face with large masses of the enemy's infantry and cavalry, supported by field guns; it was the moment for the supports to arrive; but as they were not close enough to be available at this critical moment, the attacking brigade was soon afterwards forced back to the foot of the slope.

Meanwhile the 1st Division deployed and halted just beyond effective range of the enemies guns. On the right stood the Guards Brigade in their usual order, Grenadiers on the right, Coldstream on the left, and Scots Fusiliers in the centre; the Highlanders were formed on the left of the Division. Then Colonel Steele brought the order to advance. The troops pushed their way through the tangled shrubs, and over a low wall, obstructing their path up to the Alma which they immediately crossed. The Coldstream reached the river, where it makes a large S-shaped bend, so that the greater part of the Battalion had to go through the water three times. Owing to the many obstructions in their way, all three battalions were in considerable confusion when they arrived at the foot of the southern bank. Colonel Upton, having halted the Coldstream, called out the markers to the front, quickly assembled the companies upon them, and then wheeled the Battalion into line before making any further advance.

Meanwhile Codrington's brigade was engaged in a very unequal struggle with the enemy. This was apparent to General Bentinck, who immediately ordered the Scots Fusiliers to hurry to their relief, before they had been given sufficient time to reform the line, and while the ranks were still disordered and the companies mixed up. They eagerly complied with this order. However a backward rush of some of the Light Division struck them with tremendous force. In spite of the gallantry of the officers, who, running forward, endeavoured to rally the men, three companies were swept back by the retreating brigade towards the river, while the remainder halted, opened fire and held their ground.

As this was going on, the other two Guards' battalions, now completely reformed and in proper order, advanced steadily forward up the hill. Coming into alignment with the Scots Fusilier Guards, the left company of the Grenadiers was wheeled back and fired across the front, while the Coldstream, without changing position, opened upon the Russians as soon as they had the opportunity, and the latter retired.

Kinglake in his history of the campaign commented upon the Coldstream Guards steadfast behaviour as follows:

The Battalion was drawn up in line with beautiful precision; because of the position of the ground on which it advanced, it had been much less exposed to fire and mishaps than either of the other two Battalions of the Brigade, and it had not been pressed forward, as each of the other two battalions had been, to meet any special emergency occurring on its front. Therefore it fell to the lot of the Coldstream to become almost a prim sample of what our Guards can be in the moment which precedes a close fight. What the best of battalions is, when, in some Royal Park at home, it manoeuvres before a great princess that the Coldstream was now on the banks of the Alma, when it came to show its graces to the enemy. And it was no ignoble pride which caused the Battalion to maintain all this ceremonious exactness; for though it may be true that the position of a line in peacetime is only a success in mechanics, the precision of the line on a hillside with the enemy close in front, is the result and the proof of warlike composure.[14]

To our left, protecting the flank of the British Army, were the Highlanders in echelon of battalions from the right; and this magnificent corps, handled with great ability, fired into the hostile columns that passed them on their way to the epaulment and contributed in no small degree, to lighten the task of the Guards.

Pressing on forward, the British artillery took up positions and fired either upon the enemy's guns or into the solid masses of his infantry. The first onslaught of the Light Division had shaken the enemy, and now when opposed to the steady advance of the Guards and Highlanders, he did not long maintain the contest. The Russians were unable to fight in line and remained throughout the whole day in dense columns, which prevented the Russians from using their muskets, and offered a large target to our fire.

Moving as if on parade, the Guards in line, kept up a continuous and well-aimed stream of lead, at short ranges, into the masses in front of them, while the Highlanders, in echelon, succeeded in striking the right flank of the enemy. Unable to bear down on the thin lines that opposed them, the Russians wavered, and, with a ringing cheer, our men charged home, and drove them from the field. The British Army had cleared the formidable position held by the enemy. The Russian troops fled the field, and their retreat was so precipitate that it was not even covered by cavalry or artillery. The defeated enemy was not pursued, as Marshal St Arnaud refused to follow up the victory.

The Coldstream casualties were two officers and twenty-seven men wounded. Captain Cust, ADC to Major General Bentinck, died of his wounds immediately after the action. Captain F. Baring had his arm amputated.[15]

Notes

1. Hamilton, Lt Gen Sir George, *The Origins & History of the First or Grenadier Guards*, vol. 3., John Murray, 1871, p. 184.
2. Ross-of-Bladensburg, Lt Col, *The Coldstream Guards in the Crimea*, Innes, 1897, p. 45.
3. Maurice, Maj Gen Sir F., *The History of the Scots Guards*, vol. 2, Chatto & Windus, 1934, p. 56.
4. Springman, Michael, *Sharpshooter in the Crimea*, Pen & Sword. 2005, pp. 69–70.
5. Tipping, Capt A., 'Letters from the East during the Campaign of 1854', MS, pp. 29–36.
6. Ross-of-Bladensburg, p. 72.
7. Hamilton, vol. 3, pp. 184–6.
8. Maurice, pp. 62–77.
9. Hamilton, vol. 3, p. 184.
10. Scots Fusilier Guards.
11. Hamilton, vol. 3, pp. 185–98.
12. Ross-of-Bladensburg, pp. 76–94.
13. *Ibid.*, p. 74.
14. Kinglake, A.W., *The Invasion of the Crimea*, vol. 3, Blackwood, 1866, p. 426.
15. Ross-of-Bladensburg, pp. 76–94.

CHAPTER 5

The Battle of the Alma – Other Personal Accounts

Captain Tipping's Account of the Battle[1]

Captain Tipping, Grenadier Guards, in his 'Letters from the East', describes his experiences of the battle:

We were under arms an hour before daylight this morning, and we have now after dark, about 16 hours from the time we turned out in the morning, got into position, so that we may lie down and take out rest on the summit of a hill. God's mercy kept me safe today, when death was on every side. Poor fellows, torn to pieces by the most dreadful fire maintained in a murderous manner for several hours. Our gallant Regiment turned the fate of the day, as regarded our position. The Regiment before us was nearly annihilated I am told.

The poor fellows fell on each side of me, in all directions, some cut and smashed in the most appalling manner, but providentially I escaped, though balls and bits of shell in dozens have been, for at least an hour today, buzzing around my head like mosquitoes on a summer's evening. We have lost 107 men in our Regiment and five officers more or less wounded, some very slightly. One shell burst close to me, when I could not just help stooping involuntarily, and a piece big enough to cut my head into bits, just passed over me. Morrison [soldier servant] tells me that he happened to look round at the moment and it just cleared my head. He also escaped without a wound.

Wednesday 20th September

We were under arms at 6:00 a.m. and took ground to our right towards the French; after gaining about a mile in that direction, we were ordered to halt. We remained for about an hour, lying down on the ground, while a reconnaissance was made to the front. We were then ordered to march, the Light Division in advance, our Division next. The 2nd Division was in line with us. The 3rd and 4th Divisions remained as a reserve in the rear. In this order we marched for a considerable time, and it was not till 11 o'clock that we came in view of the village of Alma, and the heights overlooking it.

We could plainly see thousands of bayonets, glistening in the sun's rays on the top of the hill, and crowning some rising ground on the highest point of which was an unfinished building, which was evidently surrounded by a mass of troops. After halting for about half-an-hour, we again marched forward and now perceived smoke and flames issuing from the village in such dense masses, and from so many quarters at the same time that no doubt could exist, as to its having been fired by the enemy.

The further we proceeded, and the heavier became the roar of the cannon, and the great ponderous round shot came bounding along the ground like cricket balls. As the men saw them approaching, they opened their ranks, and the balls went hissing past in their resistless force. Having advanced rather too fast, we now received orders to lie down, so as to give time for the other divisions to form line. The recumbent position affording a better chance of escape, than that of standing upright, and while we remained thus prostrate, the shells came rushing through the air, some of them burst just before us, some over our heads, and others in rear. It was just about this time that poor Cust was struck, and his leg carried completely away, a loss which he survived but a very short time.

The smaller the space we placed between ourselves and the batteries, towards the very teeth of which we were now marching, the hotter became the fire. We were now within reach of the riflemen, who commenced making sad havoc in our ranks. Every now and then, a rattle close at hand, induced one to turn to the right or left, as it might happen, and then one saw some poor Fellow rolling over, his bayonet and musket clanking as they fell to the ground.

And then another hundred yards brought us to the vineyard which was bounded on one side by a low wall and on the other by the river. There we saw a line of red coats lying under the wall, and thought of course that they were all wounded men, who had dragged themselves there as a partial shelter from the pelting storm of bullets. However I was sorry to see some few amongst them apparently unwounded and uninjured, except in the nervous system. One poor fellow, who had lost both legs, raised a feeble cheer, as we scrambled over the little vineyard wall, and throwing up his shako cap into the air, shouted out 'Go it beauty Guards. Go in and win.' This must have been pretty much his last cheer, poor fellow. We scurried through the vineyard, and down to the river, under a perfect hail storm of bullets, crossed the river and scrambled up the opposite bank.

We had passed through a vineyard, all entrenched and prepared for months beforehand, and then had to jump into and cross a river, some swam, some rushed over the bridge. I saw a ford, where, for a few yards, the stones were so high that one could cross ankle-deep. Grapeshot, six-pound round shot and literally musket balls like hail stones, came down upon us in the vineyards and river. On every side were bullets by thousands, I am sure one may say this without exaggeration. Nine of my company dropped. One poor fellow, exactly before me, receiving the bullet which would otherwise have been mine.

Notwithstanding all entreaties, Colonel Hood, displaying all the time the utmost coolness and decision, waited patiently till all his men were in line. He then gave the word to rise. Up we jumped all together, and formed a steady line on the opposite bank. After crossing the river, we found right in our faces a Regiment of Russians, charging down the Hill, and firing right into us, over the heads of the 95th, which were in full retreat towards us. They were pursued by the Russian infantry, which were delivering a murderous fire into them. We found the poor fellows had exhausted all their ammunition, and were obliged to retire. We opened to let them pass through and fall behind. At that moment we received another awful volley of bullets from several battalions of Russians, who are about half way up the opposite hill. Many men fell now.

The order to fire was then given to us, and the Regiment being all in line, gave a cool, deliberate aim at the advancing column, and poured into them such a shower of Minie bullets, as rather checked their onward pace. Still on they came, our men coolly reloading, as if it were only a drill in Hyde Park, and discharging another withering volley, at about 150 yards distance. That concentrated and well directed fire completely staggered the Russians, and in addition to this, Sir Colin Campbell had just brought his brigade of Highlanders over the crest of the rising ground, to the left of the battery, which had done such execution upon the Fusilier Guards.

It was here that young Burgoyne fell wounded in the leg. I'm told this morning that he has lost his leg. Our Regimental Colour, which he had been carrying, was immediately picked up by another Ensign in the Regiment. He had not long taken possession of them, before he received a bullet through the left side of his coat, grazing the flesh, but not doing any serious injury [Lieutenant Hamilton]. His sword turned the ball, which he found between his shirt and his body, after the action.

It was painful to be obliged continually to order the men to close up, as the gaps were made in the ranks by the falling of their comrades; however as fast as they could load, we kept up a continual fire upon the enemy, whom to our great delight, we now saw turn round and commence a retrograde movement up the hill, towards their encampment of the morning.

Volley after volley were poured into the retreating foe, telling fearfully amongst so dense a mass. Two heavy pieces of artillery were now brought up, and deliberate aim taken by them upon the retreating masses, which, at a few hundred yards distance, were rushing up a gorge in the most glorious confusion.

Our gallant Regiment stood in line as if in Hyde Park, the enemy coming down to within eighty or hundred yards, and there was firing from behind the Hill as well. We delivered our fire, and they dropped by dozens, another, and another volley, and the cool determined stand we made in that awful bottom, cut them down in crowds, as they came on.

At last a cheer on the right announced that they had turned. We drove them up the hill, killing them all the way up and captured a great brass gun. We pursued them until the artillery overtook us and committed fearful destruction, as the enemy retired up the opposite hill.

The first shell fired from one of the two guns just brought up, exploded right in the middle one of retiring battalions, and for half a minute, cleared a place all around. The vacant places of those who fell, being soon filled up, when another, and another dropped amongst them, and we could have continued for some time longer, reducing their numbers by scores at each volley. The enemy were beaten, and well beaten too, and both that, and every other grave error committed, will be forgotten in the glorious results of such a hard fought and desperately resisted attack on the strongest place the Russians possess in the Crimea, of course excepting Sevastopol.

It was then between 5 and 6 o'clock, and we could not pursue them for having been so long at work; our cavalry being quite outnumbered by the enemy.

We remained on the ground, to send back for the wounded, for an hour and a half, and then marched up in the dark, to the top of a hill, to prevent the possibility of being attacked at night.

The whole extent of the position must have been about 2 miles and a half in length. Not more than 12 or 14,000 British were actually engaged, but the two other divisions were supporting, if we had been obliged to fall back. They hardly fired a shot. The Russians are in full retreat to Sevastopol. They have brought in a Russian General and made him a prisoner. He says, 'We expected to see brave men but not Devils.'

Lord Raglan came up to the place, where we are bivouacked today, he confessed that Busaco[2] was nothing to this in point of strength and position. In fact I believe he had thought too little of his enemy, and was taken aback by the tremendous position, which had been fortified for months. They were so certain that it would require three weeks of sapping and engineering for us to take it from them, that they had invited a number of ladies to come out from Sevastopol to the Heights, and to see the manoeuvring below. Our having driven them out in three hours has quite astonished their weak minds.

I believe the real strength of the position on the Alma, being unknown, was a most fortunate circumstance, and tended much to the success of the attack. The prisoners, who have been taken, confirm this opinion, and say, we were all mad or fools, to attempt to take the place in the manner we did. Our generals could hardly have been aware of its strength. The enemy had skilfully concealed one of the strongest batteries, by firing the village, and it was these formidable entrenchments that we stormed and took.

A letter from Menshikov to the Czar, which we intercepted, says in speaking of Alma, 'I can hold this place for three weeks, against hundred thousand men.' It was taken in three hours. We had only 12,000 of our men actually engaged, but the sort of reckless daring, in going right up to the very guns of the battery, so astonished the natives that they were far more flabbergasted than if the usual mode of attack had been resorted to by sapping, and approaching by entrenchments. I believe the moral effect has saved us much and established such a wholesome fear, that they will attack us now with but half the pluck that they showed at Alma.

A Russian general whom we have captured says that they estimate their loss at from 4000 to 5000 killed and wounded. I was mistaken in thinking that our killed outnumbered theirs At the time I wrote, I could judge from what was before me, and as the field of battle was about 5 miles in length, you may imagine that I could go over a limited portion of it. I think our loss is about 2000.

1 October, Kamara

The French and all concur in our having had almost insuperable obstacles to surmount, and they say that our soldiers accomplished more than was ever done before. The Russians had 32 pounders covered by earth-works, in fact all their weapons had been prepared for weeks. They had 102 guns, all in position and fortified. We were perfectly ignorant of the strength of the position, I believe our very ignorance was providential, for they were so astonished at the bare fact of our attempting to attack such a fortress, without siege guns, or the usual preparations for such an undertaking, that it increased their notion of the invincibility of the allied forces, and perhaps may in the end prevent so stubborn a resistance at Sevastopol, as we expect.

Captain Wilson on the Battle of the Alma

Captain Wilson, Coldstream Guards, in his book *Our Veterans of 1854 in Camp & before the Enemy* makes the following observations on the battle:[3]

September 18, 8 p.m.

The soldiers, in highest spirits at the prospect of the coming battle, are singing lustily, round the watch-fires, 'Rule Britannia', and 'The British Grenadiers'. Noble fellows! They will pull us through anything, in spite of anybody!

Let us enquire how it happened that, while the French, whose transport fleet was small compared with ours, landed in the Crimea with a complete service of hospital carts and mules, and, moreover, were so well furnished with bat-horses, that the administration undertook the carriage of the regimental officers' baggage (at rate of one horse between five officers). The English army, sustained by the most magnificent fleet of transports the world ever saw collected, went forth to battle unprepared; its regimental officers limping along under the unfamiliar weight of their luggage; with its sick unprovided for: those paltry stretchers and their concomitant drummers being downright mockeries. Most of this destitution may doubtless be set down to a simple cause, viz, military inexperience-ignorance of the requirements of war.

Let us hastily survey the field of battle. The Russians were posted on a range of hills, which, taking root, so to speak, on the sea-shore, stretches eastward for about five miles, and terminates in a bluff forming the right of their position. Upon well-chosen spots of the exterior slopes of the ridge (which is deeply scored with ravines) entrenchments, armed with 24-pounder, and 32-pounder brass guns, had been thrown up, numerous field-batteries of 9-pounder and 32-pounder howitzers being in support. This artillery – in all nearly ninety-six guns, we are told, had been so judiciously distributed, so that our flanks must wince under an enfilading fire.

Along the northern base of the hills, at a distance of perhaps four hundred yards, flows the Alma, an insignificant stream, everywhere fordable. Its banks are unequal, averaging on the left (Russian) side six feet, and being, in general, nearly level with the water on the right (Allied) side. Vineyards and orchards fringe the edges of the river but the right edge alone is studded with houses, which are set wide apart, amid gardens. On the point, where a little bridge conducts the post-road (from Eupatoria to Sevastopol) across the Alma, is clustered a handful of huts, called the village of Bourliouk, its site being nearly opposite the centre of the Russian position.

The enemy possessed advantages over us. His entire front was covered by a river, he was posted on the summits of rocks, from which the fall to the waters' edge was broken, and occasionally precipitous. In the nooks and crannies of the cliffs, in the chinks of the ravines, in the vine thickets, his sharpshooters lay hidden – good marksmen, eager to test the bone-fracturing virtues of their boasted Liege rifles; yet, more, the presence of divers tall poles in particular localities, showed how carefully the Russian Artillerymen had marked the range of their guns – omens of a warm reception for us were those neatly-painted posts. In the matter of artillery we were, as regards weight of metal, not in gunners' skill, inferior to the foe, the British Horse Artillery having only a few 9-pounders, co-mingled with their pet 6-pounders.

Marshal St. Arnaud conceived a plan of attack. Part of the English Army was to manoeuvre against the enemy's right, with the object of turning that flank. General Bosquet's corps was to engage the enemy's attention on the left. The bulk of the Allies were to force the centre of the Russian position; this plan broke down. Lord Raglan hesitated about carrying out his share of the details. Time slipped by, and in consequence, our operations resolved themselves into the simple head-foremost tactics, characteristic of British general-ship.

[**Author's Note:** There was confusion between the allies over this plan. Raglan understood that the French would turn the Russian's left flank and only when this had been done would the British advance straight ahead.]

The united armies now marched on the same alignment. The British were 'in contiguous double columns, with a front of two divisions'. Ahead were sharpshooters, and left flank was looked to by riflemen, backed by the Cavalry under Lord Lucan. The order of march, then, may be stated as follows:

        Rifle Brigade   ↑   Rifle Brigade

Light Cavalry – Artillery – Light Division – Artillery – 2nd Division – Artillery Artillery – 1st Division – Artillery – 3rd Division – Artillery 4th Division

The impatiently waited signal was made, and the entire front of the Allies presses forward. At this juncture, the village of Bourliouk bursts into flame; the Cossacks have fired it.

On our side, the Light Division (Brown) and the Second Division (Evans), having deployed into splendid lines, step steadily towards the river; we (First Division) having halted on the extreme verge of the enemy's range, also formed line (as a matter of precaution) and then 'stood at ease'.

By this time, a tremendous cannonade was pouring on the advancing troops. And now, the round-shot, its duty done in front, or else having missed aim altogether, came sneaking towards the supporting divisions with such a gentle glide, that the men could hardly be persuaded to lift a leg, to allow the dying missile to pass unobstructed through their ranks. Not withstanding the awe of the occasion, the antics of a pretty little Maltese terrier, belonging to the jolly drummers of the Coldstream, drew loud laughs from the light-hearted soldiery. Whenever a ball hopped along the ground with more liveliness than usual, little 'Toby', darting from his bed among the drums and fifes, would give tongue in chase as friskily as though he hunted a mouse in the barrack-square of Fort Manoel [Malta].

The 2nd Division (beautifully manoeuvred by Evans over difficult ground) having pushed through the now blazing Bourliouk, is struggling up to the arm-pits in water. The iron rain splashes around – a crimson scum floats on the sluggish stream.

It is obvious that the 'Lights', have a duty, beyond the strength of their thinned ranks. In fact, Brown's danger is imminent, Lord Raglan, therefore orders the Duke of Cambridge to lead the Guards and the Highlanders to the relief of the Light Division.

Never was the command, 'line will advance', more gladly received. The three service battalions of Guards – Grenadier, Coldstream, Scots Fusiliers – under Major-General Bentinck, have the right of the line; three regiments of Highlanders – 42nd, 79th, and 93rd – led by their old warrior chief, Sir Colin Campbell, formed the left wing.

Suddenly, just as we reached the gardens bordering the Alma, a murderous storm of round shot and shell broke upon us; we crouched for a few moments behind the embankments of the vineyard; but the virulence of that diabolic artillery was no short livid spurt; so, onwards, through thick and thin. Right through the tangled shrubs tear the glorious battalions; they plunge into the river. They sprawl up the steep slippery banks on the other side, they are floundering through another vineyard, interspersed with fruit trees, and intersected with deep dry ditches; all the while, the air swarms thicker and thicker with projectiles. We are in a very hell nothing to be heard, save the humming of shells, the whiz of round-shot, the rattle of grape and canister. The trees crash and split around, the ground is torn up under our feet, our comrades are beaten down.

During those terrible moments, the conduct of the soldiers was wonderful; scarcely a man of them had ever seen a shotted-musket fired before, except at a target, and yet, they looked as cool, as self-possessed, as if 'marking time' in an English barrack-yard. Indeed, the tumble down of mess-mates only gave rise to the quiet observation, 'There goes old Tom,' 'Our Dick's done.' What a true nobleman does the Briton stand forth, when the tug of war, or adversity comes.

Our way lies over the dead and dying of the 7th, 23rd, and 33rd. Piteous murmurs for water or for help, arise from mangled bleeding forms, but we may not notice them. Scattered remnants too of that brilliant Light Division come rushing through our ranks, but those few officers of theirs, whom the bullet has spared, immediately rally this debris in our rear. Confusion can only be momentary with such soldiers; still it is evident we had not moved too soon.

Cheers, such as British throats alone can send forth, burst from Guards and Highlanders. The game seems in their grip; the cannons are just ahead, and the fire slackens sensibly; albeit, it is heavy still, so heavy that dozens of our fellows continue to be struck down, and the centre battalion of the Guards Brigade, the Scots Fusilier Guards (which faces a point blank discharge of grape and round shot) is so rudely encountered, that it recoils for an instant – only pour mieux sauter. And now, a thick wedge of grey-coated, helmeted foot shows on the slope to the right of the grand battery; it waits an opportunity of hurling an overwhelming mass upon our thin line.

Another round of deafening cheers, and file firing is commenced right into that close-grained column. Every soldier takes deliberate aim; the distance does not exceed sixty paces; hence, the Minie has an easy game, and works miracles.

CHARGE! With thrilling hurrahs the line of steel dashes forward. There rides Sir Colin foremost of the plaided ranks; there are Upton, Paulet, Dawson, Hood, showing the way to the bearskins. The 'Ruskis' await not the shock, they face about, and off at 'the double', leaving, on the ground, hundreds of dead and wounded. Forward! Friend and foe are trampled on alike; the very Colours of a regiment of Brown's, which had been smashed to bits by the feu d'enfer, when closing with its prey, are trodden under foot.

Pell-mell the Grenadiers break into the 'big battery', but with the exception of a gun or two, it is empty. And now the summit of the height gleams with

British bayonets. Heaven be praised! The 1st, 2nd, and Light Divisions have won the English half of the victory.

'Where is our artillery?' 'What a chance', are cries a thousand times repeated. The southern slopes of the blood-stained ridge, and the valley beneath, swarm with retreating masses – some brigades in confusion; others, in square order, rough customers still. They escape us! At last, whipping, spurring, jolting over the carcasses of the dead and dying, up gallops a field-battery. How we cheer it! Open Fire! Capital! Gaps are mowed through the rear guard. Every shot leaves horrid marks; but for all that, we have missed the chance of doing Menshikov a crushing hurt.

The Allies have succeeded at all points. Within four and a half hours, English 'pluck', and French dare-devilism have stormed and carried a line of heavily-armed crags; so strong by nature, so amply provided with men and metal, as to be deemed well nigh impregnable.

Such was the ever memorable 20th of September, on which the Russians lost about 5000 hardy soldiers, three guns, a large quantity of muskets, drums, knapsacks, and so forth, besides leaving in our hands many hundred prisoners, among whom were two general officers.

The day after, no sooner was the British Grenadier allowed to pile arms, and fall out, he acted nobly – worthy of himself. He went mercifully among the poor moaning, bleeding Russians, giving to them drinks of water out of his scantily filled bottle.

It was pleasant to hear that night the talk around the watch fires. The excited soldiers eagerly asked one another, 'What will they say in England about the battle? Nobody could complain as how we haven't done our duty anyhow.' 'Shall we get a medal?'

It is almost certain that if the First Division had moved to the relief a few minutes sooner, the Light Division would have been enabled to hold their ground, and thereby would have been foremost, as they richly deserved and there will to be, in sweeping the Russians out of their strong places, but as it was that culminating point of glory was reserved for others. Look at the loss sustained by Brown, total casualties were 989.

The Alma was a soldier's battle, a direct attack by lines on ordnance defended heights, which Menshikov expected to maintain against all comers for three weeks at least. With the exception of Bosquet's brilliant stroke at the enemy's left, there was but little manoeuvring. It was all hammer and tongs; and pluck, perseverance; the Minie and the *carabine a tige* did the business. Great honour is due to the ranks of the Allied Armies, who despite mountains, water, and heavy guns, drove 40,000 veterans like chaff before the wind in little better than four hours.

Of the officers killed, none had more sincere mourners than Captain Cust, Coldstream Guards, ADC to General Bentinck. He expired immediately after the amputation of the thigh on the evening of the 20th. Cust was no common man, he had all the attributes of the good soldier. He was acute, energetic, and of a singular bold, independent spirit. He abhorred meanness and chicane. His manly nature ever impelled him to side with the weak against the strong. He was a frank enemy, as a friend he was true as steel. His charity was liberal and unostentatious. Is it so surprising that Horace Cust's memory should be held so dear?

[**Author's Note:** His grave can be found on the north side of the River Alma.]

In consequence of the shameful penury of the hospital arrangements, most of our poor bleeding fellows lay throughout the night of the fight on the ground, just as they had dropped, and many I fear were not satisfactorily cared for before the morning of the 22nd. It was piteous to see a few clumsy arabas jolting towards the beach, crammed with arm-less, leg-less men, fresh from the surgeon's knife. It harrowed one's heart to listen to the cries and moans issuing from these unhappy loads. The French being decently provided with orthodox ambulance wagons, mule-litters and a service of hospital-orderlies, tended their casualties in a manner more consistent with humanity.

The great general never contents himself within the veneered lustre of unsubstantial glory, to beat his antagonist is not enough for him; the foe must be routed; to this end he redoubles his blows on the backs of the fleeing battalions, he permits to them no breathing time, he hovers continually on their flanks and rear; thus is a retreating army converted into a rabble, driven here, there, and everywhere. Unfortunately the allied chiefs did nothing of this sort. Satisfied with a brilliant feat of arms effected by their matchless troops, and forgetful of the precepts of Napoleon, our commanders pulled up in mid-career; hence a golden opportunity of crippling the Russians slipped through their relaxed fingers.

Why Menshikov was not followed up on the morning of the 21st, is a mystery. With the exception of the Light Division and a brigade of the 2nd, neither our own, or the French forces had suffered very materially. Does not history teach rapidity of movement in war to be the mainspring of ultimate triumph? No one denies that audacity, promptitude, and brains usually carry the day even against odds.

Captain H.F. Drummond's Letters on the Battle of the Alma.[4]

Captain Drummond, the Adjutant of 1st Battalion Scots Fusilier Guards, writes of his experience of the Battle of the Alma:

Bivouac (near the River Alma), September 21st, 1854:

We had a very hard action yesterday, crossing this river and attacking and taking an entrenched camp on the top of a steep hill. We had a large vineyard full of holes, burning houses, and felled trees to advance through up to the river, under such a fire of grape, canister, and round shot and shell as astonished us.

We rushed through the river where there was just a space of three or four yards under a cliff. We were forming the men into line again when they hollowed out forward; and up we went like a pack of hounds up the hill, when the 7th and 23rd were literally jammed back right through our line, and carried half our men with them; for a certain person high up thought the day was lost, and gave the word 'retire', which indeed we were forced to do until the Grenadiers and Coldstream line came out of the river, and we hooked on in the centre, and carried their camp with great slaughter, taking only three guns, but killing a great many; then up came the Highlanders on our left, outflanking them, advanced firing, and then away they went *pele mele*. We gave a parting shot and a cheer.

The Queen's Colour-staff was shot in half, and had twenty-four bullets through it. Berkeley has his leg broke, Gipps wounded in the hand, Chewton shot through and through, and stabbed when down, but not yet dead. Haygarth shot in the shoulder, not expected to live; Astley shot through the neck, Annesley in the jaw and palate, Buckley in the neck, Bulwer through the hand, and Ennismore through the leg; Hepburn through the arm, and Black Dal [Dalrymple?] with a spent ball in the leg, just enough to make him limp, but no skin broke: dear old Scarlett had a near escape – a shot took away the clasp of his waist-belt, and he never knew it till the evening. As for me, I had a shot through my bear-skin cap, and my horse killed under me with three bullets; so I may be thankful it was no worse. Hamilton's horse is wounded, and Ridley's killed, so we were pretty well touched up. Sir G. Brown said he never saw such sharp practice even in the Peninsular. We have eleven sergeants and about 180 men killed and wounded; the Coldstream only one officer and twenty-five men, as they were not in the thick of it.

We drove the enemy out of a most formidable position the day before yesterday. We have taken Mentchikov's carriage and dispatches to the Emperor, in which he says he would keep us in check at least three weeks in that position. We took an entrenched camp in less than three hours, and drove 40,000 men away, with immense slaughter. Our battalion had to charge the entrenched camp in front, consequently our loss was the greatest of our brigade; we have had eleven officers wounded, twenty men killed, and 161 wounded.

Bivouac, Sept 28th 1854

We had a most brilliant affair on the River Alma on the 20th. The enemy occupied a most formidable position on some heights above the river with several strong batteries and entrenchments with thirty-two and twenty-four pounders, and masses of men commanding the fords of the river, the bank of which is in some instances twenty feet high and quite steep.

We marched up in columns until about 500 yards from the river, when the Light and First Divisions deployed into line; the Light [division] advanced first and then us; they cannonaded us until we got to within 200 yards of the river, in some thick vineyards, amongst burning houses, felled trees, through which it was impossible to preserve a good line, when, I suppose, they thought they would beat us back by a murderous fire of grape, canister, rifles, shells, and round shot, but our men gave a cheer and dashed on through all the broken ground into the river, which we forded, as yet not having fired a shot, and having been exposed to a most destructive fire.

The Light Division had crossed just before us, and we were scrambling out of the river under the bank, not yet quite formed, when to our astonishment they, the Light Division [Buller's 2 Brigade] formed squares in front of us, and began to retire, for just in front of us was such a battery as none of us expected – about 500 yards off.

The Brigadier advanced us out at once to their support, before the Grenadiers and Coldstream were out of the river, and then began our part of the fun. We blazed into them with our Minies and marched on straight to the entrenchment under such a fire, and we got half way up, and in another minute should have been in the place, when the remains of the 7th, 23rd and 33rd (keep this private) retired (instead of halting and laying down and letting us go over them) right through our battalion, and regularly swept part of our right wing away and a part of our 5th and 6th companies, and then we had a desperate fight.

For we fired right into the entrenchments while these regiments formed up behind us, and the Russians came right out of the place upon us, thinking they could drive the Guards off; but by this time the Grenadier line came up on our right, and the Coldstream on our left, and then with a shout of joy we went – the whole brigade – up the hill into the ditch, and massacred them in crowds; they bolted pell-mell. We poured in such volleys as astonished their weak minds, killing and wounding hundreds; in the meantime the Highland brigade in line on our left brought their left shoulders up by battalions in echelon, and their firing on the flank was quite beautiful. The enemy retreated in disorder right across the plain, deserting a most splendid position in the rear.

If we had only 3000 cavalry we should have captured a quantity of guns and an enormous number of prisoners; as it was we actually had no more breath or legs to pursue them far. This takes a long time to tell but a little time to do. We have suffered severely in wounded – about 190, including officers. Ten officers and 100 men have been sent on board ship, all severely wounded, except Dal, who I expect will rejoin in a few days. The courage of our fellows is beyond praise. Ennismore was actually charging up hill on one leg and his sword, with his other leg shot through, when I sat him down and tied up his leg with a handkerchief. Close to the entrenchment Berkeley was shot cheering his men on (close to me) in the most gallant manner; and dear old Chewton was riddled with shot and behaved like a lion. As for the two ensigns [carrying the Colours], Lindsay and Thistlethwayte, they were my children – under my eyes the whole time – and their coolness, steadiness, and deliberate courage were admirable. I was obliged to shoot three Russians close up to them. They never moved or flinched, but went steadily on, as if on parade; a species of cool bravery in such young fellows as I think only exists in Englishmen.

[**Author's Note:** Officers wounded were Lieutenant Colonels Berkeley, Dalrymple (Black Dal?), Hepburn, Haygarth; Captains Astley, Bulwer, Buckley and Gipps; and Lieutenants Viscount Ennismore and the Hon. H. Annesley. Captain Lord Chewton died of wounds several days after the battle.]

I sent you a list of casualties by the last mail, I send you another now. Altogether thirty may be killed; poor Sergeant Dobbie was killed dead, and the two Lanes died like heroes close to me, shot together; indeed, the whole right section of the 4th Company was blown clean away by the fire; every sergeant killed or wounded.

Three out of four of the sergeants with the Colours were wounded, and the commanding officer has made McKechnie, in consequence of his gallantry with them; giving Bye the other colours [promoted to Colour Sergeant].[5] Sergeant Cosmo Gordon, Corporal Reynolds, Sergeants McKechnie[6] and Boyce were among the most conspicuous for their gallantry, and, I beg to bring them under the recollection of Sir C. Hamilton [Commanding Officer], for favourable mention to Colonel Moncrieff [Regimental Lieutenant Colonel]. Among the privates it would 'be invidious to mention any, but the magnificent behaviour of old Douglas, the reduced Sergeant, Neal the 3rd Company, and John Doull was very beautiful.

Lord Raglan said that evening, the only position he could liken it to was Busaco [Peninsular War], the strongest position he ever saw taken. So the only thing is for us to be thankful that our poor fellows were not killed outright. I believe they are all doing well; poor dear Haygarth and Chewton are the worst, but doing well. You would crack with laughter if you saw me with my trousers split and torn, my coat all black and dirty, and mounted on a little ragged pony I picked up, for they killed my horse under me in the entrenchment. Ridley had his horse killed, and Sir C. Hamilton's wounded and lived two days; three horses out of four killed.

We remained two days on the heights above the river, burying the killed, and sending the wounded on board ships. Our loss was about 2000 killed and wounded, and 100 officers. The Russians left about 1000 dead, and 1500 wounded to us; but lost, besides, according to all accounts, about 5000. The country all the way to Sebastopol was strewed with arms, packs, coats, boots, and the bushes all full of deserters, in short they have had quite enough of the red devils, as they call us.

18th October 1854

Jem Blair and Jem Murray have arrived, but I have not seen them. Poor Old Chewton is dead; he behaved like a lion, and was shot and stabbed when he was wounded and on the ground. I myself caught a scoundrel stabbing one of our poor wounded fellows, and shot him dead; he clutched his firelock to knock me down, but I was too quick for him with my pistol.

God knows I love you all to the extent of my heart and at times long to see you all, but a higher duty calls me here, and all such feelings for family must give way to duty, to Queen and country. This is, and has been, a very hard and trying time, and I never knew campaigning was such real hard work.

Extract of a Letter by Captain Gipps, 4th Company, SFG, later General Sir R. Gipps, on the Battle of the Alma.[7]

On reaching the Russian bank of the river we found ourselves much protected from the enemy's fire and then endeavoured then partly succeeded, in getting the men into their places in their companies in line. In another moment we should have completely accomplished this, but General Bentinck again rode up and ordered us to advance. 'Forward Fusiliers, what are you waiting for' this was what he said. After this was impossible to restrain the men up the ascent we went in imperfect formation and not even our bayonets fixed.

My attention was called to this by the men themselves who asked leave to fix them; we were totally unsupported on either flank. The Coldstream and also I believe our own left Company had not crossed the river owing to it being deeper to the left and Colonel Hood had not allowed the Grenadiers to advance until he had reformed their broken ranks. We notwithstanding continued our march up the incline. The Light Division seeing us coming, naturally concluded the brigade was entire, and fell back to allow us to pass through and were themselves hotly pursued by the Russians.

Our formation already imperfect was even more broken by the rush of the Light Division breaking through our ranks, nevertheless we advanced to within, I should say, 20 yards of the Russian redoubt, in our progress bayoneting those Russians who left the shelter of the redoubt in the pursuit of the Light Division. Up to this moment we had continued to advance but now finding our flanks unsupported and masses of the enemy on our front, we halted and commenced firing, as yet we have not fired a shot, waiting for the Grenadiers and Coldstream to arrive, well knowing their eagerness to be with us, and that in a few moments at the most we would see them at our side. At this moment someone [alas, who was it?] came up to our commanding officer and told him to give the word for us to retire and then and then only did we give way to the overwhelming masses in our front – this order to retire was repeatedly given and retire we did, but almost immediately we observed the Grenadiers advancing up the hill, seeing this the Officers at once knew that our orders to retire must be a mistake and instantly gave orders to advance again. It must be remembered that from the time we broke our ranks in order to scale the vineyard wall our formation was never complete. The Light Division has still more broken us and the numbers we had killed and wounded made it impossible for the men at once to gain their places so as to make anything like a front to advance with. Consequently the Grenadiers and I believe the Coldstream passed us and a short time elapsed before we had regained our formation to advance with them.

Colonel Hood observing this halted the Grenadiers and gave us time. It is impossible to judge of time in the excitement of an action and under such fire as we were exposed to, that I hardly dare say how long we where regaining our formation, but were I obliged to hazard a guess, I would say five minutes. This is the only part of my narrative as I had any doubts of, excepting where I speak of the intentions and motives of others or where I have by making use such words as 'I believe' or 'I think' implied doubt. The rest of the action is simplicity itself.

The Brigade of Guards, now complete, advanced up the hill, took the Russian redoubt and the next thing we saw was the enemy in full retreat. At no time was there any gap between the Grenadiers left and the Coldstream right after they had advanced from the riverbank that other troops could have filled, because though part of the time we were in confusion still we were there, and in this Mr Kinglake is misinformed.

I forgot to say that we were joined by a few parties from the Light Division who instead of retiring through us, advanced with us but to what regiments they belonged I do not know.

Extract from Lieutenant R.J. Lindsay VC, later Lord Wantage, on the Battle of the Alma.[8]

The Colours were well protected by a strong escort, four non-commissioned officers and eight or ten privates; one amongst them I especially remember on account of his cheery face and perfect confidence-inspiring, trustworthy demeanour. Sergeant Major Edwards always took credit for having selected Reynolds as one of the escort to the colours, but he chose him on account of his size. I always remained Reynolds' friend, and backed him through many a trouble. When the Battalion came home, I was fortunately able to place him in an excellent situation, which he held till the day of his death.

When the Colours were attacked Reynolds did some execution with the bayonet, and Hughie Drummond, who had scrambled to his legs after his horse was killed, shot three Russians with his pistol. Berkeley was knocked over this time, and all the non-commissioned officers with the Colours excepting one Sergeant. The Colours I carried were shot through in a dozen places, and the colour-staff cut in two. Poor old Thistlewayte had a bullet through his bearskin cap. As is frequently the case with troops in their first engagement, the elevation given to the Russian fire was, fortunately for us, too high for the deadly execution which might have been given to it. In my own case I neither drew my sword nor fired my revolver, my great object being to plant the standard on the Russian redoubt, and my impression is nobody was into the earthworks before I was.

Conclusion

The Battle of the Alma was undertaken without a proper assessment of the enemy's strength in its well-chosen position. Lord Raglan failed to maintain central command of the battle by riding through the skirmishing lines to a hill, from where he directed artillery fire on the enemy.

Because of his absence, the 1st Division was not advanced in time to support the Light Division in its attack on the enemy position. Brigadier General Bentinck could see the need to support the Light Division urgently, to maintain the forward thrust of the attack. Therefore he ordered the Scots Fusilier Guards forward to support the attack, before the Battalion had the opportunity to dress their ranks. Thus, when the troops of the Light Division retired through their ranks to regroup, they drove the Fusilier Guards back with them, as they were unable to open their ranks and let the retiring soldiers through and to maintain an orderly line of battle. The advance of the Grenadiers, Coldstream and the Highlanders enabled the Fusilier Guards and much of the Light Division to regroup and to move forward in the attack, which broke the enemy and won the battle. This is another occasion when the British soldiers' bravery and determination made up for the generals' lack of military skill.

After the battle the Army remained too long dealing with the wounded and burying the dead, instead of following up the defeated enemy. This task could have been given to the sailors to perform, leaving the Army free to follow up the retreating enemy. Sevastopol's defences were recognized by its defenders to be too weak to withstand an attack. However the divided command and the illness of Marshal St Arnaud made this course of action impossible. We have no idea what would have happened if the British had attacked Sevastopol, without the support of the French who dares wins?

Sir John Burgoyne, the Engineer-in-Chief, advised Lord Raglan that a bold assault on the southern quarter of Sevastopol could hardly fail to be successful, provided it were done at once. The south side was poorly defended and as it contained most of the city's docks, stores and barracks, the allies would have to take it sometime. The north side, however, contained a series of mighty fortresses, which would result in a hard and bloody siege. He argued that this was worth the risk of a flank march, which Napoleon thought were contrary to all the principles of war.[9]

Then the allies carried out a dangerous flank march to move their troops from the well-defended north side of Sevastopol to the less heavily defended south side, in the face of the enemy. At times they were very vulnerable to an attack by the Russians, who could see what they were doing. However Menshikov had marched his army into the interior, so there may not have been troops available for such an action. Clausewitz writes that war is won by the side that makes fewest mistakes. The failure of the Russians to attack the allies, during this operation, was a major blunder, which is equal to the allies' failure to press home an attack on Sevastopol.

Notes

1. Tipping, Capt A., 'Letters from the East during the Campaign of 1854', MS, pp. 38–56.
2. In September 1810 Wellington took up a strong position on the Mountain of Busaco, where the approaching slopes were rough and easy to defend. Massena attacked this strong position and was defeated.
3. Wilson, Capt C.T., *Our Veterans of 1854 in Camp & before the Enemy*, Street, 1859, pp. 126–49.
4. Drummond, Maj H., *Letters from the Crimea*, Norris & Son, 1855, pp. 36–71.
5. Promoted to Colour Sergeant.
6. Lieutenant Lindsay, Sergeant McKechnie, Sergeant J. Knox and Corporal Reynolds were all awarded the Victoria Cross for their gallantry in the stand around the Colours.
7. Letter written to the Colonel of the Regiment in the possession of the Regiment.
8. Wantage, Lady, *Lord Wantage VC, KCB, A Memoir by his Wife*, Smith Elder, 1907, p. 35.
9. Wilson, pp. 161–2.

CHAPTER 6

The Flank March

Lieutenant Colonel Ross-of-Bladensburg Describes the Flank March[1]

The Allies decided that they would not operate against the North of Sebastopol, but they would attack it from the side and would form a secure base in the harbours of Balaklava and Kamiesh. To carry out this operation they had to march their armies from the River Belbek to the southwest corner of the peninsular, quite close the fortress they intended to capture. The ground over which they had to march was unknown. They had left behind them the broad open plains, where they could march in battle array, ready for emergencies; they would now be approaching a woody, difficult and intersected country, and had to adopt long columns of route in moving across it. According to the information in their possession, moreover, a hostile army was sheltered somewhere within the lines of Sebastopol; it was believed to be securely posted behind the entrenchments on the northern plateau. They did not wish to meet it there, and, to avoid doing so, they were obliged to have recourse to the only alternative and to commit a bad military error. They exposed the right of their long columns and their rear to imminent danger, and, courting disaster, invited the Russians to fall upon them, in a position where a partial defeat might prove fatal to their existence.

On the 25th the main body, preceded by a regiment of cavalry, a troop of horse artillery, and the battalion of Rifles, left the Belbek, and the perilous flank march commenced. It was carried out in a manner which would have given the fullest advantages to the enemy had he availed himself of them. The general direction was kept by consulting the compass; but the difficulties of the country, the thick woods, and the haste which urged us forward, disarranged the order of the troops. At one moment, indeed, the headquarters, leading the whole advance, were followed by a large procession of 30 guns without supports, and offered a tempting and easy reward to Russian enterprise. But, slow though we may be to recognize it, a miracle does sometimes take place, and in this case it shows it in the fact that the extraordinary march proceeded onwards without the slightest mishap. Not only this, but the British even captured some 20 carts from the enemy. Though they failed to get hold of the horses, which were cut away directly we came into sight.

This meeting came about in a curious way. It happened, as we have seen, Prince Menshikov far from taking post on the northern plateau, was refitting his defeated army in the town of Sebastopol, south of the roadstead. He came to the conclusion that he ought to preserve his communications with the interior of the Crimea, and support the advance of his reinforcements he expected from Bessarabia. At dawn on the 25th, therefore, he, too, emerged from his retreat, crossed the Tchernaya at Traktir Bridge, and, advancing to Mackenzie Farm, marched towards Bakhchi Serai. Thus it came about that the two contending armies, moving on the same day, and for some time advancing towards one another by the same road, crossed each other's path, and that neither had the slightest conception of what the other was doing.

It was fortunate that, in this curious game a blind man's buff, Menshikov did not strike our columns of route full in the flank; as it was, we just happened to ram into the tip of his tail, for as the headquarters staff, stumbling suddenly on the last portion of the enemy's baggage train, as it passed unconsciously by, stood wondering at the sight, a few of our guns hurried up to the rescue, unlimbered, and secured some of the unhorsed carts. Among the booty was a carriage belonging to one of the Russian Commanders, in which were stars, crosses, medals, uniform, French novels and a portfolio of coloured prints, the morality of which will not bear discussion.

The experiences of the First Division on this route should not be admitted. After waiting, ready equipped for two hours, the men at length moved off at 8.30 in the morning, and plunged almost immediately into the forest.

Captain Tipping's Comments on the Flank March[2]

At present they seemed determined to resist pertinaciously and we have Prince Menshikov in our rear with an Army, which is at this moment advancing to cut if possible our retreat to Balaclava, should we require one.

We are living upon hard ship's biscuit, and a daily ration of salt pork, about the size of your fist, nothing in fact but a lump of lard. I was fortunate in procuring a small bag of Rice, and some arrowroot in Balaclava the other day, so that I am better off than many.

October 10th Hospital Ship

Once at least, but often twice every night, we were suddenly beat to arms, by the appearance of the enemy somewhere, and the outlying pickets firing. When ill, the sudden surprise during sleep is an unpleasant sensation. One jumps up, and buckles on sword and pistol almost mechanically from being so accustomed to it, in three minutes we are ready for anything. Until last night, I have not had my clothes off for 26 days, except once to bathe, for being 2 miles from any water, it is too precious to use for any extensive wash, and even if we had a supply of water, we have no utensils for the purpose beyond our cooking kettles.

You may just imagine the state we are in, after so many tremendous marches under a burning sun, without anything approaching to a shade.

We have now had tents served up to us in the proportion of two for all the officers of the Regiment, and fourteen for the whole of the men; they could not find conveyance for more. The fact is the authorities never intended the expedition to last for more than a fortnight or three weeks and thought that whatever happened, we might rough it for that time; but circumstances have totally changed the aspect of affairs, and from the vast quantity of materials to be dragged up from the ships, before the siege begins, it may last probably till the end of the month.

The cold salt pork and biscuit are most indigestible, this food, with hard work, cold nights, disturbed rest, intense heat in the days, and chills in the wet dewy nights, can only be stood by the iron constitution.

October 27th
Colonel Hood, who commanded the Regiment, is indeed a severe loss to the service. He was beyond all comparison the best officer in the Brigade, and more fitted to command the Regiment on active service than any man I know.

Captain Wilson Describes the Confusion that Took Place on the Flank March[3]

Everybody who has seen beaters pushing their way through a thick cover may form a faint idea of the difficulties which beset, and the obstacles which retarded our progress. The heat was overpowering, not a breath of air percolated the dense vegetation. You scrambled on with arms uplifted to protect the face against the swinging back-handers dealt by the boughs; and now your shakoe was dashed off, now the briars laid a tenacious hold on your haversack, or on the tails of your coatee. It is as much as you could do to see the soldiers immediately on your left and right. For the time, military order was an impossibility, brigades and regiments got intermixed. Guardsmen, Rifles, and Highlanders struggled forward blindly, all in a ruck. There was much suffering, and some stout soldiers dropped involuntarily to the rear, to be heard of no more.[4]

After four hours or more, the troops emerged on a lane blocked by the cavalry and baggage, and squeezed through. A little later they heard an explosion, and, pushing forward they came upon the scene of a singular meeting that took place between the headquarters staff and the rear of the enemy's army. Continuing along a tolerably good road, they approached the Valley of the Tchernaya, and, crossing it at Traktir Bridge, they finally bivouacked near the village of Tchorgun at 10 o'clock at night, completely exhausted, parched with thirst, and their clothes much torn by struggling through the wood. Indeed they were fortunate, for it was one in the morning before the last British division reached its halting ground.

Next day the movement continued; and the cholera that accompanied our troops without intermission burst out with a renewed malignity, and struck its victims down on the road side along our line of march. After three hours, the division reached Kadikoi, about half a mile from Balaklava; while our ships, approaching, threw a few shells into an old Genoese Fort which commanded the harbour, which was held by a handful of Greek troops in the Russians service; after a mere show of resistance they surrendered without difficulty.

Thus the flank march was completed, and during the whole of a difficult and dangerous operation, lasting two days, the Russians stood by absolutely passive, and the Allies were entirely unmolested. Not a company was cut off, nor was a gun taken. This was the more remarkable since, perceiving the movement from a high tower in Sebastopol, they are accurately informed of our plan at midday on the 25th. Prince Menshikov must also have known it, from the meeting that took place between the hostile armies near Mackenzie Farm. It was indeed fortunate that we had so forbearing an enemy.

Communications having now been fortunately re-established with the fleet, the British occupied the Bay at Balaklava, the French that of Kamiesh, where their respective bases of operations were formed. Thus we were placed on the right of the new line fronting northwards, and we were again posted upon the exposed flank.

About this time [25 September], an event of importance occurred to the French. Marshal St. Arnaud got so ill, that he was obliged to give up his command, and to leave the seat of war. General Canrobert succeeded him, a valiant, honourable and straightforward soldier, but one little fitted to take upon himself the onerous responsibilities of his new position.

The idea seems to have been pretty general among the troops that the flank march was intended to shift the position of the united armies from a strong front of Sebastopol to a weaker side and that the attack was only delayed until we got close to the southern defences of the town. It was confidently expected that the assault would soon be delivered, and the landing of the siege-train did not put an end to that hope. As days went by, however, it began to be realized that operations of a slower nature were to be begun, and that a siege, not an assault, was to be undertaken. The surmise was entirely correct; though the Chiefs of the Army still held to the beliefs that, when a bombardment by siege guns had taken place, the defences would be destroyed, and the town would fall before winter set in.

Lord Raglan personally seems to have been disposed to make an immediate attempt against the enemy's lines, without incurring this further delay. This view is suddenly shared and supported by Sir George Cathcart and Sir George Lyons. The Russian fortifications were slight and weak at the end of September, when the Allies got within striking distance, and, though we should be stronger against them as soon as siege batteries were constructed and armed, yet the time required to do so could be utilized by the defenders in strengthening their works that the advantages and delay would accrue to them than to our detriment. General Canrobert, however, was cautious and was disinclined to run any risks, just as the supreme command was vested in him by the French Emperor. Others, amongst the British advisers at headquarters, held the view that it was dangerous to deliver an attack unless prepared by artillery fire. Lord Raglan was forced to concur.

The Russian command left in Sebastopol after Prince Menshikov's departure, was in a state of great depression, and believed that the town could not hold out against a vigorous assault. The entire Garrison amounted to 35,850 men, made up of various elements 1 single battalion of regulars [750 men], militia, gunners, Marines, seamen, and workmen. Of the latter, there were 5000, a useful body to create a fortress, if time was granted but useless to repel an immediate attack. All the sailors set free from the imprisoned fleet, totalled 18,500, of whom a fourth part only were well trained or even decently armed.

The South side, moreover, does not lend itself easily to good defence, and on the 25th of September, this long line was imperfectly defended. On the British section, there were four works, which were unconnected by walls or entrenchment, known as the Redan, the Malakoff Tower, the Little Redan, and No. 1 Battery, near Careenage Bay. Of these the Malakoff was 'a mere naked tower, without a glacis, exposed from head to foot, unsupported by the powerful batteries which were destined to flank it, and uncovered as yet by the works which afterwards closed up around its base'. The whole of the South side of Sebastopol, moreover, was armed with 172 guns, of which by far the greater number faced the French and only a few the British position.[5]

The Russian chiefs took every measure to fortify their position, directly they understood that the allies were approaching the south side in force. The greatest activity prevailed both day and night in the garrison and amongst the inhabitants, and as the works designed by the Russian engineer officer Todleben were rapidly thrown up.

The Allied Commanders never interrupted its operations, nor did they make any demonstrations to try the quality of the defences. They contented themselves with distant reconnaissances, so that in a short time the entrenchments were greatly strengthened, especially the Malakoff and began to look more formidable than had been the case before July; the armament also was changed, the lighter guns giving way to heavier ordnance drawn from the ships and arsenal.

Lieutenant Colonel Wilson's Comments on the Flank March[6]

It was current in the Army at that time that the semi-circular advance on Balaclava was undertaken at the suggestion of the Engineer-in-Chief, Sir John Burgoyne, who had made up his mind that a bold assault on the southern quarter of the town could hardly fail of success, provided it was done at once before the enemy, whose obstinate military character he knew, had time to rally. Assuming the correctness of the report referred to, time is certainly borne witness to the sagacity of the veteran's view. Would that they had acted on his recommendation.

After dodging about in the wood for better than four hours, with no other guide but the compass looked to by a member of the Quarter-Master-General's staff, we suddenly debouched with what thankfulness on the road, which was specially reserved for the cavalry and the baggage. It was with no slight ado that the battalions trickled by files through the hocus-pocus of materiel, clogging the narrow lane; however thanks to the activity and the intelligence the men always displayed in difficulties, we shot through sooner than might have been expected.

The troops were by this time in a sad plight, besides being weary and foot-sore, the dust and vertical glare had begotten in them a raging thirst and their water bottles were empty long ago. Suddenly the loud report of an explosion, followed by a dense volume of smoke rising from out of the trees a little way ahead, startled us into renewed exertion.

'The Ruskis are yonder!' cried the rank-and-file. At once the flagging 'fours' close up; sergeants are no longer required to reiterate 'Keep your places, men.' The magic perfume of burnt powder has dissipated every ill. It was delightful to observe eyes, which a moment ago were dull and glassy, flash flame.

The cause of the excitement was that Lord Raglan, while riding a little ahead of the Army had dropped on the extreme rear of a Russian division. Both parties were equally surprised at this unlooked for meeting. The enemy blew up an ammunition tumbril, cut the traces of the beasts that dragged the commissariat carts, and made off helter-skelter.

The First Division may reckon itself fortunate, for long and trying as our day was, thirteen hours afoot, it will not bear comparison to the rear divisions, which did no bivouac until five hours after we did.

The harbour of Balaklava is so narrow at its mouth, that two large ships can barely enter it abreast; but a little further on it outspreads to a width of twelve hundred feet. Its length may be about a mile; in depth it varies from six to eighty fathoms.

From us, English military cookery gets less attention than it deserves. We know our worst enemy in war to be DISEASE, because it is notorious that, through that poisonous influence ten soldiers perish for one whom the sword kills; if then, we would have our Army efficient in the field, we must neglect nothing that can by any possibility bear beneficially on the sanitary condition of the troops. We must be careful to camp them on healthy sites, to have them properly clothed, to keep them as far as practicable out of the sun, wet and cold; and we must seek, too, that that their food is wholesome. There we must assure him that their rations are nourishing, digestible and palatable, something more is requisite good cookery which among our soldiers is an unknown art. Uneducated cookery deprives man of the enjoyment of eating. It robs him of the major portion of his nourishment, and the deficiency of nutriment entails loss of strength, and loss of strength invite disease, and disease impairs the serviceability of an army. I cannot doubt that bowel complaints, dysentery, diarrhoea and indigestion, which so raged in the

Bulgarian and Crimean camps, were generated by partially cooked or over cooked food, the absence of vegetables and of lime juice, and the quantity of salt pork habitually consumed.

Bad news, Marshal Saint Arnaud is dying. Mark this fierce soldier in Bulgaria, he is everywhere, reviewing troops, visiting hospitals and inspecting camps. See him in the Crimea; on the dawn of the Alma morning, they lift him pale and wasted into the saddle; in the evening his hour of glory they bear him fainting, through downright bodily weakness, to his simple tent. By the death of this indefatigable captain, France and England were robbed of a commander of surpassing energy and audacity. Had that energy and audacity been spared to the allies, a tremendous game might have been played.

One cannot fail to be struck with the excellent condition of clothing of the French troops. The battle and the march seemed hardly to have rubbed that gloss off it. What a contrast to the discoloured, threadbare suits of our fellows.

A salutary change in the ordinary habits of the troops dates from the outbreak of cholera in Bulgaria; before this, both camps echoed from morning to night with cursing and swearing; in vain the clergy strove to correct the evil, but they could gain no ground against this familiar vice. But suddenly a ruthless moralist entered the tents, good and bad went down beneath the silent hand of the destroyer cholera, and, for the first time the man began to ponder what the clergymen had been telling them. Thus it came to pass that swearing almost disappeared from the regimental vocabulary.

Cholera has considerably increased both in intensity and in generalness. After all this is not to be wondered at, considering that the untented troops are exposed to the searching night dews which drench us as thoroughly as rain. Many regiments, having quitted Varna, with their proper compliment of captains and subalterns, may soon find it no easy matter to show one officer per company. May the inconveniences of this short-handedness teach the folly of trying to make peace prescription harmonize with war exigencies.

Notes

1. Ross-of-Bladensburg, Lt Col, *The Coldstream Guards in the Crimea*, Innes & Co, 1896, pp. 97–108.
2. Tipping, Capt A., 'Letters from the East during the Campaign of 1854', MS, pp. 57–8.
3. Wilson, Capt C.T., *Our Veterans of 1854*, Street, 1859, pp. 162–7.
4. *Ibid.*, p. 163.
5. Kinglake, A.W., *Invasion of the Crimea*, vol. 3, Blackwood, 1866, pp. 123, 194 & 347. Sir Edmond Lyons urged an immediate assault on the Malakoff hill, which was then unoccupied, and advised the immediate construction of a battery there, which would make it necessary for the fleet to take care of themselves. The capture of the Malakoff in September, 1855, caused the immediate fall of Sevastopol.
6. Wilson, pp. 162–81.

CHAPTER 7

The Inkerman Position, the Russian Forces and their Plan of Attack, and the Allied Forces

The Inkerman Position

The allied forces had two tasks to perform: the besieging of Sevastopol and the protection of the allied army, against the threat from Prince Menschikov's army, which had marched into the countryside at the time of the allied army's Flank March.

The topography of the ground, over which the battle was fought, played a major part in the outcome of the battle, as Patrick Mercer describes in his book, *Give them a Volley and Charge!*[1]

In 1854 the whole of the position was thick with stunted oak and thorn bushes which made both movement and observation difficult. While little had been done to clear fields of fire through the brush, many tracks had been worn by both local people and, more particularly, the infantry who traversed it daily on picquet duty. Most contemporary accounts make mention of the brush but few dwell on it as much as it perhaps deserves, for those who fought there must have accepted it as a not very remarkable feature.

It is important to realize, however, just how significant it was, for in places it made bodies of men who were very close to one another practically invisible. It greatly impeded the cohesion of the solid Russian columns, and lent itself to the skirmishing tactics of the British whilst hiding the paucity of their numbers. Protruding from the ground were outcrops and boulders of lime which meant that when scrambling up slopes every step had to be watched. Furthermore, there were slopes everywhere which were sometimes bare and craggy, sometimes gently wooded glens, and sometimes miniature jungles. In short, it was a piece of ground that made command and control almost impossible, particularly when, to make matters additionally difficult, it was covered in a thick blanket of fog.

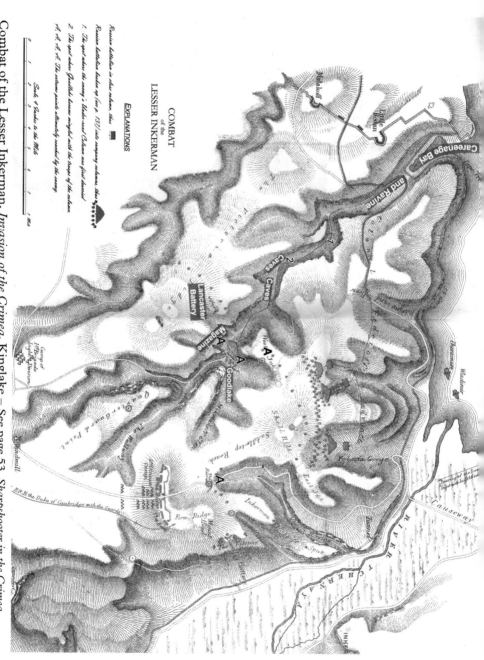

COMBAT
of the
LESSER INKERMAN

EXPLANATIONS

Russian batteries in their various positions.

Russian batteries broken up (say 15?) into company columns; then

1. *The spot where the enemy's Under-and Column are first deceived*
2. *The spot where Quarles's column mingled with the troops of the column*

A.A.A.A. *The various points ultimately reached by the enemy*

0 1 2 3 4 5 6 7 1 Mile

Scale of Yards to the Mile

Combat of the Lesser Inkerman, *Invasion of the Crimea, Kinglake* – See page 53, *Sharpshooter in the Crimea.*

In more detail, starting from the north-west corner of the battlefield, that closest to Sevastopol, the Sapper Road headed east from the city along the plateau before dipping north-east down St George's Ravine. From there it continued along the southern shore of the roadstead before joining the Post Road just before the Traktir bridge over the Tchernaya. Looking south from the Sapper Road the plateau looms above riven by two deep ravines. The more easterly one, the Volovia Gorge, culminates in a shelf of flat ground which then rises into another knoll known both as Cossack Mountain and Shell Hill which was to be the centre of Russian operations on both 26 October and 5 November. Spreading out either side of Shell Hill were two shoulders known as West Jut and East Jut; the latter falls away to its south-east into a major landmark of the battle, Quarry Ravine. Halfway down the slope of East Jut ran the so-called Post Road whilst on the floor of Quarry Ravine a rougher track ran which joined the Post Road just below the British positions.

Moving farther east and south from Quarry Ravine, a mighty finger of land, sheer for its last 200 yards, points north-east: this is Inkerman Spur. No one who went to the extremities of this spur could leave other than by retracing their steps or abseiling off the side. The south-eastern face of the spur was bounded by the verdant St Clement's ravine which culminates in another shelf known as the Kitspur. Some of the most savage fighting on 5 November was to occur in and around this ravine and the earthwork known as the Sandbag Battery at the top of it, so it may be worth pausing for a while to look at the implications of assaulting up a slope such as this.

The incline is steep and the ground loose and rocky underfoot, the most exhausting sort of ground to climb. Whilst the slope is not quite steep enough to require one to grasp at the brush for handholds, a fit man would have found it a stiff climb from the base to the edge of the rocky shelf above. When such a man was encumbered with 30 or so lbs of ammunition and equipment, carrying a musket and bayonet, and with adrenalin born of fear pumping around his system, the climb would have been exhausting. Once the attacking Russians reached the lip above, that is, when they were at their most breathless, it was here that they would have been faced by the defending British, which may go some way to explain why the Russians always hung back as they breasted this rise; the British attributed it to the intimidating power of their defence; doubtless this was partially true but their breathlessness would also have rendered them particularly vulnerable at this point.

Rising above the Kitspur and Inkerman Spur was the main British position which was shaped like a back-to-front letter L. The north-south spur was referred to as Fore Ridge and the west-east spur as Home Ridge, the whole feature being slightly lower than Shell Hill some three-quarters of a mile to its north-west. Running north-south up and over Home Ridge and being abutted to its west by the finger valleys of the Careenage Ravine was the Post Road. The Careenage Ravine ran directly south-east from Sevastopol's roadstead and provided deep and covered access from the city straight into the rear of the British position. At its south-eastern extremity it divided into lesser ravines, the Mikriakoff Glen heading east-south-east and the Wellway leading right up to the Post Road itself. The Careenage Ravine was bounded to the south-west by Victoria Ridge at the south-eastern edge of which lay a windmill that was much used by the Russians as a landmark.

So much, then, for the ground over which Russians, British and French were destined to fight, but of crucial significance were the defences which the British had thrown up to protect this open flank. The vulnerability of the Inkerman position had been clearly identified by the British, and a whole infantry division had been stationed there to protect it. However, it is clear that until events after Balaklava unfolded, there were few who fully appreciated how easily the whole of the allied cause might be unhinged by a determined attack in this quarter. Without doubt, everyone's hopes lay in a quick capitulation of Sevastopol which might be brought about by every effort being bent towards the prosecution of the siege.

Accordingly, too few troops were dedicated to the defence of the Inkerman position; the overstretched and battle-depleted 2nd Division was expected to hold a position which was close to the enemy and required probably twice the number, leaving maximum numbers of troops to get on with siege operations.

The effect of demanding too much from the 2nd Division was that they did not have enough men or time to prepare their defences properly – everyone had their work fully cut out providing picquets for the mobile defence of Inkerman, as well as finding troops for both carriage of supplies and trench work. Conditions were summed up by one officer:

> We are all nearly worn out with exposure to the intense November cold, constant fatigues, indifferent food and the loss of nearly every night's rest; three out of four have I been up, and the poor men scarcely ever get a night in their tents – not bed – for all lie on the ground; we have not taken our clothes off since landing, and even when they have a night all are under arms soon after 4 am and remain standing in the cold some hours till daybreak. Such is our life.[2]

The Russian Forces

Kinglake states that, from figures quoted in General Todleben's book, the Russian Forces on the Inkerman position were as follows:

General Soimonov, Infantry	18,829
General Dannenberg Cossacks	100
General Paulov, Infantry	<u>15,806</u>
	34,735
A battalion of Sappers	750

Artillerymen for 135 guns, including 54
guns of position and 81 pieces of light
artillery, at an average of 35 men for
each gun.   <u>4,725</u>
                                             40,210

Prince Gortchakov's army of about 22,000 in horse, gun and foot, with no
less than eighty-eight guns, was threatening the allies' right flank by occupying
ground from the Balaklava plain to the banks of the River Tchernaya, and not far
from the Inkerman ruins.[3]

The Allied Forces

Kinglake states that the Allied Forces on the Inkerman position were as follows:[4]

1st Division Guards Brigade	Div Comd – Lt Gen The Duke of Cambridge Bde Comd – Maj Gen H. Bentinck 3 Gren Gds – 501; 1 Cold Gds – 438; SFG – 392	1,331
2nd Division	Div Comd – Maj Gen J. Pennefather 1st Bde Comd – Bt Col J. Warren 2nd Bde Comd – Brig Gen. H. Adams	2,956
3rd Division	Div Comd – Lt Gen Sir Richard England 1st Bde Comd – Brig Gen Sir John Campbell 2nd Bde Comd – Brig Gen. W. Eyre	281
4th Division	Div Comd – Lt Gen Sir George Cathcart 1st Bde Comd – Brig Gen T. Goldie 2nd Bde Comd – Brig Gen A. Torrens	2,217
Light Division	Div Comd – Lt Gen Sir George Brown 1st Bde Comd – Maj Gen W. Codrington 2nd Bde Comd – Brig Gen G. Buller	649
	Guards roving piquet	<u>30</u>
	Total	7,464

Little Inkerman – The Russian Plan of Attack[5]

Kinglake states that the Russians were so elated by their one-sided version of
the Battle at Balaclava, that it was decided to carry out a sortie against the 2nd
Division, located on the south of Mount Inkerman.

The attack would be made over the same ground than the main attack. However
the British defence against the first attack made by Lieutenant General Sir George

De Lacy Evans would be very different to the defence by the British against the main attack, when Major General John Pennefather was in command. The first attack was defended from the main position on Home Ridge, while Pennefather initially reinforced his picquets and fought the battle there, reinforcing his troops from the main position.

The Russians were confident that an attack, mounted from the Karabel Faubourg, would not be seen by the Allies. Such was the mastery by the Russians of the ground to the north of Mount Inkerman (by troops on the ground and by fire from his batteries) that the attack would move from east to west over the mountain, and then begin to advance towards Shell Hill. The enemy was sure that he could carry out this plan without being seen and attacked by the 2nd Division picquets. They would then be driven in, the Russians would establish a position on Shell Hill, and after that the main position on Home Ridge would be attacked.

Although the 2nd Division was supported by the Guards Brigade and the 4th Division, and also by General Bosquet, who moved his Zouaves closer to the British position, its strength was only 2,644 men, the remainder being in the trenches. It had, however, strong artillery support from its own two field batteries, B and G, commanded by Captains J. Pennycuik and J. Turner. The Duke of Cambridge, in very good time, sent up one of his field batteries, H, commanded by Captain Wodehouse to support the 2nd Division.

At about midday on 26 October 1854, Colonel Federoff, with an attacking force of six battalions, around 4,300 men and six light guns, moved out from the Karabel Faubourg, crossed the Careenage Ravine by its viaduct, ascended along the Sapper Road to the brow of Mount Inkerman and marched eastwards across the front of our picquets until the head of his column reached the Volovia Gorge. They then turned right and the column of march was converted into an order of battle (see map).

They advanced toward a picquet of the 49th Regiment, which resisted the enemy with great courage. Lieutenant Connolly fought the enemy fiercely, and after the battle he was offered and accepted a commission in the Coldstream Guards. Later on he was awarded the Victoria Cross.

Evans refused to reinforce the picquets, keeping his forces on Home Ridge as he wanted to use the natural strength of the ground and his eighteen field pieces to destroy the enemy.

A separate column meanwhile was ascending Careenage Ravine, which ran along the left flank of the British position, which up to that time was not visible to the defenders of that flank. Captain Goodlake, Coldstream Guards, and his thirty sharpshooters of the Guards Brigade, which included the ten best shots from each battalion, were situated at the end of the ravine, close to the British lines (see map).

Captain Goodlake and Sergeant Ashton advanced along the ravine to guard against an ambush and to examine the caves. While they were inside a cave, a party of Russians, 600–800 strong, became visible to the sharpshooters who fired on them and retired along the ravine. Goodlake and Sergeant Ashton burst out of the cave and fought their way down the slope. Owing to their grey overcoats and flat caps, they were able to lose themselves in the mass of grey-coated Russians who were advancing along the bed of the ravine. Assisted by the thickets of brushwood, they were able to make their way unmolested to the front of the column. As the column came to a halt, confronted by the sharpshooters, Goodlake and his Sergeant dashed across the space between the two parties and joined their men. The Russians were unable to advance further and after a lengthy combat they remained where they were. Later on Captain Markham of the Rifles and his men joined the sharpshooters and inflicted more casualties.

For his bravery and success in holding the left flank of the British line, Captain Goodlake was awarded the Victoria Cross and Sergeant Ashton was given a commission in the Rifles.[6] Another Coldstreamer awarded the Victoria Cross for bravery on a sharpshooting operation was No. 3968 Private William Stanlock.[7]

Colonel Federoff was grievously wounded and his troops were repulsed by the artillery and soldiers of the 2nd Division. Apart from the sharpshooters, the Guards Brigade was not involved in this operation.

Captain Goodlake, Coldstream Guards – Extract from a Letter to his Parents, 6 November 1854[8]

I have 30 volunteer men from the Brigade who act under me (Sharpshooters). We go out and shoot Russians and picquets. I killed 5 men, one at 300 yards through the head and an officer at 30 yards. Most exciting! I and a Sergeant[9] were nearly trapped in a cave but we made a bolt for it and got away with a bullet through my coat and he was shot in the arm.

Captain Higginson, Adjutant of 3 Grenadiers – Letter to Captain Hatton, Regimental Adjutant[10]
Writing about the Little Inkerman action:

Heights above Sevastopol
October 27th 1854

My dear Hatton
I tore open your letters of the 9th & 13th. We had been longing for a sight of the despatch and an account of the way the despatch was received in dear old England. I seized the newspaper and hollered to the men, who were standing near and read them the account Lord Raglan gives of the advance of our Brigade and read them the paragraph in which he so well alludes to sickness and privations that they had undergone.

I never saw fellows look so pleased as our Grenadiers did, but they had hardly time to talk it over before one of Sir De Lacy Evans's aide de camps rode up saying that the Russians were advancing in very strong force up the hill in their front and that the picquets of the 2nd Division were driven in. We were under arms immediately, few though we were for we had 200 men away on outpost or covering parties so that we could only take him 270 men to support his Division, already reduced to 1000 available men from the number of picquets it has to find.

Four immense columns of Russians pushed boldly up the hill and as our field batteries could not get to work at first, they met with only the feeble resistance of our outlying picquets. But as battery after battery arrived and shot shell and spherical case fell upon these dense columns their pace slackened; still they advanced until it was time for the Minie to open on them. Then the 30th & 49th rattled away at the intruders, while additional guns redoubled their fire; there could only be one conclusion as you may imagine. A halt, a shaking and a rout followed closely on each other and then came our turn; the 30th & 49th advanced and followed the enemy right up to Sevastopol. While a Lancaster gun, which by good fortune commanded the valley through which they had to retreat, tore up whole sections of theirs like so much brown paper.

We ourselves, though for a short time under their fire, were held in reserve. We never fired a shot, so all the credit for this brilliant little affair is due to Sir De Lacy Evans and his Division. Our loss I am told is 3 officers wounded and 50 men killed and wounded. The Russian loss is fearful. Up to a late hour last night we were bringing in their wounded, who lay in heaps. Not less than 500 men must have been put *hors de combat*, and the remainder will, I think, think twice before they attempt the English position again.

After waiting for nightfall in the plain watching the Russians establishing themselves in our redoubts, which those wretched Turks had suffered them to take, we retraced our steps to our camp somewhat heavy at heart at the loss that our poor cavalry had suffered.

You may imagine that the arrival of our letters and the little brush with the columns that *would* attack our positions acted quite like a tonic upon our men. You know the result. Little did they know that less than 2000 Englishmen were more than a match for their huge columns.

As for the siege I confess I am puzzled. All accounts agree that the state of the garrison is deplorable and the French continue drawing their parallels closer and closer so the crisis is at hand. In the meanwhile we are kept on the qui vive by that army in our rear, which cannot be less in numbers than 30,000 men, while more are expected daily.

I should not be surprised to hear that Balaklava was not to be abandoned. It is not necessary to us and requires a large force to cover it.

You will be glad to hear that the Battalion is decidedly improved in health. I mean <u>general</u> health for our sick returns do not show much diminution. We have had no casualties since I last wrote save one man who was slightly wounded in the leg yesterday. Reynardson [Commanding Officer] is far from well but his pluck is indomitable. He is really at the moment of action and danger far more decided, *however*, and encouraging in tone than when on an ordinary quiet parade.

Our Sergeant Major has been away very unwell but returned yesterday. I cannot speak sufficiently of Sergeant Major Algar. His energy and vigilance are my mainstay and he too, poor fellow, has been far from robust.

We are very short of officers, as many are still on the sick list though none seriously. I hear we are to have a draft immediately. We want Ensigns, recollect that several of the wounded from Alma have rejoined us from Scutari and the others I hear are doing well.

Adieu. I cannot tell you how pleased and happy we are at hearing you are proud of us! Pray give my best regards to Colonel Wood and all friends.

I am yours sincerely
George Higginson

Do not suppose because we do not speak about Hood that we do not think about him!

Unfortunately, the British did not realize that the Russian action was a reconnaissance in force to discover the layout and strength of the British defences, and also to find out how they reacted to an attack on their front. They felt that the Russians, after such a defeat, would not try to attack again. This assumption was incorrect as they found out on 5 November.

Notes

1. Mercer, Patrick, *Give them a Volley and Charge!* Spellmount, 1998, pp. 43–6.
2. Davis, *Sherwood Foresters' Annual 1934*, letter, p. 215.
3. Kinglake, A.W., *Invasion of the Crimea*, vol. 5, Blackwood, 1875, pp. 49–50.
4. *Ibid.*, Appendix IV, p. 489.
5. Kinglake, vol. 5, pp. 1–19.
6. For a longer account of this operation see Springman, Michael, *Sharpshooter in the Crimea*, Pen & Sword, 2005, pp. 51–8.
7. *Ibid.*, p. 57.
8. Springman, p. 77.
9. Sergeant Major Joseph Ashton, Coldstream Guards, was promoted to Lieutenant in the Rifle Brigade on 28 February 1855, backdated to 8 November 1854. Caldwell, George and Cooper, Robert, *Rifle Green in the Crimea*, Bugle Horn Publications, 1994, p. 226.
10. Letter held in the Regimental records at RHQ Grenadier Guards.

CHAPTER 8

The Battle of Inkerman, up to the Intervention of the French Army, 5 November 1854

Battle Timetable

Alexander Kinglake in his book, *The Invasion of the Crimea*, divides the battle into seven periods. The principal events, relating to the Guards Brigade, are given below.[1]

First Period
0545–0730

	Russian	Allies
0545–0600	Soimonov's army (19,000) to Shell Hill. First contact with British picquets.	Troops alerted and formed up on Home Ridge. Pennefather reinforces picquets.
0700	Enemy under-road column advances up Careenage Ravine. Both Soimonov & Paulov (16,000) attack.	Coldstream to man Sapoune Heights. Grenadiers & SFG . to 2nd Division front.
	Under-road column is driven back by Clifford (2nd Div) and by fire from Grenadier picquet.	Grenadier picquet engages under-road column on left flank.
	Russians occupy unoccupied Sandbag Battery.	Brig Adams attacks with 41st and recaptures Sandbag Battery.

At the end of the first period, the Russian attacks have been held all along the line. Soimonov's army, with the death of its leader, takes little further part in the battle. The fog lifts, making it easier for the Russians to find their way on unfamiliar ground, but giving advantage to the superior British riflemen.

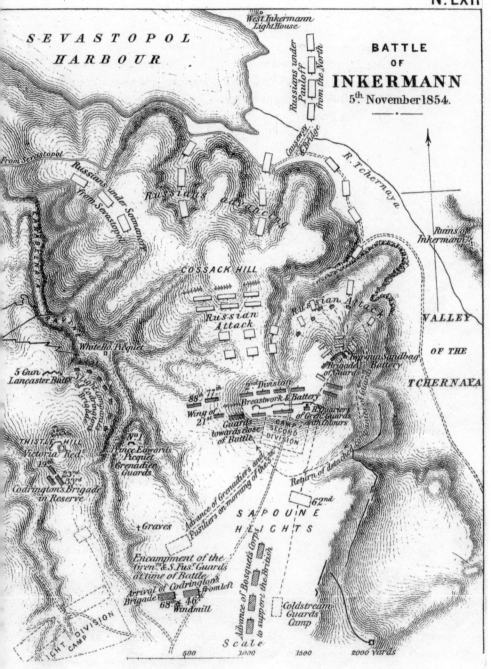

Within the map:

SEVASTOPOL

HARBOUR

West Inkermann
Light House

Russians under Pauloff
from the North

BATTLE
OF
INKERMANN
5th November 1854.

From Sevastopol

Russians under Soimanoff
from Sevastopol

Causeway Bridge

R. Tchernaya

Russians advancing

Ruins of
Inkermann

COSSACK HILL

Russian
Attack

Russian Attack

VALLEY

White Ho. Picquet

OF THE

TCHERNAYA

5 Gun
Lancaster Batts.

Light Companies of
Codringtons
Brigade

Breastwork & Battery

Brigade
of Guards

Sandbag
Battery

38. 77th

2nd Division

Wing of
21st

Return of Gren. Guards
with Colours

THISTLE HILL

Victoria Redt.
19th

No 1
Prince Edwards
Picquet
Grenadier
Guards

Guards
towards close
of Battle.

CAMP
SECOND
DIVISION

Return of detached companies of Guards

23rd
33rd

Codringtons Brigade
in Reserve

Advance of Grenadiers and
Fusiliers on morning of the 5th

62nd

Graves

SAPOUNE
HEIGHTS

Encampment of the
Gren. & S. Fus. Guards
at time of Battle

Advance of Bosquets Corps
to support the British

Coldstream
Guards
Camp

Arrival of Codringtons
Brigade from left

68th   46th
Windmill

LIGHT DIVISION CAMP

Scale

500   1000   1500   2000 Yards

attle of Inkerman, opposite p. 215, *History of the Grenadier Guards.*

Second Period
0730–0830

	Russian	Allies
0730	Gen Dannenberg takes command. Okhotsk, Yatutsk & Selinghinsk Regiments attack Sandbag Battery.	Adams forced to abandon the Battery & is mortally wounded.
		Grenadiers recapture the Battery, but find it untenable & abandon it.
		SFG repel attack from St Clements Ravine.
	Okhotsk Battalions recapture Battery, but are driven out.	Grenadiers recapture Battery & resist Okhotsk attack.
	One Yakutsk Battalion counters Cathcart's outflanking move. Another Battalion gets into position on Fore Ridge, threatening troops at the Battery.	'The Gap' opens between the Battery & 2nd Div. Cathcart (4th Div) refuses to fill 'The Gap'. Torrens Brigade descends the slope followed by many troops from the Battery. This is the 'False Victory'.
		The Duke of Cambridge escapes capture at Battery; Asst Surg Wolseley leads charge to prevent this.
0830		The French attack & reach the base of Inkerman Spur.

At the end of the Second Period, the intervention by the French has stabilized the area of the Sandbag Battery. Repeated attacks on Home Ridge have been repelled. The British had, however, lost half of their original strength of 4,700, while Dannenberg still had 9,000 men in reserve, 8,000 men in the fighting line, and 100 guns in batteries on Shell Hill.

Objective

The objective of this chapter is to explain the record of the Guards Brigade in this battle. At the Battle of Inkerman, the Guards Brigade held their position on the right flank of the allied front, supported by such Regiments as the 95th, and other soldiers from line regiments, against an enemy which varied between four and ten times the allied troops. Similar Homeric struggles were taking place on the battlefield elsewhere. These took place at the Barrier, and on the 2nd Division position on Home Ridge, especially during the assault of the 'massive trunk-column' on this position. Similar struggles took place on the allies' left wing.

Success on all these fronts made certain the repulse of the Russian Army. Failure on one front only would have almost certainly resulted in defeat. Every regiment that bears this battle honour on their Colours can take pride that their bravery and fighting spirit made a signal contribution to this victory.

Captain C. T. Wilson, Coldstream Guards

In his book, *A Regimental Officer, Our Veterans of 1854*, he gives a very comprehensive account of the battle from the point of view of the Guards Brigade:

> The evening of the fourth was miserably cold; and sleety rain fell incessantly. In the front all was still. At 2:00 a.m., on the 5th, the foremost sentries in the outlying picket reported that they heard the noises of wheels in the Valley of Inkerman. It being supposed by the piquets that the rumbling came from peaceable carts on their way to the town. They should have realized that this was the movement of artillery.
>
> At 6.30 am, as the light was glimmering through the fog, the whole Guards Brigade went into action.[2]
>
> On the fourth of November, the enemy received strong reinforcements. That night Russian forces attacked our piquets. No sooner was Shell Hill free of our men, than the Russians dragged their batteries onto its top and began to open fire. It was while our troops were in the act of getting under arms, that the 32-pounder howitzers and 24-pounder guns, in position on Shell Hill, commenced discharging "their devilish glut."
>
> Never, surely, did soldiers make ready to fight, and to die, under more tremendous circumstances. Upon the plateau hung a fog, an impenetrable wet blanket, so thick that it was next to an impossibility to make out an object twenty yards off; on all sides, too, the roar of deep-throated ordnance; and, beating full against the files as they mustered, ripping and crunching battalions 'ere well formed, an iron maelstrom.
>
> What a blessing we had veterans in our ranks in this extremity, otherwise, it had been a rueful day for England. Adams shoves back battalion after battalion, as they come swarming up, through the brushwood, on the Sandbag Battery.
>
> We now turn to another part of the field. The camps of the Divisions, we left so furiously contending, were considerably nearer the Inkerman valley than was the Guards' camp; hence the Household Brigade came later into action.
>
> On the morning in question, the tent, of which I owned a sixth part, was occupied by only two officers beside myself, the rest of its tenants being on

picquet in Canrobert's redoubt; we thought little of the noise. And then, as it increased, we arose to pull on our boots and put on swords and revolvers to be ready for the 'fall in.' Suddenly was heard the cry, 'STAND TO YOUR ARMS!' We fell in, and in three or four minutes on the word of command,' Left four deep, quick march,' The Coldstream Guards marched away towards the noisiest sounds of battle. The Grenadiers and the Fusiliers, camped somewhat nearer than the Coldstream to the flank attacked, were a little ahead of them. A handful of brave soldiers -- only 17 officers, 34 sergeants, 14 drummers, and 373 rank and file of the Coldstream marched to the Sandbag Battery.

With the Coldstream in place, a thread of about 1300 Guardsmen was thrown across the assailed Ridge. But fresh soldiers are at hand, and such soldiers – the veterans of the British Guard. With ringing cheers, 450 Grenadiers came bounding on; bayonets charged, they rush at the battery, now full of Muscovites. The blow is irresistible. In a horrid minute the little enclosure is black with corpses, and throbbing with wounded. The Grenadiers now split into three divisions: one party occupied the battery; the other two formed at right angles on both flanks. The [Scots] Fusiliers on arriving prolonged their comrades' line to the left; the Coldstream, as they came up, lengthened it on the right. Thus the narrow strip of height, on the peak of which arose the two-gun work, was thinly edged by the *tria junctura in uno*[3] ranged two deep The Duke of Cambridge and General Bentinck had the command.

This was a battle in which matchless 'private soldiership' was all important. The Hill was immersed in vapour; and a man could scarcely see the length of his own company; no man could tell with precision what was going on 50 paces on either side of him. The ground on which we stood was rough and sprinkled with bushes. Below us, on the right, was the Valley of the Tchernaya, and a very sea of mist. On the left, yawned a deep ravine, separating us from where the 2nd Division struggled.

One column attacked the Sandbag Battery, and which being without a banquette or step, on which the defenders might stand to fire over the parapet, was indefensible according to ordinary rules; but this outrageous, abnormal emergency admitted of no rules, so we regarded the miserable work as a very true citadel and clung to it tooth and nail; other columns at the same time assailing both flanks.

Owing to the thickness of the fog, the Russians could approach within thirty yards of us without being clearly perceived. This was no disadvantage to the English; for at such close quarters, the Minie played with terrific effect on the serried masses, blasting them like flashes of lightning. No human nature, however disciplined and stubborn, the Muscovite military nature is both, could make head against that hellish musketry. After a minute or two of sharp firing, the columns would get troubled; waver a little; and then turn to the right about, and retire; nevertheless, we were not left unmolested for an instant; no sooner had one corps made off, than its supporting battalion started up before our view, with the same dull stereotyped yells, the same obstinate but soulless action. Although, in consequence of their massive formation, and the admirable weapon, with which they were smitten, the enemy suffered comparatively far more, than our own dispersed line; yet, at a very early hour of the morning the British losses were heavy.

Scarcely had we well fallen to, before I saw the Coldstream Adjutant, Elliot, no man was ever more deservedly beloved, stretched dead, and the favourite 'grey' – poor little Bashi-bazouk – standing bleeding by his master's side.

As my company took ground to a flank, the colour-sergeant was felled with a bullet through the side. Never can I forget the look that dying man cast upward at me as I passed on: it was horrible in its intensity. Every moment, on every side, comrades were dashed down.

As time wore on, and the ranks lessened, nearly every semblance of order on the battalion scale vanished. All the officers and non-commissioned officers, the gallantry and intelligence with which the latter did their duty could not be surpassed, had now power to do, was to keep the soldiers of their respective companies partially together. Tactics, of course, there were none. The exigency outstripped art; brute valour and moral constancy were the sole arguments applicable to the situation. Front, right, and left, every Englishman saw, or felt a foe. This foe must be kept at arm's length, or all was lost, and, under the remarkable circumstances of the case, he could only be withstood by individual exertion, by an exhibition almost superhuman of Anglo-Saxon 'pluck', and by the shattering bullet of the Minie. Therefore, wherever danger was, British soldiers stood, clustered in sparse knots, fighting each on his own hook, like so many lions at bay.

Some people talk of the English private 'requiring to be led by the officer', a mistake. On that blood-puddled ridge there was neither leading, nor being led. Every heart, no matter whether noble or peasant, answered to the call of duty as became a man; every arm struck as became a man; every Grenadier, Coldstreamer, Fusilier, Linesman[4] died, as it is meet a Briton should die, for his country. In place of being under the necessity of cheering on his men, the wary officer had rather to curb their impetuosity, to keep them from being carried by heroic fury too far after the retiring enemy. Of this truth, I had signal proof later in the day.

One might as well attempt to describe the manoeuvres of a faction fight in Tipperary, as to narrate the details of this death-struggle. All to be said is, that amid a dense fog raged wholesale murder; the mortal strife was hand to hand, foot to foot, muzzle to muzzle, butt-end to butt-end.

It must not be supposed that we always stood rooted on our ground and that we never budged. No, the fight rested not steadfast for an instant. It was now backward, now forward, now sideways. Here, a Grenadier party, after a frantic tussle, would be forced by overwhelming swarms out of the battery; there, a knot of Coldstreamers would arrest the advance of an entire Russian battalion; in another place, a cluster of Fusiliers, rallying after a repulse, would fling themselves upon a column, and, with the sheer might of strong hearts, arms, and steel, send it slap-dash over the height's crest. This ceaseless wrestling to and fro accounts for the Sandbag Battery being occupied alternately by men of the different Guard regiments (or, more properly speaking, by mixed parties of the three regiments', larded with brave 'liners'). This was the *modus operandi*.

Whenever Paulov succeeded in ousting one band of defenders from the work, a comrade batch, the nearest at hand, would rush in, and by a combination of bullet, bayonet, and gun stock, thrust forth the intruders. As these isolated engagements took effect beard to beard, officers had occasionally opportunities of testing the sort of stuff out of which their swords had been forged. Wilkinson's cutlery[5] stood the trial well – not so the handiwork of less careful armourers. At any rate, I can assert that my recreant blade, which had been bought from the tailor who rigged me out on appointment, bent like a thing of pewter over the thick skull of an unpleasantly forward Calmuck. To all expectant ensigns of my acquaintance do I exhibit this goose-begotten tuck, with the hope that its disloyal curve may be unto them warning against an inconsiderate and all-in-the-lump purchase of their equipments.

The 'Colts', which were either decently capped, or had escaped the malign influence of the wet night, did their owners faithful service; but such pistols as had suffered from damp, or were furnished with miserable American caps, bought at Constantinople, could not be depended on. Out of my five barrels I could only persuade one to do its duty; from that one, however, went a lucky, but not mortal ball.

Time marches so marvellously fast in battle – hours fly like minutes – that it is utterly impossible for men plunged in the melee, to form an idea of how they stand with the clock. I have, therefore, no notion at what period reinforcements reached us. All I know is, that, toward the close of the fight, I saw many linesmen fighting intermixed with guardsmen. One occasion, being hard pressed on a flank, I ran to another band of our fellows to obtain help. Among those I appealed to, was a soldier of the 20th Regiment; to my shout, 'Fall in there my good fellow,' the honest man, under the impression that he was being ordered away altogether, replied, 'O yer honor, don't be after sinding me off, I'd like to go on fightin wid the guards.' When it was explained that he was simply asked to lend a hand and rifle to some guardsmen, who were in jeopardy hard by, the gallant Patlander said not another word, but sprang into the desired position, and fell fighting like Leonidas.[6]

No lull in the battle-storm. Despite melting ranks, despite the fresh regiments which continued to stream up the hill side, despite the growing scarcity of ammunition, the English clung to their battery with the grip of despair. If, by chance, the bull dog's hold was for an instant shaken off, the next moment his teeth closed tighter than ever on the sand bags.

So immense was the importance of the little tongue of land on which we stood at bay – among other advantages, the mastery of it, would have enabled the Russians to operate with withering effect on the right flank of the 2nd Division, which could only just withstand the weight of the front attack – that Paulov made mighty exertions to gain a footing. The fewer the bearskins visible, the greater the number of flat caps that thronged up. The Guards, occupying the redoubt, by standing on the carcasses of the slain, were enabled to fire over the parapet at the enemy fermenting underneath; or, as cartridges grew scarce, to smash out their brains with musket butts, and to heave big stones down upon them.

The Russian officers behaved like true soldiers. They were ever in front of their less adventurous rank and file, urging them on with voice, and uplifted sword; nay, they rushed freely on certain death, with the view of inflaming the sluggish spirit of their followers. I saw one glorious fellow leap with an hurrah from the parapet of the battery into the midst of a chevaux-de-fries of bayonets. A private soldier followed; while one would wink, the two was dead, pierced to the back-bone in twenty places.

And now, half the Brigade, a grandiose title for 1,300 men, strewed the ground; some slain outright, others bleeding to death, others vainly imploring to be carried off the field. Oh that I must write 'vainly', but in the devilish turmoil not a man, whom God had shielded, could be spared to carry away the wounded. The honour of England, nay, the very safety of the Army demanded that all living should be breast to breast with the Russians.

At one moment I caught sight of three officers of my acquaintance, stretched side-by-side almost. Two, Butler and Neville, had done for ever with human misery; the third, Pakenham of the Grenadiers, lived still; I heard him faintly beg for a stretcher, heard him murmur how he had been basely stabbed after his fall. I looked about for the drummers, whose duty it was to succour the wounded, but a sudden press carried me nearly off my legs, and I saw that brave soldier no more.

It is known that the 4th Division (Cathcart) on approaching the battle was split into two independent bodies. The 1st Brigade (Goldie) marched to the left of the Inkerman Road, to the support of the 2nd Division. The 2nd Brigade (Torrens) led by the gallant Cathcart in person, proceeded to the extreme right for the purpose of strengthening the Guards. It would appear that when Sir George reached the rear of the imperilled 'Brigade', he found them struggling to regain the battery out of which they had been lately driven.

Now, the morning was still so thick, the confusion so confounded, that a newcomer was not at all likely to form a correct idea of the real complexion of matters. Perhaps Cathcart underestimated the force with which the enemy acted; perhaps he thought (as many would have thought under the circumstances) a stroke at the Russian left or rear to be the most judicious assistance he could render his over-taxed countrymen. Be that as it may, at the head of two or three companies of the 68th, and some 200 men of the 20th and 46th, he plunged into a hollow, a little to the right of the battery.

The result is notorious. Hardly had the devoted troops quitted the hill-top, than they found themselves enveloped, hemmed in, pinned down by deep columns. There was no retreating. For a while, the soldiers fought with the rage of desperation, and then – destruction. The general and his *alter ego*, Seymour, fell dead, hit with many bullets; Torrens and Maitland (aide-de-camp) were badly wounded, and the few soldiers, not shot down, were scattered hither and thither in hopeless flight.

Meanwhile, the Guards, who, in the rush and trampling, and skull-cracking of the strife, had been ignorant of Cathcart's ill-fated diversion in their favour, seemed at their last gasp, every minute found them less able—not a jot less willing – to repel the enemy. Hardly a man had tasted food that morning, hence, individual strength began to flag; where companies had contended, now only sub-divisions struggled, hence, collective power was ebbing fast. Nor was this all, ammunition had become frightfully scarce; in many cases, indeed, the soldiers had none left, so they were reduced to rifling the pouches of their fallen messmates; and when that resource failed, to pounding away at the ugly Calmuck visages with stocks and stones.

I have said that the men needed no pricking on, 'no inspiring example', on the contrary, that the officer had more frequently to draw the rein than to ply the spur. Of this truth, a remarkable illustration was now afforded me. The group, with which I was connected, had forced a superior number of Russians into hurried flight down the hill-side into the valley. With this good fortune the brave fellows ought to have been content. Not so, however, immediately the 'Muscov' showed their heels, I saw several soldiers break away from the right of my party, and pursue the fugitives. It was plain that, unless the hunters were quickly halted, they hasted to destruction. Therefore, shouting 'halt! halt!' I ran after them.[7]

As well might a penny trumpet strive to make its puny pipe heard amidst the crash of Costa's orchestra,[8] as my small voice in that mortal uproar. Down the steep we went: the dogs of war hot upon the trail, I calling them off with impotent vehemence. We reached the valley in disorder. Scarcely had our feet touched the plain, before some of Liprandi's riflemen sprang up from amongst the bushes, and blazed full in our faces. A few men dropped. At this moment, several soldiers of the 46th and 68th—remnants of Torrens's crushed brigade—joined us: we all turned about; and began to re-ascend the hill. The rise was precipitous, the ground slippery; distant field-pieces let fly grape at us, without, however, doing much hurt; *tirailleurs* kept peppering our backs; not a round left in our pouches.

Every minute guardsmen and 'liners' rolled over, some struck with lead, others done for through sheer exhaustion. It was a dire emergency—press on, or die. We had got about half-way up the height, and were beginning to think ourselves safe;

and yet the worst was to come. On a sudden, a shower of bullets from the hill's crest, right above our heads, amazed us; the soldiers around me cried out, 'Why, our own chaps are firing on us; we be mistaken for Rooshians.' Looking upward, I beheld, through the vapour which still hung upon the plateau, a black line of infantry, which I also took for countrymen; and so, with one accord, we roared, 'Hold hard, for God's sake: we are English!' The louder we shouted, the heavier rained the balls about our ears. Dismal predicament a set of panting wretches clambering up a mountain, between two fires! We still toiled upward, and then it became plain that the troops shooting at us from above, were Russian, that by some mishap had gotten possession of our old position on the ridge. As soon as I ascertained the fact, I formed my *omnium gatherum* into single file with an interval of several paces between each man, and desired the soldiers, instead of advancing straight to the front, to turn sharp to the left, and proceed along the hill's side, inclining gradually towards the summit.

My object was to gain the rear of the enemy, our only chance of avoiding cold steel or bonds. As we ran in this string for our very lives, a man fell wounded near me; the thump of his fall made me turn round; as I did so, two Russians started up from behind a bush, and, with bayonets fixed, dashed at the poor shuddering fellow, but the Grenadier, nearest him had marked their damnable intent and, before a word could be said, I heard the muzzle of a musket ring upon the breast-bone of one ruffian; I saw a gory point, protruding between his twitching shoulder-blades. With a last effort, the transfixed raised his firelock to strike at his assailant, and, in that attitude, tumbled heels over head down the steep place; the second miscreant escaped.

I have said we lacked ammunition. We now actually stumbled upon enough and to spare. Stretched right across our path was a dead ammunition mule, evidently killed by a shell, as also had been the Turkish driver, whose corpse lay close by. Heaven be praised, the panniers were untouched! I shall not attempt to describe the ravenous avidity with which the few men that remained with me seized upon the Godsend. In an instant, the panniers were broken open, and pouches, pockets, caps crammed with cartridges.

The Grenadier Guards
Colonel E.B. Birch Reynardson, the Commanding Officer of the Battalion, wrote to Colonel Woods, the Regimental Lieutenant Colonel, after the Battle.[9]

Before Sebastopol
Nov. 7th 1854

Dear Colonel
I must write you a few lines in the midst of much business in hand to inform you of a general action which took place on Sunday morning early at ½ past 6am between the Russians, who attacked us in very great force at first our 2nd Division and the Brigade.

The Russians during the night had managed to place a large quantity of guns on a Hill commanding the position held by the 2nd Div and with (they say Polish & Russian prisoners) of 56,000 men, we are told under Prince Constantine, himself; these troops principally from Odessa. Our informant says with provisions for 4 days, and they were certainly well primed with Raki.

When we got to the scene of action which was about an hour after it commenced we were under a very severe fire of shells and some shot from the overwhelming force of Russian artillery & as we had not got into position, they were doing great mischief *on crowning the height*. We found one of our redoubts taken by a very large force of Russians, who were pouring a tremendous fire into us as we advanced. There was nothing to be done than to take this position from them, which our Gallant fellows did in very good style; the fire now was worse than Alma & our poor fellows began to fall.

Sergeant-Major Algar amongst the first shot through the head! He died next day – a sad sad loss to us. (Sergeant Norman takes his place and Powley next to him.)

At this time my charger was shot from under me, four shots in her neck and chest & I think in the girth – and another in the loins, so I had to go thus the rest of the day on foot – all our horses were soon *told off* – and the staff being [word(s) missing] from loss of horses, and themselves wounded amongst them General Bentinck in the arm. We were pretty well left to ourselves. Once from the overwhelming forces of Russians and their turning our flank from such insufficiency of support, we were *obliged* to retire behind the breastwork and the redoubt was retaken by the Russians.

However we soon went at them again and after a very sharp fire, and when short of ammunition, pelting them with stones, we succeeded in driving them down the Hill. I ordered the Grenadiers to charge with the bayonet, but not to go down the Hill after them on any account. However they were so flushed with success, they did overdo it, and the consequence was we were <u>almost</u> outflanked again, and were obliged to retire behind the breastwork again to refresh ourselves from the fatigue and get a fresh store of ammunition, for we had long been without it in some parts of our line.

I cannot speak <u>too highly</u> of the <u>individual conduct of all</u> the officers, who were important in their endeavour to keep up a good front and nobly as our gallant fellows behaved, it would have been no *help* to have attempted to hold the position much longer, had not our reinforcements come up, and in which the French rendered very great assistance.

I grieve to say that in this attack we have lost three officers – Lt Col Pakenham, Sir R. Newman & Capt H. Neville; wounded Sir J. Ferguson, Percy, Tipping, Barford – contusion, Hamilton – contusion. How any escaped is to me a perfect marvel.

A spent ball hit my arm and went through my cloak and a shell smashed my Grenadier Cap, as it did at the Alma. So I have indeed to thank God for his Mercies to me.

I have just seen General Bentinck, who is going away for three months. Upton [Coldstream] has the Brigade of course.

We have just found some of our missing men were killed, which will be in the return. We are now 5 Companies of 30 files each!!!! So your 80 men will be of little *reward* to us. [If we] have any more loss we shall soon be wiped out of the list altogether. As yet we have had to bear always a heavy share of the work.

Sir G. Cathcart was killed by too free exposure of himself I fear. Torrens Wounded: Genl. Adams, Dr Osmond and Genl. Bentinck; Upton not much hurt, but the staff also have suffered very much.

I told Percy I should not forget the gallant manner he tried to rally our men and did rush up almost single handed and unbacked [by men] to the redoubt, and was the means of returning them to the assault, where he got a blow over the head.

However I must say all behaved admirably and it is difficult to particularize. I made Palmer [later awarded the VC] a N.C.O. from the gallant manner he followed Sir C. Russell, [later awarded the VC] who offered to lead them at a critical time, if they would follow him. He [Palmer] was the only man who was near and bayoneted a Russian who would have otherwise killed Sir C.R. Russell. Higginson [Adjutant] has seen your letter.

We seldom have any rest and as all our men & officers suffer more or less from the horrid bowel complaint of this country; if we cannot get less work and more rest we shall soon be a sorry lot.

The Coldstream were a good deal cut up. The Fusiliers very little in comparison. Poor Blair [SFG] died this morn; Walker [SFG] was also wounded slightly in the neck; there seem to be few who escaped altogether. I can't remember the names of the 8 officers of the Coldstream who were killed. Just been told we are to be in readiness to turn out, and having sent a party to bury the Dead have just 100 men!!! disposable.

I expect John Bull has overrated our powers and thinks we are invulnerable; whereas the Russians can supply their army I fear to any amount. I am so glad Nicoll is coming out as we are sadly short of medical advice. Poor Bradford [Lt Col] is so rheumatic, he cannot crawl about scarcely; he is most plucky and does his best but could not get on in the Affair the other day, as he had no horse. I must recommend him to get leave for a few days or weeks, and that may entail a medical board, but he is of very little use.

I am believe me yours most truly
Ed. Birch Reynardson.

I hear I am to congratulate you on the birth of a daughter. I hope doing well.

P.S. Late tonight Laurence (Asst Surgeon) & 1 Sergt. & 32 men just arrived, after buffeting about in the sea for a fortnight; their clean appearance are a strange contrast to our tattered fellows here, who many of them have hardly trousers to cover themselves.

My last return says:	Off.	Sergts	Drums	Cpl	Pts
	3	4	1	4	66 Killed
	6	6	1	11	127 Wounded
Missing					
	9	10	2	15	197

Just had a turnout & false alarm; it seems we are never to sleep with our uniforms off. I have done so once since we landed at Eupatoria.

8th. We expect to move our ground today nearer to Lord Raglan to give us a little rest & change; for here we are turned out for everything and our men horrified to death which in weak state from [word(s) missing] and shortness of numbers would soon [word(s) missing].

Captain George Higginson, the Adjutant of the Battalion, wrote to Captain Hatton, the Regimental Adjutant, after the Battle:

The morning of the 5th Nov. broke misty and chill. After a foggy night, as I lay preparing to get up at about 6 o'clock, having slumbered since 5 when our outlying piquet relief had *started*, I heard shots in the direction of General Evans camp on our right. I darted out of the tent and to my horror saw some heavy guns blazing at his position from the heights just in front of him up which they must have carried them during the dark night. Of course we were under arms and off to the assistance directly of the 2nd Division and in less than a quarter of an hour we were hotly engaged.

The Russian force appeared to be enormous and soon drove in the 2nd Division regiments, already enfeebled by previous losses. The battery for two guns in front of the position was carried (there were no guns in it) and the Grenadiers were ordered to charge and retake it. Our fellows responded with a cheer, fixed bayonets and went at it at the double. Away went the Russians out of the battery and down the hill, closely pursued by the Grenadiers; then followed a mistake in general opinion nearly fatal to us, but I must retrace my course.

Just as we reached the battery, Bentinck was wounded and all our chargers were killed at least Reynardson's, Hamilton's [Colonel & mounted officer] and mine were, so that we had no mounted officers; for Cadogan had been obliged to dismount owing to the rough ground. Consequently it was impossible to check the pursuit as soon as we ought and in vain did we shout to some 60 or 70 fine fellows, who were chasing five times their numbers down a slope which was almost a precipice. The Russians still masters of the high ground on their left, stood their ground and as strange to say no support came to us and we had been fighting now 2 hours with our weak brigade against ten times our numbers.

We had to retire and reform. This was done beautifully about 100 yards in rear of the battery which of course the Russians again reoccupied, thereby cutting us off as we reformed our men, who had followed down the hill.

Then we saw the French coming in on our rear, so again we went at the battery, Percy leading with some of his men, he himself being full 10 yards ahead of anyone. Again the Russians flew out of the battery and fell back again upon their supports which came pressing in up the valley, on the left the head of which valley you must try to comprehend, badly as I explained it, outflanked the battery altogether.

Strange to say the French did not come in support as we had hoped but were detained for some reason or other by Canrobert, I fancy on account of the appearance of the Russians on their flank.

It now became to be serious – our ammunition failed and there was no reserve to hand and the havoc made to our bearskins by the Russians, reduced us as a battalion to not more than 100 men, not including the men who had gone in pursuit and whom we thought annihilated.

Again therefore we left the battery, keeping a good line towards the left flank and filing up the hill until we found that the Russians had driven back the Regiments of the 2nd Division on the left of ourselves and were actually above us and between us and a large redoubt which covers the height just in front of Evans' camp.

I looked at the Colours I thought for the last time and I believe everyone down to the private soldiers thought that the poor old 3rd Battalion was doomed.

Not a round of ammunition was left and we were being peppered on three sides.

Then followed perhaps the brightest achievement Englishmen are capable of, sticking close to the Colours, which Turner and Verschoyle carried like heroes, the men went up the hill at the charge and literally charged home a distance of not less than ¼ of a mile to the upper redoubt. God alone knows how thankful we were when we sprang through the embrasures and fell utterly exhausted in this secure rallying place. For in the meanwhile the French had arrived in very large force and tackled the Russians most nobly.

Ten minutes rest set us to right and we filled our pouches with cartridges and longed for news of our missing comrades. We had been lying in comparative safety, for nearly an hour. I say comparative for the Russian shot and shell only shaved our heads instead of taking them off; then up rode the Duke, who almost cried with delight at seeing us and the Colours; he had given us up for lost and was mourning over the annihilation of the regiment.

By this time the Zouaves and our finest aspects of the Light Division assisted by some heavy guns, which had been wheeled up by hand, had driven back the enemy and made the victory complete, so nobly begun by our 2nd Division and our very weak brigade.

We got the order to move off to the left in rear of some French guns which required support and you may fancy our delight at finding Cadogan & Percy with the main body of our missing men who the latter had led round the foot of the hill up a bye road to our rear. The way these fellows cheered at seeing the Colours again would have done your heart good.

We had another two hours to wait under a most galling fire of artillery until the Russians were finally routed, and when we returned to camp it was 4 p.m. so that we had been fighting nine hours and a half! The Russians had at least 42,000 men opposed to us, against which the 2nd Division and our Brigade were pitted for three hours without support.

And now for the melancholy part of the history – Pakenham, Henry Neville and Newman fell – their first wounds were not severe and I grieve to add that they were brutally butchered by the enemy. Newman's body was not found till yesterday and was scarcely recognisable. Pakenham poor dear fellow, I saw the last of and until the arrival of the clergyman, for he lived till 10 that night, tried to administer that consolation which alone can give ease to the dying. Neville was carried to the General Hospital and I was greatly upset that when I went there at night, they would not admit to me that his state was so critical. Tipping & Sturt are both severely, but not dangerously wounded; they are both shot in the thigh.

Percy has a slight wound in the face and Fergusson has a contusion on the left wrist, which will disable him perhaps for a month. Hamilton [the Colonel] has a wound in the foot but happily a slight one and dear old Ralph [Bradford] has a slight contusion.

We went into action as near as may be 430 men out of which we have lost the enormous number of 60 killed and 163 wounded (you will see by the return).

You will see in the return of poor Algar's death how little one thought to count on the future. The beginning of this letter shows this most sadly. His loss is not only great it is irreparable. He lived a few hours but was insensible the shot having gone right through his head. I am of course at a loss for a sergeant major.

Norman the senior pay sergeant is acting but with many good qualities has not the calibre of a sergeant major. You must send me Ireland or some good man as soon as possible.

[**Author's note:** Regimental Sergeant Major John Algar was shot in the head and died of wounds on 6 November.]

I might go on writing for hours about this bloody battle but must refrain beyond repeating that I am confident you will hear on all sides that, if it was possible for the 3rd Battalion to behave better than they did at the Alma, it was on the 5th November that they did.

I leave to the Commanding Officer the pleasing task of telling you how nobly the officers led and rallied their men. I cannot however omit mentioning the coolness of Burnaby who had only arrived the day previous from Varna and was for the first time under fire. He has quite re-established our good opinion of him and excited general admiration. My poor little mare struggled on long after she was wounded but fell at last from loss of blood but true to the end.

The Russian loss is perfectly awful and the field of battle is a more horrible spectacle even than that of Alma. The estimate of dead is by some even rated as high as 10,000.

As for future proceedings I cannot pronounce any opinion. Wiser heads than mine are puzzled but I imagine that something decisive is intended as the French siege attack's further parallels [trenches] are close to the Russian batteries and their mine is reportedly ready.

We have been so much employed in burying the dead and attending to our outposts and the wounded that we do not even know who is to command us.

Bentinck's wound is only slight and he is to have the 4th Division, I hear from someone, as soon as he is well, as Cathcart was killed. As for the losses of the poor Coldstream in officers I shudder to think of it. Bentinck and 11 officers of the Brigade HQ all well yesterday and only 2 alive today.

Farewell my dear Hatton I have again been mercifully spared to write you an account of our doings and when there are so many gaps in our once full ranks I almost doubt that I can have *been spared* unwounded through the struggles.

Pray remember me to all friends and pray thank Colonel Wood for his letter to me of the 18th.

Ever yours most truly
George Higginson

The Duke behaved like a trump.

Captain Tipping, Grenadier Guards

His letters relate his experiences at the Battle, until he was wounded in the groin, but the bone was uninjured. He was put on board the hospital ship, *Colombo*, was for a short time in Scutari Hospital, and he was then finally evacuated to England, arriving at Southampton between 17 and 18 December 1855.[10]

Colombo Steamer – Nov 7th

We had a most terrific conflict. Shortly often a break they took us in our rear, at a weak point of our line, concentrating overwhelming force at this Point. They took a redoubt from us, in which we had about 60 or 70 men of the 55th Regiment, I believe. Two battalions of 8 to 9000 Russians advanced from two directions at the same time. We charged down upon the Battery, which was in possession of the Russians and drove them out. They rallied and charged back in overwhelming numbers, and we were obliged to retire. They got into the battery, of course, there was no withstanding such fearful odds. Another company of Grenadiers came over the Hill. We rallied the men, and charged at their head. In ten minutes afterwards, crowds of our fellows were killed. We expelled them. We have lost fearfully.

At the time I was shot, the Russians were close to us, not more than 30 yards. They were in tremendous force, and we attacked them with a handful of men, and were assailed by showers of balls. They had been made half drunk to increase their ferocity; they stood delivering such fire, as almost annihilated our Regiment in the course of half an hour. We were totally unsupported, and attempted to do what I would bet my life, no troops in the world but English, would have attempted.

We had to attack a redoubt or fortification filled with Russians, and strongly supported by a battalion of the best troops they have, which arrived only the day before. This battalion was just under the fortification on the side away from us. Our side was of course lined with as many of their sharpshooters as could load and fire upon us over the parapet. They cut us down so fearfully, that we stopped firing, and charged them with the bayonet, driving them out at the other side, and then fired into the thick of them, they were all jostled together to get out of the redoubt, killing crowds of them.

They soon discovered the weakness of our force, there being only three companies of our Regiment engaged. All our left wing were just over some rising ground, and were I believe attacking artillery, so when the enemy found that we had no Regiment either of Horse or Foot to help or support us, up they came in a mass of columns, and drove our poor miserable little force out of the redoubt again, having sent a division round to attack us in rear.

We retreated out of the redoubt for about three minutes to give the men breathing time, and charged it again, but they were too many for us, and would not move. Three of us got underneath the parapet, and there they were with the muzzles of their guns, close to our heads, but could not depress them sufficiently to shoot us, and the moment their heads came over the top, we had either a revolver or sword to receive them with. They then heaved huge stones upon us. Colonel Percy was very much hurt by one of them.

It was just after this that I got my wound. The Colonel's horse had been shot under him, and he came up on foot, and said that a good flank fire might be obtained, from another part of the fort. I got some men to fire from the spot indicated, as soon as possible, and had been there for about three minutes, in a most exposed spot, when I was hit. On every side of me, fellows were falling, how anybody can have escaped I cannot conceive. There must have been at this point I am describing, 10 or more probably twenty Russians, to one of our men. I know literally nothing of the battle in a general way, I can only speak of the part I was engaged in, and afterwards. I was in too much pain to get any details. Balls passed through several parts of my clothing, before one took effect.

Colonel Pakenham, and Sir Robert Newman, and Neville, all fell much about the same place, and the barbarians came up and bayoneted them on the ground as they lay.

So ended the second part of the battle. The next chapter describes how the French Army came to the assistance of the Guards Brigade.

Notes

1. Kinglake, A.W., *Invasion of the Crimea*, vol. 5, Blackwood, 1875, pp. 87–99.
2. Wilson, Captain C.T., *Our Veterans of 1854 in Camp & before the Enemy*, Street, 1859, pp. 280–312.
3. The then motto of the three regiments of the Brigade of Guards.
4. A soldier from a line regiment.
5. Wilkinson Sword was founded in 1770 as a gunmaker. Henry Wilkinson was a highly skilled technician, who took over the business in 1848 on his father's death. He undertook extensive studies into the nature of steels, from which he became an expert in the construction of swords. He died in 1861; the company then became James Wilkinson & Son, which evolved into Wilkinson Sword. Until the beginning of the First World War, they remained noted gunsmiths, while increasingly being in the forefront of sword development and marketing (W.S. Curtis, Past Chairman, Crimean War Research Society).
6. King of the Spartans, and the leader of a small army of Spartans, resisting the Persian invasion at the Pass of Thermopylae. When he found out that they had been betrayed, he and his small army charged the Persian army and they were all slaughtered.
7. Number 8 Company, 1 Coldstream charged too far and had to be led back. Wilson, pp. 294–6. Number 8 Company, 3 Grenadiers, commanded by Lieutenant Colonel Lord Henry Percy, also charged too far and had to be brought back to the British lines, through the enemy. For this and other brave actions at the Sandbag Battery, Lord Henry Percy was awarded the VC. Hamilton, Lt Gen Sir George, *The Origins & History of the First or Grenadier Guards*, vol. 3, John Murray, p. 232. Colonel E.W.F. Walker, commanding 1 SFG, charged down the slope with his Battalion and was ordered to return to the Sandbag Battery. Maurice, Maj Gen Sir F., *The History of the Scots Guards*, Chatto & Windus, p. 98.
8. Sir Michael Costa (1810–1884), composer and conductor; Director of Music at Covent Garden theatre from 1846; conductor of Philharmonic concerts, 1847–54; knighted, 1869; director of Italian opera from 1871.
9. Original letter in the records at RHQ Grenadier Guards.
10. Tipping, Capt A., 'Letters from the East during the Campaign of 1854', MS, pp. 91–119.

CHAPTER 9

Inkerman – The French Army and Victory, November 1854

Third Period
0830–0915

M arshal Dannenberg concentrates his attack with twelve battalions (6,000 men) on Home Ridge. Major General Pennefather has 3,000 men. Helped by the French, the attack of the massive trunk column is repulsed. A great crisis is averted by a handful of troops, in an infantry equivalent to the charge of the Heavy Brigade.

Fourth Period
0915–1030

	Russian	Allies
0930	Russian artillery is concentrated on our troops at the Barrier.	The French are attacked in the area of the Sandbag Battery.
		Two 18-pounder guns are put into action at the junction of Fore & Home Ridges.
		They concentrate their fire on the enemy artillery on Shell Hill.
		Bosquet arrives with 2,000 infantry on the right flank.

The long-deferred arrival of the 18-pounders is the turning point of the battle.

Bosquet's arrival secures the difficult right flank, the defence of which absorbed so many troops in unnecessary fighting for the useless Sandbag Battery.

Fifth Period
1000–1100

Russian	Allies
The Russians attack the French on the Inkerman Tusk, drive them out and reoccupy the Sandbag Battery.	Bosquet advances to the Inkerman Tusk, and is then forced to withdraw to Fore Ridge.
The Selinghinsk battalions at the Sandbag Battery are routed, and driven back to the Tchernaya.	Bosquet orders the Zouaves to attack the Sandbag Battery, where they are joined by the Coldstream in a successful attack.

At the end of this period, General Canrobert concentrated the French forces in the area from the Kitspur to Home Ridge, and made no further moves against the enemy.

Sixth Period
1100–1300

Russian	Allies
The Russians begin to waver as their guns on Shell Hill begin to suffer from the fire from the 18-pounders.	
	Pennefather confident of ending battle if reinforced; 18-pounders out of ammunition.
	Canrobert won't advance.
	Raglan determined that the Russians will not occupy Shell Hill. Orders attack which causes Russian batteries to limber up & withdraw, which precipitates Russian retreat.
Dannenberg decides to withdraw.	

The offensive spirit of the British infantry was never better seen than at this moment. Pennefather, with no more than 750 men left, tired after a long battle, staged an attack against enemy reserves, on commanding ground, and thus causes the Russian commander to abandon the field.

Last Period
1300–2000

Russian	Allies
The Vladimir battalions advance in mass to cover the withdrawal, and are broken up by the fire of the 18-pounders.	Canrobert refuses to join in the pursuit. Todleben considered this to be a wise decision. Had tired troops attempted to follow up beyond the range of their heavy guns, they would have come under the guns of the town defences and of the ships, and would have suffered heavy casualties.
Prince Menshikov orders Dannenberg to halt the retreat. Dannenberg replies that if he does, the army will be destroyed.	
All enemy artillery is withdrawn from Shell Hill. The withdrawal is now covered by fire from steamships in the Roads.	

Canrobert occupies West Jut with two battalions and one battery.[1]

Out of their attacking force of some 40,000, the Russians lost 10,729 men at Inkerman, killed, wounded or prisoners, including six generals and 256 officers.

Captain Wilson, Coldstream Guards[2]

March! By this time, we were some little distance to the rear of where the Russians stood, when they commenced firing upon us, and were close to the brow of the height. The crisis, therefore, was at hand. Should we escape, or should we be knocked on the head? The odds, I own, seemed rather in favour of the grim alternative. For all that, we put our trust in Providence and kept going. At length, my little band – it had dwindled to next to nothing – topped the ridge. The fog has passed away, there is broad day-light now. But where are the English? Gone; and in their stead large bodies of the enemy. A bad lookout. We're in for it.

Hark, the *pas de charge*! the toll of fifty drums! the bray of fifty clarions! We're saved! We're saved! See, clouds of Zouaves, and Algerians! Bosquet's Light Infantry! As they come bounding towards us, we flourish our muskets with rapture in the air. We cry 'Thank God!' We cheer – how we cheer – '*Wive francis.*' (Such was the unscholarly pronunciation of the benediction.) The French reply with equal heart, '*Vive les Anglais! Les Anglais sont les plus braves soldats du monde!*' And, on every side, hot Zouave hands are stretched forth to clasp ours. We mix with the glorious ranks, and now the grand, the ecstatic moment of a life – VICTORY! TRIUMPH! The warrior whirlwind sweeps on; the Zouaves, with flashing eyes and deep-mouthed oaths – a tiger herd; the 'Turcos' hoarsely screaming and wildly brandishing their rifles. The officers point with their swords to the ever-memorable battery ahead, our goal for the last time, shouting '*En avant mes braves.*'

We are received with a scathing fire from behind the sandbags; it lashes the fury of the *Zu-zus*. By the gorge the torrent floods into the work. The panic-struck Russians are shot, stabbed, bludgeoned, trod under foot by scores, in their endeavour to escape. The place is as a slaughterhouse – blood and groans, and shrieks for mercy; but there is no mercy. At times like this, man is no Christian, but a ruthless savage.

The Zouaves clamber over the parapets of the work, and on after the flying enemy! My God, a hideous sight! The little space in front of the battery (i.e. toward Inkerman) is literally heaped with dead and wounded, so thickly heaped, that nowhere could we get clear footing: our path lay wholly over stiffening carcasses, or fainting wounded.

We were now made to lie down under the edge of the plateau, directly in front of where the Second Division camp had stood only a few hours before. Ahead, our artillery was blazing away, and getting infernally blazed at in return. Although our present position was not an enviable one – shot, shell, case-shot, and grape flew about like hail, too often cutting down good fellows, for whom bayonet and bullet had had mercy previously; yet did it afford us a little rest, which we sorely needed.

Let us return to the time when, in order to touch upon the doings of the Guards, we left the Second and Light Divisions grappling with 'the children of the mist'. It will be remembered how Sir George Brown, with the first note of alarm, sent the 1st Brigade, Light Division, to the uttermost left, that they might hold the slopes adjacent to the town, and cover the English 'right attack' (battery).

The 2nd Brigade of the same division took post more to the right, thus giving the hand to the Second Division, which maintained the centre, i.e. the ground of their own camp.

The Fourth Division, on nearing the scene of action, was divided; its 1st Brigade, under the lamented Goldie, backing up Pennefather on the left of the Simpheropol Road – the 2nd Brigade, as we know, 'doubling' to the relief of the Guards, fighting on the extreme right of the battle. The Third Division (England) could only afford two regiments to the aid of Brown, the rest being employed in or near the trenches, under the orders of the vigorous Eyre.

It must not be supposed that these positions were taken up scientifically, or according to deliberately issued orders. No, they were taken up at random, as troops arrived to fill them. The enemy was here, there, everywhere; consequently, as regiments, in the greater number of instances mere detachments, just relieved out of the trenches, hurried up, they laid on wherever their arms appeared to be in greatest request at the moment. In short, they threw themselves into the first gap that showed itself.

The artillery got into position with all speed; but it was soon manifest that, notwithstanding the skill and courage of our gunners, their 9-pounders and 24-pounder howitzers could not cope advantageously with the superior number and larger calibre of the Russian metal, viz. 24-pounders and 32-pounder howitzers, in position, and field-batteries, consisting of more 12-pounders than 9-pounders. Crimean experience should rid us of all conceit in showy field-day galloping about with pop-guns. To obtain practical results, we must take ugly, heavy metal into our service. Notwithstanding, the Royal Artillery heedless of the immense losses they were sustaining in men and horses, fought on with the same unswerving constancy as their comrades of the bayonet.

The struggle on this part of the field (left and centre) was of a piece with the struggle of the Foot Guards on the right. Here as there, disjointed bodies of British held their own against the deep masses surging upward through vapour-loaded brushwood, under cover of the fire from Shell Hill.

It may be asked, why did not the French render assistance? Because, for a long time, our allies were in a situation of great perplexity and danger. On the left of their siege works they were hard pressed. Taking advantage of the mist which prevented the signals of the sentinels on the look out being perceived, a corps of about 5000 Russians rushed upon the batteries, opposed to the Flag-Staff Bastion; for a while the *coup* prospered. Four mortars were spiked, our allies were thrown into some disorder; but they rallied quickly; and, after a hot conflict, drove their assailants whence they came, with heavy loss.

Yet more, it should be borne in mind that, during the greater part of the morning, it was impossible to ascertain which was the real attack, and which the feint. The plateau is of wide extent. It was shrouded in fog. The roar of cannon, the rattle of small arms was heard in all directions; as far as could be made out, the enemy were advancing from the N.E. and W. For example, Liprandi's army-corps (under Gortchakov) stood *en bataille*, in the valley of the Tchernaya. For a time, the plan of its General was unfathomable. Would Balaklava be attacked? Was the rear of the Allied position to be stormed?

Now, so long as doubt existed as to the particular point against which the Russian force in this quarter would be driven, it was obviously out of the power of Bosquet (especially responsible for the safety of the Anglo-French rear) to detach elsewhere any considerable body of his troops. Nevertheless, at the very outset he did tender to the English such aid as he could spare; but, under a misconception of the nature of the fight, then commencing on the right, that aid was unfortunately declined. In fact, it was not till time had stripped Gortchakov of his false colours, had unmistakeably shown that the horse, foot, and guns marshalled on the banks of the Tchernaya, with all their big looks, meant nothing serious, that the French *corps d'observation* could possibly move to the succour of the English.

About eleven o'clock things looked desperate. Our artillery was overmatched, our Infantry broken into fragments. A vast number of officers had gone down. Unless speedy help came, all was lost. Suddenly the tide turned; the sun pierced through the fog. The omen was a happy one.

With the hope of resisting, on something like fair terms, the enemy's crushing fire, Lord Raglan ordered two 18-pounders (the heaviest metal we possessed outside the siege works) up to the front. Colonel Gambier was severely wounded while exerting himself to get these pieces dragged to the edge of the heights, a difficult task, owing to the losses we had sustained in horses, and the miry, cut-up condition of the ground. Whereupon the command of the guns devolved on Colonel Collingwood Dickson. He was one of the ablest young officers in the army, who by his vigour and skill in this crisis, largely contributed to the coming victory.

And now, Bosquet having seen through the swagger of Gortchakov, was free to befriend the British. He changed front. With the Zouaves and Algerians he struck a terrible blow at the Sandbag Battery; while his troops of the line and field guns advanced to the support of the exhausted but inflexible regiments, holding the left and centre.

Here was the turning point of the battle. With reinforcements came recoil. Although the Muscovites were over and over again rallied, and brought to the scratch by their brave officers, they no longer made headway, nay, they lost ground every minute. Before long, it was plain that they were falling back at all points.

However, those ninety cannon still thundered on; the English and French field-pieces still fought them without success; but when Dickson, after surmounting difficulties, which would have appeared insuperable to a man of inferior talent, and less determination, had gotten his 18-pounders to bear upon the artillery in position on Shell Hill, a change came over the state of things in that quarter.

His opening discharge of the eighteens must have struck home, for almost immediately after it, the enemy's fire grew unsteady, a few more rounds crashing into the midst of guns, gunners, and horses; and the Russians, limbering up, retired behind the crest of the hill. Not yet were they beaten. More than once they re-appeared to dare our shot, more than once they had to hide from its blasting accuracy. Indeed, so dogged was their purpose that it was past four p.m. when their last battery rumbled away for good and all, leaving the plot of ground, to which the 18-pounders had applied their force, marked with one hundred corpses, more than fifty dead horses and a score of upset tumbrels.

The retreat was now general. The more distant Russian brigades withdrew in good order; not so those nearest the Allies. So long as they were sheltered by the fire of their artillery, the assaulting battalions did stoutly, they rallied several times, but, when the might of that tremendous arm began to tail, they lost heart; they turned to the right about, and the English and French drove them at the bayonet point down the slopes into the valley.

There, all was wild confusion. The narrow chaussee [road] crossing the marsh was alive with a vast rushing mob; which some of our field-guns kept racking with plunging shot. Horrible must have been the butchery. Entire sections must have been scranched [ground to pieces].

At half-past four p.m. the soldiers' battle was won. Of the 8,000 Englishmen that fought on this immortal day, 43 officers, 32 sergeants, 4 drummers, 380 rank and file were killed; 101 officers, 121 sergeants, 17 drummers, 1,694 rank and file were wounded; 1 officer, 6 sergeants, 191 rank and file were missing. Total loss. 2,590.

Numbered with the dead were Generals Cathcart, Strangways (of Leipsig renown), and Goldie. Reported as wounded were Generals Brown, Bentinck, Adams, and Torrens.

I subjoin [add] a few figures, which tell, with eloquent simplicity, the Alpha and Omega of the Guards: how 'the Brigade' stood when battle was joined, and how it answered the roll at half-past four o'clock p.m. In the first place, there went forth on that morning:

	Offrs	Sergts	Drums	R & F	Total
Grenadier Guards	22	24	17	438	501
Coldstream Guards	17	34	14	373	438
Scots Fusilier Guards	20	23	17	332	392
					1331

Secondly, there fell, foot to foot with the Russians, of:

	Offrs	Sergts	Drums	R & F	Total
Grenadier Guards, killed	3	4	1	71	
Grenadier Guards, wounded	6	6	0	138	213
Grenadier Guards, missing	0	0	0	4	

	Offrs	Sergts	Drums	R & F	Total
Coldstream Guards, killed	8	3	0	59	
Coldstream Guards, wounded	5	6	2	114	173
Coldstream Guards, missing	0	0	0	0	

N.B. The 8th Company of the Coldstream, out of 62 R and F present in the battle, lost 22 men killed, and 19 wounded. Total casualties, 41; i.e. two-thirds of the effective strength. The eight officers killed were Lt Colonels Dawson and Cowell, Captains Mackinnon, Bouverie, Elliott, and Ramsden; Lieuts Greville and Disbrowe. The five wounded were Colonel G. Upton, Lt Colonels Lord C. Fitzroy and Halkett, Captain Fielding, and Lt Amhurst. The four who escaped unhurt were Captains Stronge and Wilson, Lieuts Tower and Crawley.

	Offrs	Sergts	Drums	R & F	Total
Scots Fus Guards, killed	1	2	0	47	
Scots Fus Guards, wounded	8	8	2	105	152
Scots Fus Guards, missing	0	0	0	0	

Grand total of loss in Brigade of Guards – nearly half of the officers and soldiers actually engaged.   538

The despatch, which informed England of this dearly bought victory, commended the services of many of the living, and blazoned the merits of many of the dead; but from that encomiastic scroll, there was, at least, one remarkable omission. To the memory of Colonel the Hon. Vesey Dawson, shot through the heart while in command of the Coldstream Guards, was conceded not a passing word of eulogy, or of regret. It is melancholy to reflect that on this humble page should stand the only record of how as brave a soldier as ever drew a sword, as noble a gentleman as ever earned the love and respect of his fellow-men, fought and died.

The 6,000 French actually in line, lost about 1,760 men of all ranks; hence, the total casualties of the 14,000 Allies who worsted Menschikov, Dannenberg and two Arch-Dukes, on November 5, 1854, mounted up to 4,850.

Lord Raglan reckoned the number of Russians concentrated for the attack at not less than 60,000. Of these, he believed 5,000 were left dead on the ground, and 10,000 either wounded or made prisoners, which gives 15,000 as the sum total of the enemy's casualties. A Russian writer, in the main a fair one, disputes the correctness of this estimate. He calculates the number of his countrymen actually engaged, or ready to have engaged, at about 29,700, and will admit a loss of only 3,000 killed and 6,000 wounded; total

9,000.[3] With respect to statements so discrepant, we should probably deliver no improper verdict, if we decided that there was a slight exaggeration on one side, and some abridgement on the other.

With the tactical part of the Battle of Inkerman, military criticism has little to do. There was a surprise. There was no manoeuvring. The time for professional craft had slipped away unperceived. Fierce action, stubborn 'pluck' alone might save the day. While you slept the enemy reached your gate. You started up 'twixt waking and sleeping'. With muddled wonder you tumbled into the murky morning. Yon closed with the Muscovite anyhow and everywhere. You waged a murderous 'Donnybrook Fair'[4] fight in the dark. In the end you got the best of it. Voila, tout.

To what causes are we to assign this memorable success? First and foremost, to the indomitable persistence, with which the regimental officers and soldiers maintained the battle, until the arrival of French assistance. Secondly, to the effective fire of the Minié rifle, 'ce feu violent des carbines', as General Dannenberg described it.

In what order did the combatants fall to? The British worked in thin loose lines; the Russians in columns of companies. Only a few paces intervened between the opposing muzzles; hence, the English Minié having for its target a human mass, a large proportion of bullets reached the core of that mass, each well-aimed bullet, killing and mutilating in its course several men; but the rude firelock of the Muscovite, directed at a mere human thread, could at best hurt one soldier. The superiority of our weapon certainly told immensely in our favour. With many eminent military qualities the Russian wants dash. His courage would seem to be passive not active. Unexpectedly received, on gaining the brow of the plateau, with that feu violent, he halted, and began firing in return; thus placing himself at a disadvantage, thus neutralizing the tactical effect of his columns, the functions of which ought to have been fiercely aggressive. Had he, at the commencement of the battle, pushed those columns resolutely forward, it follows, nearly as a matter of course, that, by the sheer momentum of his heavy masses, the British lines would have been broken through, and trampled down utterly. It would have been a question of weight alone. As it was, no devotion, no exertions on the part of the Russian officers, could, at the outset, spur their battalions to one grand combined rush.

Amen to Inkerman. To England and France that 5th of November will be a day of national pride for ever. To their armies it brought salvation and glory. But Russia it set wailing and gnashing her teeth: to her army it bore unmitigated disaster and bitterness of spirit. Not merely did she lose thousands of her bravest sons, that was a small matter; but a desperate and subtle effort, the end of which, to the eye of human wisdom, seemed vengeance and annihilation of the invader. Officer-like skill, soldierly daring, numerical superiority had gone for nothing. English, French, despised Turks, still troubled the soil of Muscovy.

Captain Alfred Tipping, Grenadier Guards

I believe only 8000 of our men were engaged and about 6000 French. The French came to our assistance late in the day when we were getting the worst of it, and they certainly supported us nobly and saved the position. We should probably have been driven back, and our whole camp taken, had not the French come up and given us a hand.

I was then lying on the ground, and saw some troops moving towards our position, which had been so warmly assailed. I do think the sight of those Zouaves coming up, gave me more intense pleasure I had never before felt. Poor fellows. They marched and saw through the smoke, a body of men close to our position. They took some for us and unfortunately got near them. They were Russians, who delivered a murderous volley, and cut them down dreadfully, however this reinforcement so cheered our half beaten poor fellows, that they redoubled their fire and between the Zouaves and our men such a slaughter of Russians took place, when I'm told, you could not count the dead bodies on the steps of the Hill, down which they were driven.

I knew that Neville was mortally wounded, from the way in which he fell. He was shot just before our first charge into the Fort, and was brought out alive in the evening with the bayonet wounds, but it was a gunshot wound which killed him, poor fellow, as it had injured his spine.

We were carried off the field, and laid down on the ground close together. He [Neville] died in dreadful pain, having just begged me to get him some eau de cologne. I was not sorry to see him released, as his agonies were frightful, and with a spinal injury, there could be no hope. I shall not soon forget that night!

Poor fellow, he had been for hours groaning most piteously, when quite suddenly the groans ceased, and I felt sure, though I could not see for it was quite dark, that his sufferings had come to an end. I think it was about 10 or 11:00 pm. The night was bitterly cold and damp, so that I thought that he had better remain where he was, lying close to me, till morning, rather than allow the tent to be opened for the purpose of removing him. However about half an hour afterwards, I heard someone pulling at the string which fastens the door of the tent; so I hollowed out to ask who it was, and found it to be the Duke of Cambridge, who was walking about the camp anywhere, trying to see what he could do for the wounded fellows, who were lying about in all directions, undergoing operations etc. He asked me how I was going on, then turning his lantern upon poor Neville's face, which was pale and motionless, he asked me who it was. I told him and he appeared much shocked, and went out, sending a fatigue party to carry poor Neville away. I made his servant give me his watch, purse etc, which the next day I gave to his cousin, who came up to see him. They rolled him up in his blanket, and carried him out, and this was last view I had of my old friend.

Amputations of legs and arms were going on within a few yards of us during the whole night, and the hollowing and groaning of poor fellows, suffering with every species of wound, was most harrowing.

You will know what terrible losses we have had in the last affair and the loss of such splendid soldiers, as the guards proved themselves to be, is irreparable. It will take years to make such regiments again. I'm sorry to say, there is one of the companies mustered after the action, and all they could boast of, were 16 men, out of the strength of 100, the regulated amount of each company.[5]

Captain H.F. Drummond, Adjutant 1st Battalion, Scots Fusilier Guards was wounded at Inkerman.[6] His Father received letters from the following officers:

Colonel Walker SFG, 6 Nov 1854

I have to inform you that, in a severe action yesterday, your son was severely, but I am happy to say not dangerously, wounded. Of his heroic conduct I can bear witness. I saw him rush forward when the Russians were close upon us, and waving his sword repeatedly for his men to come on.

His great friend, Captain Scarlett, Scots Fusilier Guards, 7 Nov

Our Hugo has been wounded. He had a narrow shave far his life; the ball took his right breast and was turned by the rib, and has gone out under his arm behind.

We had a very severe time; the old story British pluck and no generalship. The official list is thirty-eight officers killed and ninety-one wounded; 126 sergeants killed and wounded; over 2000 men killed and wounded: the total 2300. The Russians have had a most severe licking.

My company lost eleven men killed outright and twenty-two wounded out of something over fifty. The Russians were about 50,000 when they made the previous sortie. I hope we shall take this place; but if reinforcements arrive for the Russians before ours, we shall be besieged instead of besieging.

Captain Drummond writes to his family:

HMS Retribution, Nov 8th [To his father]
We had a desperate battle on Sunday last. The Russians attacked the right of position with enormous masses of men (reckoned at 30,000) at daybreak. It had been a dark, wet, foggy night, and they had got upon the next hill to us, favoured by the weather, heavy batteries of thirty-two and twenty-four pounders. At day break they fired shot and shell in storm into our very tents, and, under cover of this, enormous columns advanced against our position; the only troops we had to oppose being Evans Division (call it 3000, it was not so much) and the Brigade of Guards; but we only had seven companies

of each regiment in the field, as the others were out on picket in the trenches look what a handful of men to defend the key of the position; 50,000 French three miles in the rear. We ought to have had 10,000 of them on the spot [French troops].

We went in at them at once, shot them down like dogs, repulsed them with enormous slaughter, when all of a sudden, as I was charging with our right flank company, beating them beautifully down the hill, and our men shooting to perfection, I was very much astonished at being sent flying head over heels. The rascals were close in front, and one sent a bullet into my chest to the left of the nipple of my right breast, which, providentially for me, came out under my armpit instead of going through my body; it has followed the bone all round and, I believe, has broken nothing. I cannot move my arm, the whole side is so bruised and stiff; it was very close quarters and a wonder it did not kill me it, took my breath away.

It was a very stiff fight, we had to repel four separate attacks, each time with fresh men, before we got reinforcements up. Our loss is terrible! irreparable! Nine of the Coldstream [officers] killed; we have eight wounded, and poor Jem Blair dead. England expects too much from such a handful of men; we will all fight until we drop, but we can do no more; and our army is not now above 13,000 men, our brigade being about 900, less than the strength of a battalion. Another such a victory as we had on Sunday, and the English army is at an end, unless they send us 20,000 men. Clouds of Russians kept pouring in one down another comes on. We have now licked three lots, and if three more come on we must, in the natural course of events, come to an end.

HMS Retribution, Nov 18th [To Fred]

I was on foot in the bushes with the men, driving the enemy before us; we were firing right into them, and they were retiring and firing, ten or twelve yards off, when a fellow rolled me over like a rabbit; sent head over heels, my sword flying out of my hand, and every bit of breath out of my body. So I thought to myself, there, my boy! your fighting days are over, when a Grenadier bugler hauled me off to the rear.

The battle of the Alma was child's play to the 5th of November. Such desperate work; for two hours, did our men stand alone, unsupported, and repel attack upon attack, made by masses of men, covered by a host of artillery; our guns being pop-guns to them. If it had not been for the Guards, that would have been an awful day for England, and dearly have our poor fellows suffered for their valour.

Our numbers will soon be exhausted. My battalion now musters about 300 bayonets; the brigade about 900, not the strength of one battalion.[7]

Notes

1. Kinglake, A.W., *The Invasion of the Crimea*, vol. 5, Blackwood, 1875, pp. 95–9.
2. Wilson, Capt C.T., *Our Veterans of 1854 in Camp & before the Enemy*, Street, 1859, pp. 296–312.
3. *Ibid*, p, 307. Captain Anitschkof, of the Russian Staff, states the Russian loss as follows:

	Generals	Officers	Soldiers	Total
Slain	1	42	2,927	2,970
Wounded	2	206	5,583	5,791
	3	248	8,510	8,761

The same writer gives the following 'detail' of the Russian forces on 5 November 1854:

(1) General Soimonov commanded the right army corps, consisting of 29 battalions, 38 guns = 17,500 men.

(2) General Paulov led the left army corps, consisting of 20 half battalions, 96 guns = 13,500 men. Thus, these two corps comprised 49 half battalions, 134 guns, 31,000 men.

(3) The corps destined to operate before Tchorguna under Gortchakov was composed of 16 battalions, 58 squadrons, 100 guns = 20,000 men.

(4) The garrison of Sevastopol, under the orders of Lieutenant General Moller, consisted of 30 half battalions, 16 guns = 20,000 men.

(5) There was also, on the Mackenzie Heights, a body of 6 battalions, 36 guns = 3,600 men.

4. Donnybrook means a brawl or uproar; a free for all. At Donnybrook, near Dublin, such uproars at the annual fair were common.
5. Tipping, Capt A., 'Letters from the East during the Campaign of 1854', MS, pp. 107–8, 116–17.
6. Drummond, Maj Hugh, *Letters from the Crimea*, Norris & Son, 1855, pp. 67–77.
7. *Ibid.*, pp. 71–85.

CHAPTER 10

After Inkerman

Inkerman was the most important battle of the war. Losing it could have resulted in the complete defeat or in a partial evacuation of our forces. All those who took part and who recorded their impressions of this conflict agree that the battle, fought against an enemy ten times their numbers, was won by the leadership qualities, bravery and initiative of the regimental officers and our non-commissioned officers, and the bravery and fighting spirit of the men, who refused to accept defeat, even in the face of overwhelming odds. The generals could claim no credit for the victory, as they made virtually no contribution towards achieving it.

Ground & Weather
Unlike the Battle of the Alma, which was a set-piece attack with almost total visibility over the whole front, Inkerman was made up of a series of battles. It was fought in valleys and glens, initially in a thick fog and mist. Visibility was made worse by the smoke of gunfire,[1] so that these individual battles were fought without reference to or knowledge of the other battles taking place nearby.

This noise and lack of visibility made it almost impossible to see what was happening or to communicate with the different units. There was a high incidence of casualties among generals, staff officers and mounted officers on the battlefield. The only order given by Lord Raglan to his troops was to bring up the two 18-pounder guns to overcome Russian superiority in artillery, which should have been done well in advance of the battle, as part of a defensive plan. He also asked General Bosquet for support.

It was very hard for regimental officers to issue effective orders to their troops which they could hear. For each battalion in the Brigade there are instances where the men charged down the hill towards the enemy, totally ignoring or being unable to hear the commands of their officers to halt.

Were the British Surprised?
Field Marshal Lord Wolseley, who landed as a Lieutenant with his Regiment in the Crimea on 3 December 1854, and who became an Assistant Engineer, was sure that we had been surprised. In his book, *The Story of a Soldier's Life*, he describes his views on the battle:

The Battle of Inkerman could never have taken place had any ordinary care and intelligence been shown by those, who select the positions for our outposts, whose purpose it was to watch the enemy's movements, to ferret out his intentions, and so to protect us from surprise. It was a disgrace to all concerned that we were caught napping by an enemy, whom we allowed to assemble close to us during the previous night without our knowledge. Had any general, who knew his business, Sir Colin Campbell, for instance, been in command of the division upon our extreme right that Gunpowder Plot Day of 1854, we should not have been caught unaware. No trouble was taken even to send the patrols into the valley of the Tchernaya, where a main road crossed the river by a bridge near its mouth.

We sat down quietly on the top of heights and slopes, making no effort to ascertain what the enemy were doing about a mile off at the bottom of them. In all the history of modern war, I do not know of another instance of such culpable neglect on the part of divisional commanders of all the well-known and long-established precautions which should be taken by troops in the field against surprise. We knew the enemy was near us, and but eleven days before, that enemy had made a serious attack from the Tchernaya valley, only a few miles above Inkerman, upon our short line of communications with Balaclava.

The fighting characteristics of our soldiers and regimental officers was so conspicuous throughout the Battle of Inkerman that we have been content to forget the culpable professional ignorance of those who had been selected to command them. May God defend us in future against any similar reckless selection.[2]

General Sir Frederick Hamilton, who was present in the front line as a Colonel throughout the action, was sure we had been surprised. When the Guards Brigade moved to Balaklava on 23 February 1855 to allow them to recover from their losses after Inkerman, they came under the command of Sir Colin Campbell.

As there was a possibility of a surprise attack on Balaklava, Sir Colin, who was resolved not to be taken by surprise, as the Army confessedly was on 5 November, selected an alarm post on the opposite heights, most exposed to an attack, where the Brigade assembled. Each morning at 3.00 am they took up this position, and when day dawned and the enemy was seen in the field, they marched back to camp.[3]

Lieutenant Colonel Sir Frederick Stephenson, who commanded Left Flank Company, Scots Fusilier Guards, had the following comments to make on the battle in a letter to his parents:

2nd February 1855. Mother, you ask how it was that we were surprised. Both the night and the morning were foggy. The preparations made by the enemy gave him great advantage. The outlying pickets of the 2nd Division, who

enadier Guards leaving the Tower prior to embarking for foreign service. (*Captain A. Tipping/*
wıth)

bin scene in a gale of wind.
in A. Tipping/E. Skipwith)

3. Soldiers dancing at Queen Victoria's birthday celebrations. (*Captain A. Tipping/E. Skipwith*)

4. The Invasion Fleet sailing to the Crimea. (*Captain A. Tipping/E. Skipwith*)

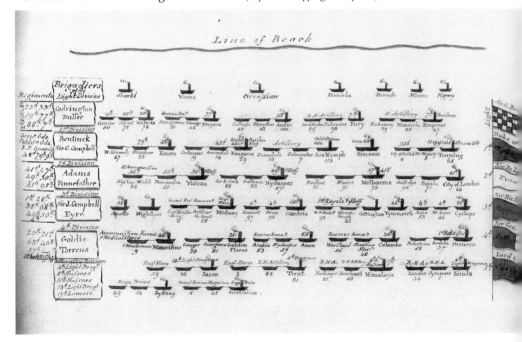

he entrance to the harbour of Balaklava. (*Captain A. Tipping/E. Skipwith*)

6. Captain Goodlake and his Sharpshooters on patrol.
(*Chevalier Desanges/ RHQ Coldstream Guards*)

7. The Guards at the Alma. *(Orlando Norrie/Private Collection)*

8. The Guards at the Alma. *(Orlando Norrie/Private Collection)*

9. The Scots Fusilier Guards saving the Colours at the Battle of the Alma. (*Lady Butler/RHQ Scots Guards*)

10. The Battle of Inkerman. (*Orlando Norrie/Private Collection*)

11. The Grenadier Colour Party at the Battle of Inkerman rejoining the Guards Brigade. (*Robert Gibb, Naval & Military Club, Cranston Fine Art*)

Battle Scene (Inkerman), Coldstream Guards. (*Orlando Norrie/RHQ Coldstream Guards*)

Captain Alfred Tipping being carried wounded from the Inkerman battlefield. (*Captain A. Tipping/ ...pwith*)

14. The Roll Call. Exhausted Grenadiers stand in the snow after the Battle of Inkerman awaiting the Roll Call. Lady Butler sketched the picture at Wellington Barracks, using soldiers from the 3rd Battalion as models. Major Higginson was the mounted officer. (*Lady Butler/RHQ Grenadier Guards*)

After the Siege of Sevastopol. (*Orlando Norrie/Private Collection*)

The Hospital at Scutari. (*Captain A. Tipping/E. Skipwith*)

17 Eugene Nightingale, ...

18. A Christmas Dinner on Heights before Sevastopol. (*William Simpson*)

19. Picture of the blanket presented by the Guards Brigade to all officers and soldiers of General Bosquet's Division for their support of the Guards Brigade at Inkerman.
(*Musee de l'Armee, Paris*)

20. Photograph of the Bentinck Medal.
(*RHQ Scots Guards*)

Lieutenant General Sir William Codrington, ~~nerly~~ Coldstream Guards, Army Commander, ~~5~~; GOC Light Division, 1854; Brigade ~~nmander~~, 1854. (*Roger Fenton/Royal Collection*)

22. Lieutenant General HRH Prince George, Duke of Cambridge, GOC 1st Division. (*Royal Collection*)

Major General Sir Henry Bentinck ~~mmanded~~ the Guards Brigade at the Battles ~~he~~ Alma and Inkerman. (*Royal Collection*)

24. Colonel The Hon. Francis G. Hood commanded the 1st Battalion Grenadier Guards at the Battle of the Alma. He was killed in the trenches on 18 October 1854. (*RHQ Grenadier Guards*)

25. Colonel F.W. Hamilton served with the Grenadier Guards in the Crimea, was present at the Battle of the Alma, at Balaklava, at Little Inkerman, at the Battle of Inkerman and at the Siege of Sevastopol. (*RHQ Grenadier Guards*)

26. Colonel Edward Birch Reynardson commanded the 3rd Grenadiers at the Battl Inkerman. He was present at the Battle of tl Alma. (*Roger Fenton/Royal Collection*)

27. Major George Higginson served with the Grenadier Guards in the Crimea. He was Battalion Adjutant at the Battles of the Alma, Balaklava, Little Inkerman, Inkerman and the Siege of Sevastopol. In January 1855 he was appointed Brigade Major of the Guards Brigade. (*RHQ Grenadier Guards*)

28. Captain Alfred Tipping served with the Grenadier Guards in the Crimea, and was present at the Battles of the Alma, Balaklava at Little Inkerman and Inkerman, and at the Siege of Sevastopol. He was severely woune at the Battle of Inkerman and invalided hom (*E. Skipwith*)

Colonel G. Uptown Coldstream Guards, ~~r~~ Viscount Templeton, commanded the 1st ~~B~~talion Coldstream at the Battles of the ~~Alm~~a, Balaklava and Inkerman, where he was ~~wo~~unded and his horse killed, and at the Siege ~~of S~~evastopol. (*Brigade Journal, 1872*)

30. Lieutenant Colonel Hon. P. Feilding, Coldstream Guards, served in the Crimea as DAQMG of the 1st Division. He was present at the Battles of the Alma, Balaklava, Little Inkerman and Inkerman, and at the Siege of Sevastopol. (*Brigade Journal, 1891*)

Colonel Francis Seymour, Scots Fusilier ~~Gu~~ards, served in the Crimea. He was present ~~at t~~he Battles of the Alma, Balaklava, Little ~~Ink~~erman and Inkerman, and at the Siege of ~~Sev~~astopol. At the Battle of Inkerman he took ~~ove~~r command of the Battalion, when Colonel ~~W~~.F. Walker was wounded. He continued to ~~com~~mand the Battalion, until he was severely ~~wo~~unded in October 1855, when he was ~~inv~~alided home. (*Brigade Journal, 1891*)

32. Major R.J. Lindsay VC, Scots Fusilier Guards, later Lord Wantage. He was present at the Battles of the Alma, Balaklava, Little Inkerman and Inkerman, and the Siege of Sevastopol. He was awarded the Victoria Cross for his bravery in saving the Colours at the Alma and for his bravery at Inkerman. In August 1855, he became Adjutant of the Battalion on the death of Major Hugh Drummond. (*RHQ Scots Guards*)

33. Guards Brigade officers awarded the Victoria Cross: Colonel The Hon. Henry Percy VC, Grenadier Guards; Major Sir Charles Russell Bt, VC, Grenadier Guards; Brevet Major Robert Lloyd Lindsay VC, Scots Fusilier Guards; Major Gerald Goodlake VC, Coldstream Guards; Brevet Major J.A. Conolly VC, Coldstream Guards. (See Appendix D for Victoria Cross citations.) (*Brigade Journal*)

should have given us timely warning of important moves by the enemy, were very remiss in their duty. During a considerable part of the night, they heard vehicles moving along the road under their posts. They took these to be market carts. This matter should have been reported to Divisional HQ which would have probably ascertained that they were artillery, being concentrated for the attack in the morning. Furthermore in the damp weather, our firelocks did not fire. At night, the ear must be more trusted than the eye.[4]

Entrenchments
Despite the fact that the enemy had launched an attack against our lines on 26 October, which was obviously a reconnaissance in force to find out the strength of our defences, no plan of defence had been drawn up and no attempt at entrenching our position had been made. Furthermore General Hamilton remarks that the Scots Fusilier Guards, on taking up their position in defence of the Sandbag Battery, had to advance through a confused mass of brushwood and trees, which, having regard to the safety of the camp, should undoubtedly have been cleared away by the General responsible for the safety of the position. These trees being allowed to remain was an oversight, all the more glaring, as their removal would have furnished a good stock of firewood for the camps, in addition to strengthening the position of the Army.[5]

After the battle the position was entrenched, but before the battle took place there was no plan in place to construct strong points to break up a frontal attack, as Wellington had done at Waterloo, by fortifying Hougoumont, La Haie Sainte and Papelotte.

Ammunition
No arrangements had been made to keep the front-line troops supplied with ammunition and troops had to search the pouches of their wounded and dead comrades, and sometimes had to resort to throwing stones at the enemy.

General Hamilton compared the usage of ammunition by the Grenadiers at the Alma and at Inkerman. At the Alma the Battalion was 700 strong in the field, they fired 9,000 rounds; at Inkerman, where the Battalion went into action about 400 strong, and were reduced to 200, they fired 19,000 rounds.[6] This figure would have been higher if the supply of cartridges had been properly organized. On at least three occasions our troops had no ammunition.

Medical
The arrangements for the sick were defective. The French generously lent their mule litters for the purpose of moving the disabled. Without this help the British could have hardly cleared the field of Inkerman of their wounded.

In May 1854 the Director General of the Medical Department sent in plans for the preparation of hospital ships, both for the transport and reception of patients, and for the establishment of hospitals at suitable points on land. The recommendations were ignored. The House of Commons, by its deliberate destruction of all auxiliary services, was to blame in this matter as in that of land transport.[7]

Advantages & Disadvantages

The British Army's principal advantage was the Minie Rifle/Musket, as its bullet could go through up to six men in a packed Russian column. The British, on the other hand, fought in line, two men deep. The British knew the ground well while the Russians did not. The ground favoured the British, as the Russians had to climb a steep hill before assaulting the British lines. In addition the mist, while allowing the Russians to approach unseen, hid from the enemy the weakness in numbers of our forces.

However, Sir John Fortescue draws attention to the problem of controlling troops and the resulting dispersal of our forces over the battlefield:

> More serious was the tendency of small victorious bodies to press the pursuit too far and to break up into knots of lost and masterless [leaderless] men. The most flagrant instance of this was when the Guards and the troops brought up by Cathcart dashed into the wooded hollows below the Sandbag battery; many officers, to use the words of Colonel Hamilton of the Grenadiers, 'only fearing that they would not be the first to enter 'Sevastopol'. The fog no doubt helped to propagate this blunder, but it was serious, for the Brigade of Guards – and thirteen hundred men constituted an appreciable fraction of four or five thousand – was not collected again until the action was practically over. They did not cease fighting, but they had ceased to be an organised body; and the like may be said of practically every battalion present. The units, as has been told, were in the first instance miserably weak; they were decanted into action by driblets; they were still further thinned by casualties. Small wonder that the remnant of the organised was minute.

The commanders of Battalions and detachment suffered heavily. Of the seventeen who were engaged on Inkerman Ridge, six were killed, nine were wounded and the two that remained unhurt had their horses killed under them.

Roughly speaking, then, the British on Inkerman Ridge sacrificed a third of their numbers. The Brigade of Guards, out of a total strength of rather more than 1,300 of all ranks, lost just over 600, the Grenadiers, the strongest of the three battalions, suffering most in the matter of men.[8]

Lord Raglan's Inkerman Despatch[9]

Lord Raglans despatch to the Duke of Newcastle, Secretary of State for War, dated 8 November 1854, contained the following comments on the Guards Brigade's performance during the battle:

The Brigade of Guards, under his royal highness the Duke of Cambridge, was engaged in a severe conflict.

The enemy, under the cover of thick brushwood, advanced in two heavy bodies, and assaulted with great determination a small redoubt which had been constructed for two guns, but was not armed. The combat was most arduous, and the brigade, after displaying the utmost steadiness and gallantry, was obliged to retire before very superior numbers, until supported by a wing of the 20th regiment of the fourth division, when they again advanced and retook the redoubt.

This ground was afterwards occupied in gallant style by French troops, and the guards speedily reformed in rear of the right flank of the second division.

After the 20th, the 95th and most of the Guards had followed Cathcart's example and charged down the hill, all that remained on the Kitspur were the Duke of Cambridge and some 150 men. Confronted by 2,000 Russians, they attempted to extricate themselves. A day later, Cambridge made his report to Lord Raglan:

The 4th Division came up in support but made a flank movement down the valley to the right of the ground held by the Guards. Unfortunately there was no support on the left & the mist being very thick & the ground extremely difficult to the eye from the thick brushwood the Brigade [of Guards] was entirely cut off from the 2nd Division & it was with great difficulty that I was able myself to get back. Major General Bentinck had been previously wounded. I had endeavoured to get our men back but could not manage this as so many had advanced down the hill with the 4th Division. I saw no men of the Guards till I rallied them in rear & on the right flank of the 2nd Division.

Here I must record the noble conduct of Assistant Surgeon Wilson of the 7th Hussars attached to this Division. He was the only Officer at hand & rallied the few men we could get together & then held the ground to the right for some time preventing the Russians from getting through & enabling a great many of our men otherwise cut off to get back.[10]

The opportune appearance of the French 6th Regiment of the Line was also crucial in stemming the Russian advance. The critical moment of the battle had passed.

Some six weeks afterwards, Cambridge felt compelled to write to Raglan both rephrasing and elaborating upon his account of this phase of the battle. He deemed it necessary because the reception afforded the publication of Raglan's despatch describing the Battle of Inkerman had, in some quarters, been decidedly lukewarm, as he explained:

The Brigade of Guards are a little annoyed that it should be supposed that they were *driven back* by the enemy & forced to retire & reform *behind the*

2nd Division … After maintaining their ground for a very long time & indeed many of them having even gone far beyond the two gun battery, the Brigade was suddenly & completely cut off from the position of the 2nd Division by a violent attack on the part of the Russians who drove back the troops on the left of the Brigade of Guards, but not the Guards themselves, [who] with a large portion of the 4th Division were engaging in a hand to hand contest, when they suddenly perceived what had occurred on their left & it was about that period that poor Sir George Cathcart fell.

After this the Guards had nothing left for it but to be completely surrounded or to force their way back through the Russian masses now on their left & pushing on towards their rear. They at once went at them with the point of the bayonet, not a man having a round of ammunition left, as we were in the act of serving this out when the above occurrence took place. Therefore though the Guards actually retired they did so facing an enemy in their left flank & rear & literally at the point of the bayonet, therefore in fact never retiring before the enemy at all but forcing their way through him till they reached the breastwork or position of the 2nd Division. I feel it my duty to represent these circumstances to you, as I fear from my want of detail I may have unintentionally been the cause of that which has pained many of my gallant friends, the idea that it could be supposed that they had been driven back. Possibly if you could do anything to place the Government in possession of these facts it would be gratifying to these fine fellows.[11]

Captain Goodlake in his letter to his parents dated 17 December 1854 complained about Lord Raglan's comments about the Guards Brigade at Inkerman:

We are all [the Brigade] awfully disgusted at the light way in which Lord Raglan mentions the Guards on 5 November. We fought by ourselves, unsupported by any regiment, without artillery, for four hours. Three times without ammunition, against the Russians far outnumbering us in a position so central that had they retreated, the enemy would have turned their flank and been all over the camp and no one could tell what would have happened.

The real state of the case is that he is living far off, knows nothing and cares less (at least it seems so) and did not like them (the press) praising the courage the Brigade showed and the admirable manner in which they repulsed these large bodies, for showing himself up in allowing so few troops to defend a position of such importance and then not being there in time to send up reinforcements, consequently the awful slaughter the Brigade sustained.

Fortunately we had seven companies on piquet or the Drummers would have had to represent the Brigade out here. So he gets made a Field Marshal[12] and we do not get the praise, which is due. It must have been a very bloody and determined resistance, by the number of officers and men the Brigade lost, which of itself will proclaim the truth. It is natural that after the supernatural courage that was displayed by our Brigade that we expected it would have been mentioned in the despatches. But to the people, who read the account in England, it will appear that we did hardly anything, instead of bearing the brunt of it, while numbers of the Line regiments were actually running away. Our camp was full of them. There is one thing, a great consolation, which is that the whole army knows how the Brigade behaved and acknowledges the unjustness of his Lordship's despatches.[13]

Captain Higginson was also very upset by the tone of Lord Raglan's despatch dealing with the performance of the Guards Brigade at Inkerman, and complained to his parents in his letters home:

12th December 1854. I will only allude to the affair of the despatch of Inkerman, at which we are all frantic. Anything so materially false as the account of our doings, I never saw. Despatches are reckoned as sound materials for an historian to work upon, and should not be hastily or timidly framed. After the arrival of the Alma despatch, I called together the battalion and read the account with much pride; but on this occasion I could not bring myself to do it, so shamefully are we treated.

19th December 1854. I do wish I could look back on a due display of activity or cordial appreciation of our condition by the staff at headquarters. Though his age and strain of work, which might have tried to the utmost the strength of a younger man, justified Lord Raglan's remaining in retirement, he was so rarely seen that the personal encouragement of the Commander-in-Chief, amounted to a few carefully-expressed 'general orders'. Copies of his despatches have reached us, and I am constrained to admit that in neither of these important records had the conduct of the Brigade of Guards been recorded in the terms of eulogy which the prominent part they took in those battles entitled them to expect. The measured language of the despatches was perused by us in silence, even the rank and file feeling just disappointment at the bare mention therein of their behaviour on those two momentous occasions. A misstatement of facts, which that document was undoubtedly guilty of is always galling. Still more so when we have reason to believe that the writer of the despatch spoke in very different terms in his private letters.[14]

Sir Frederick Stephenson's remarks in his letter to his parents confirms Captain Higginson remark that the tone of Lord Raglan's despatch does not tally with the compliments he paid to the performance of the Guards Brigade at Inkerman:

Lord Raglan says we saved the right of the position. One of our officers was paying a visit to one of Raglan's ADCs the day after the action. Lord Raglan came in and said to the ADC. 'Do you know who you are talking to, you are talking to a hero and so are all of them.'[15]

The Reverend Anton Tien, Chaplain to the Scots Fusilier Guards at Inkerman[16]

Dr Tien had an interesting experience at the Battle, relating to our troops in the Sandbag Battery:

It is with a feeling of thankfulness that I look back to Sunday 5th November 1854, that eventful day of the Battle of Inkerman, when with my valued friend, the late Captain Sir William Peel RN of the Frigate Diamond, who commanded battery No 2 Naval Brigade, we were, under God, the means of saving HRH The Duke of Cambridge and the handful of Guards under him.

At early dawn, we were aroused by the roar of cannon and artillery, not the ordinary cannonade between trench and fortress, but a quick and vigorous outburst of shot and shell, the thirty-two-pounder shells coming through the air and bursting into fragments with their harsh grating 'scrisht', the most hated of all battle sounds, and underlying quick rattle of musketry.

The attack was sudden and simultaneous all along the line from the French at Kamiesch to the English right at Mount Inkerman, about the red sandbag battery. The hottest attack, however, was on the 2nd Division Home Ridge, the Guards Brigade and a little later at the Windmill.

The Guards had already driven back down the Kitspur ravine a huge attacking party of Russians, five or six times, and they were hard pressed, being attacked by 20,000 men led by General Pavlov, while the 2nd Division was attacked by 40,000 men led by General Somoinov.

At the commencement of the attack before dawn, Captain Peel [RN] hurried to his battery, saw everything was in proper order, came back to the 2nd Division to fetch his India-rubber bed from the tent of Captain Connolly of the 30th Regiment, where he had spent the previous night, but most of the tents of the 2nd Division, especially those of the 30th Regiment, had been destroyed by the Russian artillery fire from Shell Hill.

I had just returned with the ADC [Military Secretary] Colonel Steele, from delivering the General's orders to the Turkish troops, and I met Captain Peel on the back of Home Ridge behind the headquarters. He asked me to go with him to the Red Sandbag Battery, on our way we passed through many killed and wounded Russians and English, bullets, shells and shot were whizzing in all directions.

A Russian officer, who was mortally wounded, cried 'Water, give me water to drink.' I dismounted and gave him some out of my flask, and he said with great animation, 'Tell your people to come out of that battery, they are about to be surrounded,' and in fact they were nearly cut off by a large force, composed of the Ikutsk, Sappers, and the Okhutsk and Selinghinsk Regiments. I told Captain Peel what the wounded man had said, and sure enough we saw with our field glasses, through the mist, that the Ikutsk Regiment from the high ground behind the Guards on the slopes of Mount Head, was firing on the battery as they came down, whilst the Okhutsk Regiments were advancing on the left front of the Guards.

Captain Peel conveyed this intelligence to Captain Higginson of the Grenadier Guards, and he to HRH the Duke of Cambridge, who immediately ordered the men to fall in, put the colours in the midst, and make a rush at the Ikutsk Regiment with fixed bayonets as the Russians were coming down the hillside, and cut their way through. The Duke rode past the enemy with his ADC, Major Macdonald, but not unscathed, for he was hurt by a ball which grazed his arm, and his charger was shot under him; half of the soldiery who were under him (a small body of men possibly not more than 200) cut their way through the Russians and so saved the Colours, but half the troops were killed and wounded during the rush.

So the wounded Russian's important and timely information, conveyed through Captain Peel saved the Duke of Cambridge, the handful of soldiery and the Colours of the Grenadier Guards. Captain Peel presented me to HRH the Duke of Cambridge, who still remembers my connection with the Army in the Crimea, and can recall the incident.[17]

There were so many instances of our wounded soldiers being attacked by the Russians that Lord Raglan ordered that a Court of Inquiry be held to take evidence of these criminal acts from witnesses. This took place on 9 November 1854, the Deputy Judge Advocate, W.G. Romaine acted as secretary. The opinion of the Court was that the evidence proved conclusively that the Russians had maltreated many wounded and disabled soldiers on the battlefield.[18]

The Blanket Presented to Marshal Bosquet's Division by the Guards Brigade

In the Musee d'Armee in Les Invalides in Paris is a full-size blanket, one of which was given to all the officers and men of Marshal Bosquet's Division, by the officers of the Guards Brigade, as a souvenir of the support the Zouaves gave to the Guards Brigade at Inkerman, which turned defeat into victory. On one end of the blanket there are the words 'Inkermann, The Brigade of Guards'. On the other end there are the words 'Inkermann. La Division Bosquet'. In the centre is a seven-pointed star. There is no mention of the giving of this blanket in the histories of the three regiments involved, nor is it mentioned by General Sir George Higginson, Sir William Russell or Sir Evelyn Wood, who were present in the Crimea at the time. This is surprising as it must have been a major operation to have organized the manufacture and distribution of around 3,000 blankets.

Comments on the Efficiency of the Army in the Crimea

Field Marshal Sir Henry Wood served in the Crimea as a Midshipman in Captain Peel's detachment, manning a gun battery. He transferred to the Army, won the Victoria Cross in the Indian Mutiny, and reached the rank of Field Marshal.

He comments that it is remarkable that the naval officers should have been so much more successful in looking after their men than the army officers, but the fact is undoubted that they were so. The suffering caused to the Army arose from want of transport for 9 miles: nevertheless, even without transport, something might have been done in the winter by organization, but army officers had not been trained to think of measures for supplying the men's wants.

Commodore (later Sir Stephen) Lushington initiated all the sanitary measures, which helped to keep down our sick list; it was he who organized the carrying parties, and got the warm clothing brought up [from Balaklava]. He insisted on the tents being thoroughly drained, and made shelters, the walls being rough stones, for drying the men's clothing. After he had built a wooden hospital, the next shed, which he got up about the middle of January, was converted to a drying room. In contrast with the Army's arrangements, where the soldier who up to December was supposed to cook in the little tin pot he carried on his back, the sailors had full-time cooks who were not sent to the trenches.

Every morning before the Bluejackets marched off, whether at three or six o'clock, they had to drink their cocoa or coffee on parade, to ensure that they did not go down to the battery with an empty stomach.[19]

This lack of professionalism in army officers is confirmed by General Higginson's account of his experience as Adjutant of 3 Grenadiers in peacetime. The company commanders and company officers were hardly ever present at the barracks. They relied completely on the Adjutant and the non-commissioned officers to train their men up to the correct standard of proficiency in drill. The Adjutant was also responsible for the efficient administration of his unit.

December 1851. The whole work of a battalion, drill and internal economy was the responsibility of the adjutant, who lived in barracks and never took any leave.[20]

Generals and Staff[21]

Field Marshal Lord Wolseley confirms this ignorance by officers of military matters:

What generals then had charge of England's only army, and of her honour and fighting reputation! They were served to a large extent by incompetent staff officers as useless as themselves; many of them merely *flaneurs* 'about town', who knew little of war and its science. Almost all our officers at that time were uneducated as soldiers, and many of those placed upon the staff of the Army at the beginning of the war were absolutely unfit for positions they had secured through family or political interest. There were, of course, a few brilliant exceptions but that made the incompetence of the many all the more remarkable. Our generals were old-fashioned. No new light, no useful gleam of imagination or originality, ever illuminated whatever may have been their reasoning powers.[22]

In the spring I sketched and carefully examined the ground where our troops had stood and fought on at Inkerman. I fully realized how nearly we had been destroyed, and admired more than ever the splendid fighting qualities of our regimental officers and of the rank and file they commanded. Indeed, my oft repeated study of this battle on the heights where it was fought, made me feel prouder than ever of our race, though fully convinced that our affairs were so abominably mismanaged upon the occasion that the Russians ought to have utterly destroyed us. All who that day saw our men fight were loud in praise of their regimental spirit and of the devotion of our officers to their men. It was indeed a soldier's battle, and who can praise their valour enough! What Napier wrote of it as displayed at Albuera is equally applicable to the way in which all ranks stood at Inkerman. The noblest traits and virtues of the British soldier and of our regimental officers came out there all the stronger because of the painful contrast between such qualities and the helpless, feckless ignorance of war displayed by many of our generals and their inept staff upon that occasion.

His Royal Highness the Duke of Cambridge was in the midst of the hardest fighting in and around the two-gun battery, and I have heard men say it was difficult to understand how he escaped being shot, for he stuck to his post to the last, encouraging by his example all around him.

I never thought that Lord Raglan was equal to the conduct of a great war. He seemed to lack the imagination, the military instinct, the knowledge of war's science and the elasticity of mind and body that is essential for the general commanding an army in the field. He had an extremely difficult game to play. The Government of the day, plunging stupidly into war with a great European Power of whose military strength it was apparently ignorant, had invaded the Crimea with little knowledge of its geography and still less of its rigorous climate. When disasters ensued, as is usual with politicians in power, the Ministry had striven to throw the blame upon the general commanding in the field and upon the staff who had not even been selected by him. But Lord Raglan's military virtues were many. His steadfast courage, and his kindness of heart to all about him, were striking traits in his character, whilst his well-born dignity of manner had doubtless much influence over foreigners upon all of whom God had not been so bountiful in natural gifts.[23]

It was not our rank and file who were the worst in this respect, for they had been well taught obedience, the first and most important duty of a soldier; it was our officers of all degrees who were generally ignorant of their work, and the most striking examples of military ignorance were the great majority of those who had been selected to be our generals and our brigadiers and for the staff of the Army generally.

A large proportion of these were taken from the Foot Guards, who had not then even the advantage of knowing what our Army was like outside of St.

James' and Windsor. All were gallant, daring fellows, who looked well after
their men, and never spared themselves in any way in doing so. They were
the very best material of which officers could possibly be made, and on active
service always showed themselves most anxious to learn their duty, and never
shrank from any amount of hard work. It was not their fault that they did not
know their duty as officers when they embarked for Turkey; it was the fault of
the wretched system under which they lived nominally as soldiers, but never
in barracks with their men, and having but little personal contact with them.
All that is changed now. All corps in our Army were vastly improved by their
service in the Crimea, but to none did it give such an entirely new life as to
all ranks in the battalions which constituted the Brigade of Guards in that
war.[24]

Captain Higginson also gives more evidence of army officers' lack of
professionalism:

You ask me to tell you all I know and I think, and I do not hesitate to do so. The
whole thing is resolved into one grand fault – *we literally have no Commander-
in-Chief*. We have an excellent man, it is true, fully capable as far as mental
capabilities will go; but you know that alone will not suffice, and that if the
generalissimo will not blow up the division generals, the division generals
will take the brigade-generals' reports for granted, and the brigadiers will be
satisfied with whatever reports the commanding officers of the regiments may
choose to give them. While all that, personal inspection, without which no
certainty of the proper attention having been paid to orders can be arrived at,
is *entirely* and absolutely neglected. I have known our own young officers on
outlying picket to say, 'I wish to heaven some general officer would only come
round and blow me up *well*, rather than being left here unvisited for twenty-
four hours.' In these few words you arrive at the root of the evil.

It is true that Lord Raglan may not be able to keep the commissariat mules
alive to provide for fresh meat twice a week, roast coffee, or build huts; but the
responsibility of the due performance of these duties must attach to some one.
To whom then [does it belong] but to the head? Not to be prosy, I might draw
in a few words a comparison between his position and the C.O. of a regiment
and an adjutant who wanted looking after. If the chief don't bully the adjutant,
the regiment goes to the devil, as this army has.

If Lord Raglan had insisted on Estcourt (AG) and Airey (QMG) and their
subordinates riding daily round divisions and pickets, abusing every one and
forcing both men and officers to exert themselves, much – oh, how so much of
all this misery would have been averted. But whenever these men come here
(and I can only speak of their visits to our brigade), they actually required
to be told what duties we performed, how we did them, and *where* we went!
Nothing could be more gentlemanlike than their manners, mode of inquiry

and professions of good will, and apparent anxiety to benefit; but from the unfortunate fact that they none of them *seem* to know anything of regimental system or duty, they reverse the position of instructor and instruct*ed*.

We are invited to make reports and suggestions to which, when made, not the slightest attention is paid.

22nd June 1855. There is no use in denying that the Army is disgusted, not at this our first reverse, for reverses will always happen, but through want of confidence in our leaders. We do not feel that there is any guarantee that the same mistake will not be made again and again with the same lamentable loss of life. In ten days the British Army had 160 officers *hors de combat*, and under 2000 men.

3rd July 1855. Poor old man! It was his kindness that prevented him from being a great general. Nothing but extreme indifference will carry a general through a war like this.

I look on it that we have no general living, who with the means here at his disposal, can effect the gigantic work demanded by the people, or rather the press, of England. Late experience in the trenches more than ever convinces me of this. It is quite impossible that the men can last out many weeks, employed as they now are, unless some great and unforeseen success should act as a stimulus and revive, not their determination, for they have plenty of that but their ardour.

In comparing Lord Raglan's performance as a general to that of the Duke of Wellington, it is clear that the Duke was more direct. Sometimes he issued orders directly to units. At Waterloo, he told Major General Sir Peregrine Maitland, commanding the 1st British Guards Brigade in the 1st Division to tell his troops to lie down. When the French were 25 metres away, the Duke shouted, 'Now Maitland! Now's your time!' The troops stood up, fired a volley and charged, and the French were routed.[25]

Similarly Wellington would never have ridden through the skirmishing lines, as Lord Raglan did at the Battle of the Alma, leaving Brigadier General Airey, the Quartermaster General, in command without any clear orders. The Duke was direct and decisive, and would have kept the management of the battle in his hands. At Inkerman it is very unlikely that Cathcart's disastrous foray would have taken place. The Duke would not have tolerated subordinate commanders ignoring his orders, as they believed they knew better than he did. He would have insisted that Cathcart's troops supported the Guards Brigade.

Wellington would also have been tougher with the French. He would have insisted that the French took over a higher proportion of ground, as their strength was greater than the British. Similarly he would have refused to agree to Marshal Pelissier's last-minute change of time for the first assault on the Redan. He would have also insisted that agreements once made were implemented without delay.

Trenches[26]

Captain Higginson describes his experiences in the trenches:

28th March 1855. Both men and officers have been from the very first sent into the trenches without instructions of any kind, except to hold their own; no rules for the distribution of the covering parties, posting of sentries, or placing of reserves have ever been vouchsafed, and all that is told to the officer to whom a whole 'siege attack', including battery, trench, zigzag and advanced work is given, is that so many men are to go to one, so many to another.

I am more confirmed in this opinion from what happened to myself yesterday. We now have to furnish daily 1000 to 1500 men from the 1st Division, and these form part of the 3000 men which guard the whole right attack, quarries and all. An adjutant of the day is detailed, whose duty it is to tell off the whole of the parties for the different posts, of which there cannot be less than five and twenty. You can understand the difficulty there must be in threading one's way through such a labyrinth of zigzags and parallels, directing twenty-five parties, to as many posts, all depending on each another, the most advanced being within 80 yards of the enemy.

I went therefore, to a friend of mine, a very sharp fellow in the 47th, for a lesson in the matter; for all these advanced trenches have been made since we left the front in February. You will scarce believe me when I tell you that there are, even now, no orders of any kind issued to officers in command; everything is left to the discretion of the general of the day, who delegates it to the field officer of the day, who confers with the adjutant, and they decide as they think best. Not a rule for fighting, retiring, supporting, rallying or pursuing is even hinted at; and had I not chosen to inform myself personally of the usual mode adopted by the divisions which have been furnishing the trench guards latterly, I might have been in orders for a duty I was entirely incompetent to fulfil.

Consequently I passed the whole of yesterday afternoon in the trenches with a plan in my hand well marked and numbered, and am now prepared, thanks to my friend in the 47th.

14th July 1855. I had a rough twenty-four hours in the trenches after I last wrote; the Ruskies fell foul of our working parties, and we treated them to grape most warmly. Sir Colin Campbell chose to take command himself, and as he did not know the ground, I had to guide him over the advanced works. Consequently we are great allies, and if it were possible for him to have a good opinion of a guardsman, which I doubt! I believe that 'ere individual is myself. He is a man of extraordinary powers, both of mind and body, considering his age [in his 64th year].

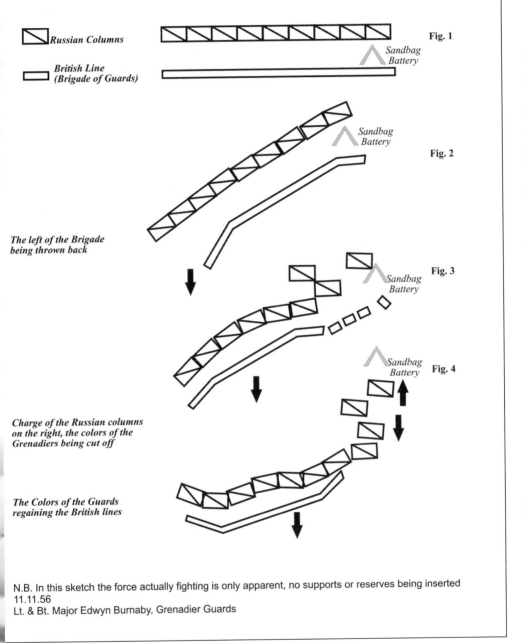

The Brigade of Guards at the Battle of Inkerman 5th Nov 1854

Russian Columns

British Line (Brigade of Guards)

Sandbag Battery

Fig. 1

Sandbag Battery

Fig. 2

The left of the Brigade being thrown back

Sandbag Battery

Fig. 3

Sandbag Battery

Fig. 4

Charge of the Russian columns on the right, the colors of the Grenadiers being cut off

The Colors of the Guards regaining the British lines

N.B. In this sketch the force actually fighting is only apparent, no supports or reserves being inserted
11.11.56
Lt. & Bt. Major Edwyn Burnaby, Grenadier Guards

Diagram of the Brigade of Guards at the Battle of Inkerman. The Colours of the Grenadiers, regaining the British Lines having been cut off. Lt. & Bt. Major Edwyn Burnaby, Grenadier Guards, 11.11.56, hand drawn. RHQ Grenadier Guards.

Recommendations for the Victoria Cross[27]

On 8 November 1856, Colonel Wood, the Lieutenant Colonel of the Grenadier Guards, wrote to Brevet Major Burnaby asking him what officers he would suggest should be recommended for the award of the Victoria Cross. He refers to the occasion in the battle, when the centre of the Battalion and the Colours were cut off. In this incident, he says that the officers and men displayed great gallantry and determination by facing about and charging through the enemy, until they reached the British Lines. He wishes to confirm that the officers present were Brevet Major Burnaby, Lieutenant Colonel Higginson, Captain Sturt, Captain Verschoyle, and Lieutenants Turner and Sir James Ferguson. As he believes that three companies were involved, he would like three recommendations so that he could forward their names to the Commander-in-Chief.

Burnaby replies, sending a sketch of the action. He explains that after holding its position for a very considerable period, the Brigade was forced to retreat by the heavy masses of the enemy. The hardest pressure was on the left flank, which was thrown back, but the whole line kept its connections. Then a furious charge on our right caused it to be broken. Through this breach the enemy advanced in such great numbers, that the Colours were surrounded and cut off. This is the incident to which Colonel Wood refers.

Burnaby himself witnessed the admirable behaviour of the small party surrounding the Colours. Seeing the enemy closing on the Colours, he rallied a few men and prevented the enemy's advance, by covering the Colours in their retreat. In doing this he lost nearly all his men, was surrounded and was himself cut off. He mentions the bravery of Acting Corporal Lucas, who saved his life in the most gallant manner. His position was such that it prevented him seeing the actions of other individual officers. He did however witness the gallant conduct of Lieutenant Colonel Higginson, who he hopes will receive the honour due to him for the energy he displayed. This recommendation was not successful.

Casualties

The casualties suffered by the Guards Brigade at Inkerman were as follows:

	Officers		*NCOs & Men*		*Total*
	Killed	*Wounded*	*Killed*	*Wounded*	*Casualties*
3 Grenadiers[28]	3	6	101	124	234
1 Coldstream[29]	8	5	84	123	220
1 Scots Fusiliers	1	8	64	106	179
Total	12	19	249	353	633

Guards Brigade

The Brigade's strength before and after the battle was as follows:

	Before			After		
	Officers	*R & F*	*Total*	*Officers*	*R & F*	*Total*
3 Grenadiers[30]	25	405	430	16	236	252
1 Coldstream[31]	17	438	455	11	307	318
1 Scots Fusiliers[32]	19	372	391	10	202	212
Total	61	1215	1276	37	745	782

Notes

1. Smokeless powder did not come into general use in the British Army until the early 1890s. It is said that after firing a broadside the captain of a battleship could not see the bows of his ship for smoke, before smokeless powder.
2. Wolseley, FM Viscount, *The Story of a Soldier's Life*, vol. 1, Constable, 1903, pp. 142–3.
3. Hamilton, Lt Gen Sir J.F., *The Origins & History of the First or Grenadier Guards*, vol. 3, John Murray, 1871, p. 256.
4. Stephenson, Sir F.C.A., *At Home and on the Battlefield*, John Murray, 1915, p. 107.
5. Hamilton, pp. 222–3.
6. *Ibid.*, p. 243.
7. Fortescue, Sir John, *A History of the British Army*, vol. XIII, Macmillan, 1930, pp. 152–3.
8. *Ibid.*, pp. 140–2.
9. Tyrrell, Henry, *History of the War with Russia*, vol. 2, London Printing & Publishing Company, 1856, p. 352.
10. Massie, Alastair, *The National Army Museum Book of the Crimean War: The Untold Stories*, Sidgwick & Jackson, 2005, pp. 111–12.
11. *Ibid.*, pp. 111–13.
12. Lord Raglan was appointed Field Marshal on 5 November 1854.
13. Springman, Michael, *Sharpshooter in the Crimea*, Pen & Sword, 2005, p. 83.
14. Higginson, Gen Sir George, *Seventy-One Years of a Guardsman's Life*, Smith Elder, 1916, pp. 215 & 226–30.
15. *Stephenson*, p. 107.
16. Handwritten account of the action by Dr Tien, from the records located at Regimental Headquarters Scots Guards.
17. This article was written when the Duke of Cambridge was Commander-in-Chief about 1880.
18. Robins, Colin, *Romaine's Crimean War*, Sutton Publishing, 2005, pp. 252–60.
19. Wood, FM Sir Henry, *From Midshipman to Field Marshal*, Methuen, 1906, pp. 58–60.
20. Higginson, pp. 56–8.

21. Wolesley, pp. 226–30 & 276–7.
22. *Ibid.*, pp. 95 & 137.
23. *Ibid.*, pp. 142, 137 & 170–1.
24. *Ibid.*, p.106.
25. Adkin, Mark, *The Waterloo Companion*, Aurum Press, 2001, p. 397.
26. Higginson, pp. 250, 274, 276–7 & 280–1.
27. Handwritten letters by Colonel Wood and Major Burnaby in the archives at Regimental Headquarters Grenadier Guards.
28. Hamilton, vol. 3, p. 240.
29. Letter from Major Edward Crofton, Regimental Adjutant Coldstream Guards, 20 July 2004, to the author, and Ross-of-Bladensburg, Lt Col, *The Coldstream Guards in the Crimea*, A.D. Innes, 1897, p. 186.
30. Hamilton, vol. 3, p. 241.
31. Ross-of-Bladensburg, p. 186.
32. Maurice, Maj Gen Sir F., *The History of the Scots Guards*, vol. 2, Chatto & Windus, 1934, pp. 102–3.

CHAPTER 11

The Winter of 1854/5 – November 1854 to June 1855

1854

6 November	Decision taken by Lord Raglan that the Army will winter in the Crimea.
7 November	The entrenchment of the Inkerman position by the Turks begins.
14–15 November	The Great Storm, the 8-mile stretch of road to Balaclava becomes a morass and is impassable.
17 December	Sharpshooting stopped, too few men available.

1855

1 January	1 Coldstream receive their knapsacks.
1 February	Guards Brigade, only some 312 men able to do duty.
2 February	Lord Rokeby arrives to take command of the Brigade.
5 February	Lord Aberdeen resigns and Lord Palmerston becomes Prime Minister.
15 February	Lime juice issued to all ranks.
23 February	Marched to Balaklava and hutted nearby. Grand Crimean Central Railway operational from Balaklava to Kadikoi.
March	Land Transport Corps starts operations in the Crimea.
10 March	Changed huts to the Heights west of Balaklava.
26 March	Railway line extended to British Headquarters on the Heights.
8–17 April	Second Bombardment of Sevastopol.
18–25 April	Railway line extended up the north-east valley to the Worontzoff Road to supply the 2nd and Light Divisions, with a westward branch to serve the 4th Division and the siege batteries.
30 April	The electric telegraph line completed to allow messages to be sent to and from London and the Crimea.

3 May	First Kertch Expedition, recalled 9 May. Changed huts to the Heights east of Balaclava.
9 May	Returned to the huts on the West Heights.
19 May	Marshal Canrobert resigns and Marshal Pellissier takes over command of the French Army.
23 May	Second Kertch Expedition takes Kertch and Yenikale and successfully cuts the Russian supply lines to Sevastopol from Rostov, the River Don and the Sea of Azov.
6 June	Third Bombardment of Sevastopol.

Winter 1854/5

After the Great Storm of 14–15 November the roads became impassable and the supply ship *Prince* was lost, with most of the Army's winter clothing.

Captain Hugh Drummond, Adjutant, Scots Fusilier Guards, wrote an account of the Great Storm to his Mother on 20 November 1854. He was on board HMS *Retribution*, recovering from the wound he received at Inkerman:

On Tuesday last, the 14th, a fearful storm began in the morning, and raged all day. We parted two cables out of three, and drifted from where we were originally anchored, half a mile out at sea to three ship's length from the precipitous rocks, hanging by one cable; our guns thrown overboard; green seas washing all over; our yard struck by lightning and shivered; indeed all hope was gone, when a violent snow-storm set in, and the wind moderated, and, by God's Mercy, we rode it out until the next day, when the weather moderated, and a tug came out of Balaclava and towed us in, a fearful wreck; rudder and bowsprit gone, boats washed away; in short, the dear old gallant *Retribution* is but a wreck.[1]

William Russell's dispatch in *The Times* about the Crimean War, dated 25 November 1854, gives a chilling picture of the condition of the Army in the Crimea:

It is now pouring rain – the skies are as black as ink – the wind is howling over the staggering tents – the trenches are turned into dykes – in the tents the water is sometimes a foot deep – our men have not either warm or waterproof clothing – they are out for twelve hours at a time in the trenches – they are plunged into the miseries of a winter campaign – not a soul seems to care for their comfort, or even for their lives. These are hard truths but the people of England must hear them. They must know that the most wretched beggar, who wanders about the streets of London in the rain, leads the life of a prince compared with the British soldiers who are fighting out here for their country, and who, we are complacently assured by the home authorities, are the best appointed army in Europe.

At the end of the year of 1854 William Russell wrote:

> Why were they in tents? Where were the huts which had been sent out to them? The huts were on board ships in the harbour of Balaclava. Some of these huts were floating about the beach; others had been converted into firewood or used for stabling for officers' horses.[2]

He summed up the effect of this incompetence on the fighting efficiency of the Army:

> What was the cost to the country of the men of the Brigade of Guards, who died in their tents, or in hospital of exhaustion, overwork, and deficient of proper nutriment? The Brigade (originally around 2,900 strong) mustered a little over 400 men fit for duty by the middle of February 1855. It would have been cheap to have fed these men we had lost on turtle and venison, if we could have kept them alive – not only those, but the poor fellows the battle spared, but whom disease took from us out of every regiment in the expedition.[3]

About the winter of 1854/5, William Russell wrote:

> A soldier is a very dear animal. A crop of them is difficult to raise and once they have been fully grown and have become ripe soldiers, they are beyond all price.[4]

Captain Alfred Tipping, Grenadier Guards, wrote in his letter to his family after the Battle of the Alma that a French officer, noting the lack of care of our men in providing them with tents to keep out the heavy dews and the absence of any proper provision for the accommodation of the sick, remarked:

> It seems to me that your soldiers are not looked after as they should be. They merit in your hands priceless care. If you have such soldiers you should look after them as you would your eyes.[5]

Commissariat, Transport and Hospitals

In the Crimea, in the absence of an efficient and effective transport and supply operation, and without a trained staff as Wellington had, even when the Army had supplies in Balaclava, it was unable to supply its front-line troops. In winter the principal shortages were clothing and boots, rations, fodder for the horses, medicines and hospital supplies, tents, huts and warlike stores. Unlike the French Army, during the summer months it had failed to build all-weather roads and central stores. It could not supply its troops adequately in winter until the railway from Balaclava to Kadikoi became operational during February and March 1855. It was later extended to the top of the Sapoune Heights, overlooking Sevastopol.

The Army's medical requirements, the pressing need for field hospitals and for effective ambulances for transporting battle casualties to these hospitals, were not properly considered. The ambulances, specially designed and built for the campaign, were useless and could not travel over rough ground. There were no hospital ships in existence.

Florence Nightingale, with her nurses, had been sent out to the hospital at Scutari by Sidney Herbert, the Secretary at War. She and the medical staff arrived at Scutari in mid November, just as the casualties from the Battle of Inkerman were arriving at the hospital. They were unaware of the existence of germs. They believed that disease was caused by bad air, miasma, generated by decay, dirt, middens, accumulations of filth and by marshes. The sanitary measures introduced by Florence Nightingale, better cooking arrangements and diet, as well as proper nursing routines, made considerable differences to the patients' survival.[6]

The First Sanitary Commission, consisting of Dr Sutherland and other public hygiene experts, which arrived in March 1855, were given executive powers by the Government to clean up Scutari Hospital. The sewers were cleaned out and running water installed. They then organized the cleaning up of Balaclava town and the harbour. Florence Nightingale told Lord Shaftesbury that the Sanitary Commission had saved the British Army.

On 17 December 1854 Captain Goodlake wrote that he was very angry about the state of the wounded. He said that the wounded were looked after disgracefully. 'There are no doctors, no nurses, no orders; all is confusion as there is no system.'

During the period from November 1854 to August 1855 he wrote about the very unsatisfactory supply position in the Crimea. On 22 November he explained that, while there were plentiful stores at Balaclava, the problem was getting them up to the troops. On 5 January he wrote that on that day his Battalion had only 128 men fit for duty.

The lack of a proper road from Balaclava to the camp, together with insufficient carts, made supplying the troops very difficult.

Sir John Fortescue commented that if they ate at all, their diet, added to the constant cold and exposure in the trenches, induced diarrhoea and dysentery. The greater the number of men who succumbed, the fewer were left to do their work, and the greater was the burden that was laid upon those few.

Raglan had begged for the formation of a land-transport corps in June 1854; but nothing had been done. The French, knowing the business of war, had a complete military department for transport and supply; the English had none. Parliament had deliberately destroyed the last vestige of a wagon train many years before; and the Ministry, as ignorant as the House of Commons, could see no greater necessity for such a thing in war than in peace.

The only forage obtainable near the spot was chopped straw, which was inconveniently bulky, and the Commissary had accordingly applied to the Treasury, before the Army landed in the Crimea, for 2,000 tons of hay; but little more than a tenth of that quantity arrived before the end of the year. The loss of twenty days' forage in the storm of 14 November 1854 was, of course, a piece of bad luck, but if the authorities at home had had any idea of the conduct of a campaign, such a misfortune should not have brought the Army, as it did, to the verge of starvation. There was no ill will among the officials at home; on the contrary, there was honest zeal and devotion. But there was also abysmal and, seemingly, invincible ignorance, with a lordly disdain for all past experience. What they could not understand was that, while a very slender intelligence may suffice to fill a depot, a very elaborate organization is needed to bring food and clothing to the body. The distance from England to Balaclava by sea was 3,000 miles, but the distance to the camp was 3,008; and it was just the eight odd miles that made the difference.

It was necessary to man the trenches for purposes of security. So men and officers went down, drenched, ragged and hungry, to crouch on the wet ground or stand knee-deep in water, did their twelve hours of duty and returned to the sodden soil under their dripping tents to find at best, a ration of salt pork and biscuit without the means of cooking it, and at worst nothing at all. There was shelter, in the shape of planks for huts, plenty of food and plenty of warm clothing in Balaclava itself, but these things might almost as well have been in Constantinople.

Yet the men of the old long-service army, to their eternal credit, passed through this ordeal without a murmur. They died by scores and hundreds daily of cholera, dysentery, diarrhoea and sheer hardship, but they stuck to their work and did not complain. The same soldiers were on duty in the trenches at least four days, and sometimes five or even six days, out of seven, but so long as they could move, they obeyed orders and waited patiently for relief by death. There were commanding officers who, by impressing the horses or ponies of all under them, and taking advantage of a favourable day, managed to bring up clothing from Balaclava by some means.[7]

Some of the Army, such as the Rifle Brigade, had been on campaign, but for the others, used to living in barracks, such as the Guards Brigade, and especially the new recruits and the new drafts, there was no tradition of cooking in the field, as there was in the French Army. Many of the unwieldy and heavy camp kettles issued to the troops had been thrown away by many units during the march to the Alma.

It was not until much later that consideration was given to the correct diet for soldiers to combat disease and to perform their tasks effectively. The valuable lessons learnt in earlier campaigns about maintaining a high standard of camp hygiene and the prevention of disease had been forgotten.

[**Author's Note:** Sir John Pringle, Physician-General to the Forces in the Low Countries in 1744, published *Observations on Diseases of the Army* in 1752. He is the father of modern military hygiene, attributing much army sickness to the air from marshes, rotting vegetable matter, fouling of the camping grounds by humans and animals, and from bad ventilation in hospitals, barracks and ships. He also advocated the frequent changing of camping grounds and organized messing for soldiers. All this wise advice was forgotten in the Crimean Campaign.]

Christmas on the Heights before Sebastopol by William Simpson

This picture (see plate section) depicts officers of the 3rd Battalion Grenadier Guards at dinner on 25 December 1854. The portraits, commencing with that of the officer in the foreground on the left, and following the natural course of the bottle, which he holds in so caressing a grasp, are those of Captain Frederick Bathurst, Captain Sir Charles Russell, Captain Charles Turner, Captain Lord Balgonie, Captain Barnaby [Burnaby], Lieutenant Colonel Lindsay, Colonel F.W. Hamilton, Lieutenant Colonel Prince Edward of Saxe Weimar, Captain Higginson, Lieutenant R.W. Hamilton, Captain Sir James Fergusson and Captain Verschoyle.

General Sir George Higginson in his book, *Seventy One Years of a Guardsman's Life*, comments on this dinner:[8]

In a large volume of sketches made by Mr. William Simpson, an artist of considerable repute, there is a drawing entitled 'A Christmas Dinner'. The tent in that drawing was mine. I had decorated it as best I could, so that I and my brother officers could celebrate Christmas with as much cheeriness as we might muster. We had secured from a French sutler at Kamiesh some fearful effervescing stuff which was called champagne, some scraggy fowls and a ham, and the evening was passed with due conviviality, and interchange of those expressions of goodwill and friendship which only the strange tenour of our daily life could draw forth. I have often in subsequent years seen in London shop windows prints from this drawing, at the foot of which is given the names of those who were present at our Christmas dinner of 1854. The fact that I am the sole survivor of that gallant company has come home to me, bringing a train of thought whereon to indulge a few reflections which may be accepted from one whose race is nearly run, by those who, among my younger readers, may be beginning a hopeful career in the regiment whose honour those good gentlemen did their utmost to preserve.

Captain Edwyn Burnaby writes in his diary:[9]

Sunday 24th December 1854
Outlying Picquet. A most horrid wet day; it never stopped raining. Fergusson came as a reinforcement, having just returned from Gabion detachment.[10] We had some 1st rate coffee in the little tent & then some hot grog.

Monday 25th December 1854

Xmas Day. Rode over the very slippery ground where the snow and ice still lay to Kamara. I met Charleton going to the front with biscuit. Our grand dinner in Hamilton's tent. 2 geese, 1 turkey, leg of mutton & mince pies which Lindsay had sent him from Missiri. A most cheery dinner. Bill Bathurst on Picquet and Turner away gabion making. [Both these officers are shown in the picture.]

On 8 February, Captain Goodlake reported that the Brigade had 600 duty men and the Coldstream only 126. After the Guards Brigade moved away from the front line to Balaclava on 23 February and no longer had to carry out trench duties, he was able to report that by 28 July the Brigade's strength had increased to 1,000 duty men.

Captain Drummond, Scots Fusilier Guards, writes to his family on 30 November and reports that he had been over to Scutari and seen a quantity of wounded and sick men.

The accounts they give one and all of the way they were treated, until latterly, is sickening, and a scandal to England. It is much better now, but the transports on the passage down from the Crimea are sent in an awful state. The finest and gallantest fellows in the army left to rot untouched, unattended to, and uncared for, and pitched overboard by dozens; sometimes literally starved. The French do all this admirably – their hospital is beautiful and the whole system and organization is good. The long and short of the matter is, we have neither one thing nor the other. England is not such a great country, as I thought she was, her resources and means are so misapplied.[11]

On 30 November and on 28 December, he sympathizes with the Duke of Cambridge's plight:[12]

The Duke of Cambridge is now living at the Embassy, a medical board sat on him yesterday, and has ordered him home, which I am very sorry for, and yet glad of, for, poor fellow if he was to go back to the Crimea he would die, like poor Thistlethwayte;[13] there is no recovery out here from that fever.

In January 1855, he writes:

Our army is in a desperate state, not a man hutted, and hardly any warm clothes issued, and a foot of snow on the ground. Ships, full of huts and warm clothing, are at Balaclava, but nothing finds its way up to camp; there is no means of transport.

What an admirable government [French], and what resources! Look how their army is found with everything, and ours with nothing. All their men in good sheep-skin coats, before we had one. If I were not an Englishman, the English army is the last service I would enter.[14]

He reports on Major General Lord Rokeby's, reactions when he took over command of the Guards Brigade on 2 February 1855:

Poor dear Rokeby was sadly shocked when he saw the remnants of the magnificent Guards. They have so over-worked our poor fellows, and underfed them, that we have now about 200 left in each battalion. If it had not been for the exertions of the officers, getting ponies, and bringing up the men's things, they must have been frozen to death or starved, the Commissariat could hardly bring them up their biscuit and pork; and as for warm clothing, every thing the men have got has been brought up by the officers on their ponies, jerseys, coats, and all coffee and sugar; and now we have got tea and tobacco, and things are beginning to mend. Alas! not until the pith of the men are dead.[15]

On 16 February 1855, he writes to his brother on his concern for the soldiers in his Battalion:

I found our men in an awful plight – only 100 left fit for duty, and some of them very shaky. Almost all have scurvy, and dysentery kills two, three, or four every day; they have been so terribly overworked and so ill-clad and fed, human nature could not stand it. All the officers are well in health and spirits, but in awful bad tempers at the loss of all the men. It might have been in a great measure avoided by giving them fresh meat occasionally, or bread, or vegetables. Bread they have never had, vegetables three or four times in as many months, and fresh meat nine times in the last two months, and their clothes, poor fellows!

However, now each has a good sheepskin and underclothing, which we never should have got up if the officers had not all slaved and worked, and bought horses themselves. You will not perhaps believe it, but the only articles the commissariat have brought up since last November are the biscuit and meat. The officers' ponies and mules have fetched from Balaclava every article of clothing, and all the tea, coffee, sugar, rice, &c. the men have had. If it had not been for the Company Officers the men would have all perished for want of clothes and the necessaries that I have enumerated. Now we have so few men left the commissariat are able to supply us with coffee, rice, and sugar.

Oh, my country! It is a miserable Government; no head – a universal dread of responsibility and everything in confusion. I hope the new Government will put order into all this chaos.

I am as comfortable as can be; a stove in my tent which is dug down three feet in the ground: a table of earth round the hole, a good bed, lots of grub, a fur coat to sleep in, a buffalo robe, good boots – in short you know I like this life, and always did. I am wretched away from my regiment, and since I have been back I am better than I was in Pera, and as strong as possible.[16]

In March 1855, he writes on the supply position and on the progress in building huts, which took place when the Brigade moved its camp to Balaclava:

Almost all the men are in huts, which we are building as fast as we can. I am still in a tent, but Stephenson Coke and I mean to get a hut when we can. It is still very cold – snow-storms and hard frosts – but, on the whole, better than it has been; and the health of the men is a little improved – those that remain; alas! There are not very many.

The furs the Governor sent me are splendid. Now I take my boots off, and undress, and put my fur coat on as a night-shirt, with the cap right over my ears, and am as warm as can be. I am all day settling huts, and building like a carpenter.

However, thank God the worst is over; we have good warm clothes, huts, and plenty of food; but what it has been this winter, defies all description, entirely owing to the want of foresight, or proper precaution on the part of our weak and wicked Government.

We are improving rapidly in health, our remaining men coming out of hospital fast; they get beer every day. We have ransacked all the ships in harbour and opened a shop, to supply them with butter, cheese, herrings, good Scotch whisky, pickles, in short, the things a soldier likes best. The result exceeds our best hopes; and the remainder of our noble fellows live in clover, and improve *a vue d'oeil*; that shows what warmth and good food will do for men – and huts and good grub.

I am happy to say that the remainder of our men are in a first-rate condition. We are getting them out of Field Hospital fast; and those that are out are strong and in good spirits; discipline is admirable; but we have had awful losses.

I pity the Russians, that is if we get anything like a fair proportion to lick five or six to one will not matter; but when it was like Inkerman, about twenty to one, that is too long odds, and very fatiguing![17]

He writes in April 1855 on the improving supply position:

Here we are in absolute idleness; nothing doing anywhere, but taking shot and shell up to the front, and building huts. The railway is open nearly to Lord Raglan's house, which is an immense assistance, and saves the men a great deal of hard work. All our batteries are ready heaps of ammunition, and such a lot of big guns.

Yesterday I got into a hut for the first time. Stephenson is in one partition and I in the other. It is a large hut divided across the middle; one half allowed for a Colonel, the other for two Captains; so dear old Scarlett and I take the other half, which will be very jolly.

All our men that are left are very well and strong in new clothes, and with lots of fresh meat and vegetables, and a roof over their heads. It reminds me of St. James's Street, to see them turned out now as smart as if they had never done anything.

There is not one case of diarrhoea or dysentery in the battalion. That shows what good food, and no more than a fair proportion of work, will do for men. They were fools as well as brutes for treating the men as they did all this winter.

We have a table with four legs that does not wobble about, and a roof that keeps the wet out. Tonight we have a turkey, like an ostrich, and mutton chops, like small bits of gutta percha so you see the condition of the officers is admirable! The morale of the men is immensely improved, for they have begun to get drunk and fight a sure sign that the Briton is himself again. Colonel W [Walker] is alarmed rather at these last symptoms of improvement. I assure him they will cease when we take the field again. We are now 258 rank and file, besides the Karani detachment.[18]

In May 1855, he writes of the improving health and standard of living of all ranks:

We now look quite like a battalion again; our last draft has made us up capitally; they are by far the finest draft that has been sent out to any regiment yet, and look like work. If these fellows survive in two years time they will be first-rate troops, like our old hands, who are dead and gone, poor fellows! In the meantime they are rough and raw, and far too young, but the most willing subordinate fellows possible.

We have them out twice a day to drill, occasionally to ball practice; they are very good at both, and have been capitally trained at home. We now have between 6 and 700 men, a sprinkling of the old ones, alas a very small one, but more than I expected we should get two months ago; some men have actually come back, who have been returned dead, and taken off the strength of the regiment for months.

We are in capital health; men well and eager, and in good condition; better fed and clad; the commissariat in a little order, and the transport corps beginning to work, but slowly. The rail keeps the army in front alive.

Here old Scarlett and I lead a most blissful life; lots to eat and drink, so snug in our half hut. I will describe: wood, of course, with a sloping roof and a partition across it, one half is Stephenson's and the other half Billy's and mine; a bed on each side and a table in the middle, the Colours hanging over the table; an old glass cupboard taken out of a house in Balaclava; on one side of the door boxes and trunks; on the other, lots of rails with hats, telescopes, swords, pistols, coats, and cloaks hanging.

I wish England was really a great country and could send us a real army, instead of leaving us in a corner with barely 20,000 men; no transport, and no cavalry; dependant on the French! But never mind, it will take longer to do, but we are sure to conquer in the end. I am just going to dinner, soup, preserved vegetables, sherry, preserved salmon, a salad of dandelions, beer, boiled pork and preserved cabbage; more beer, more sherry; roly-poly pudding! cheese, more salad, more beer, more sherry; hurrah! hurrah! brandy and water and cigars! hip, hip, hip, hurrah.[19]

On 28 May, he writes that he acts 'as Brigade Major to the troops on the heights, ourselves, 31st, Marines, and the remains of the 63rd; the Grenadiers and Coldstream remain in the old camp on the hills, the other side of the harbour'.[20] He hopes that:

The Sardinians will prove themselves as good as they look, for a more perfect little *corps d'armee* than theirs, I should think was never seen. It certainly puts our miserable republican administration to shame.

What a pity the dirty British public cut the army down so low, and then put us, short-handed, to such a work as this. We are now well supplied with everything, and the army is ready and fit for work; John Bull would sooner sacrifice his first army and pay double in the end, for his obstinacy, than consent to pay so much a year and keep his army fit for work.[21]

You cannot think how pleasant it is having old Billy Scarlett again; Stephenson, Hepburn, Scarlett, Francis, Baring, and I all mess together; so that we have quite convivial meetings.[22]

To his father, he writes on 11 June 1855:

But what is so terribly felt by the army is the wretched conduct of our country; one hangs by a thread, and that thread popular opinion, or a roguish popular government, which dreads being called to account for £. s. d; any reckless expense for a popular idea, but not a farthing for military necessity. Now we are beginning to be much better off, both in men and food, but last autumn and winter's awful lesson has sadly weakened the confidence of the army in the people of England.[23]

Military Mistakes & Problems

In May 1855, Major Drummond writes as follows:

It is notorious to all the world that there was no fortification at all, except our bodies; I wish to God there had been, for we should have saved half our men, and that, as it is well known, was the extraordinary neglect. It was repeatedly pointed out, but never corrected.[24]

There is great dissatisfaction in the army at the whole of the staff being promoted, and not a single regimental Captain; it is a crying injustice; we have promotion fast enough, but the whole of the staff, that is the Captains, regardless of whether they were in the action of the 5th or not, are promoted, when so many distinguished company officers get nothing: to men in the line this is a scandalous injustice. To what [factor] was that great victory owing? To the personal efforts of the company officers, not one of whom is promoted. Take my battalion, Scarlett is the only one promoted, the only one not in action on the 5th.[25]

All our recruits are boys, too young; our valuable old battalions, our veteran troops, are all gone, alas.[26]

To his father he wrote on 9 March 1855:

Those battles were horrible, but that no one minds, because it is fair-play; but to see the men one delights in, and is proud of, the most magnificent old soldiers, who love their officers, waste away, and slip through your fingers from wicked neglect and economy of the Government, makes one despair of getting fair-play from a popular Government.

The Duke told me I ought to have been promoted; my horse killed under me in one battle, and I myself severely wounded in the next battle; but I told him it would do me no good in reality, although it might have gratified my vanity; as I am getting so near the top of the list, I shall soon get my company.[27]

The Railway

On 23 February the 'Grand Crimean Central Railway' was operational from Balaclava to Kadikoi, and by 26 March it had been extended to the British Headquarters on the Heights. Between 18 and 25 April the line was extended up the north-east valley to the Woronzoff Road to supply the 2nd and Light Divisions, with a westward branch to serve the 4th Division and the siege batteries. On 1 April, Captain Goodlake reported that the railway could send up 112 tons a day.

The railway played a major part in the Second Bombardment of Sevastopol from 8 to 17 April. The British fired 47,000 rounds in this bombardment. On 10 March, the officer in charge of the Siege Train reported that he was 22,987 rounds short of the requirement of 500 rounds per gun and 300 per mortar. By 10 April this had been more than made up and a far greater proportion of the larger and more damaging mortar shells were delivered.[28]

Transport & Supply

Although Lord Raglan had asked for the re-establishment of a transport corps in 1854, because of delays by the Duke of Newcastle, the Minister of War, the Land Transport

Corps was not operational in the Crimea until March 1855, when it became clear that the idea, promoted by the Treasury, of using local transport was impossible, as none was available. This remedy had the disadvantage that the LTC was a military body, while the Commissariat was a civilian body. Furthermore, transport and supply were two separate organizations, which did not promote efficiency.

The Kertch Expedition

The first expedition was recalled on 3 May, due to a disagreement with Marshal Canrobert. The second sailed on 23 May to cut the Russian supply lines to Sevastopol from Rostov, the River Don and the Sea of Azov, as Sevastopol was not entirely surrounded by the Allies, especially on the northern side of the harbour. The raid was completely successful as Kertch and Yenikale, which were fortified towns on the straits between the Black Sea and the Sea of Azov, were captured. A great quantity of ships and grain were taken. The capture of these towns also enabled our ships to sail into the Sea of Azov. Captain Goodlake refers to this raid in his letter of 1 June.

The Mamelon and Malakov Towers, and The Redan

In his letter of 30 March, Captain Goodlake mentions how his sharpshooters used to operate round the Mamelon defensive tower, in front of the Malakov. It was part of the inner ring of the Sevastopol defences and was taken by the French on 18 June 1855, when they also tried unsuccessfully to take the Malakov Tower (the Round Tower), which was captured by the French on 8 September 1855. The loss of this tower forced the Russians to abandon the south side of Sevastopol Harbour and they withdrew their troops, over the bridge of boats they built, to the north side of the harbour.

The Redan was a Russian fort and part of the Russian defences, which the British failed to take on 18 June and on 8 September 1855, when the French took the Malakov. The Redan was considered impossible to hold after the Malakov was taken, so it was abandoned by the Russians.

Trenches

On 1 April 1855, Captain Goodlake was very worried that the British Army had too large a frontage of trenches to man. He wrote that the men were worked very hard in the batteries. They worked for eight hours on and eight hours off, of which two hours were spent travelling to and from the camp to the batteries. They looked much beaten.

He was also worried about the effect of trench work on the men's attitude and morale. On 14 May, he explained in his letter that the casualties arising from trench work had turned the men into 'funkers', as they were always looking for cover from grape and canister. They hung back in an assault and were, like the French, very sensible. In the past they had never thought they could be licked and never knew when they were.

Captain Higginson, the Adjutant of 3 Grenadiers, who later became a general, comments on life in the field in letters to his parents:

Under the ashes of the fire, I laid an 18 lb. shot, which gradually accumulated heat. In the evening it is transferred to the foot of my camp bed under the blankets and my damp clothes are heaped on the outside. I secure a certain amount of warmth for myself and also dry my clothes.

We have nothing more than we had when we landed, except an extra shirt or two which we got up from the ships, and an ordnance blanket which each officer had served out to him. My bed is composed of an old sack, begged from the Commissariat, which I have stuffed with a little hay borrowed from 'Squirrel', my blanket underneath, my regimental cloak over me, and sword and cap by my side; there I am! I am generally up two or three times in each night, as working parties, etc., have to be paraded, so undressing is out of the question. Fortunately I get plenty of cold water, so my India-rubber bucket serves me in good stead each morning outside our tent, I say *ours*, for Hamilton and Lindsay are tent fellows with me. My clasp knife and old fork, my school spoon and one of your silver mugs form my *batterie de cuisine*, or rather my service of plate, and my servant's mess tin boils the water.

And still we live quite luxuriously, I sometimes think, for we send down to the ships, and we have quite a little cellar of port, sherry, and brandy. I breakfast between six and seven and dine at three, if possible, finishing the evening with a bucket full of coffee or tea. Bread, milk, butter, or fresh vegetables, except rice, I have long been a stranger to, and shall no longer consider them necessaries of life; though I dare say I shall not enjoy them the less when I get a chance of a dig at fresh provisions.[29]

They overdrive the willing horse as they know that we are the last to complain; both men and officers feel that they are intended to be an example to the army, and that they must keep up that example though it results in our annihilation. We now only have 750 effective men on parade.[30]

We have no regimental horses. Everything brought up from Balaclava, fuel, comforts for the sick, clothing for the healthy, bedding for the hospital, rice and vegetables for the battalion, is brought up on horses, the private property of the officers, laden and led by men of the regiment.

We have now 130 sick and the daily allowance of fresh meat [we obtain] from the commissariat is seldom more than 15 pounds a day. We have therefore to buy sheep so that the sick can have their mess of soup. Thanks to private exertions, the men who should be the general's greatest care are properly looked after.

Fatigue parties have to be sent to Balaclava to fetch the rations for the regiments; men are employed on this duty, who have been the whole previous night in the trenches; of course they knock up and the hospitals fill; the surgeons demand medical stores and comforts; there is no transport; the sick require removal to shipboard; the clothing arrives at last at Balaclava, the quartermaster-general gives each regiment an order for its quota with the remark, 'You must fetch it yourselves for there is no transport.'

As for the French, the secret of their success lies in their never attempting anything without due preparation. They land their regiments; but never dream of employing them in arduous duties, such as trench work or redoubt making, until they are *bien installés*. Their numbers enable them to do this before they draw on their reinforcements; whereas we, having landed without a reserve, are obliged to shove each wretched regiment as fast as it arrives into the batteries, regardless of the consequences.

In the trenches, shells and bullets whiz round in disagreeable proximity, which keeps the mind and body at full stretch. The men return so beat up that rest is all they want; they do not have a fair share of the rest enjoyed by the French regiments.[31]

Florence Nightingale

At a meeting in London on 29 November 1855 to thank Miss Nightingale for her services in the Hospitals of the East, Sidney Herbert read the letter from Scutari in which a soldier described the men kissing Miss Nightingale's shadow as she passed, which suggested the poem *Santa Filomena* by Longfellow.[32]

Lo! in this house of misery,
A Lady with a lamp we see
Pass through the glimmering gloom,
And flit from room to room.

And slow, as in a dream of bliss,
The speechless sufferers turn to kiss
Her shadow, as it falls
Upon the darkening walls,
                    Santa Filomena by Henry Longfellow

In his letters Captain Tipping wrote out this poem and placed it opposite his picture of Miss Nightingale, carrying her lamp, passing through a ward at the hospital, where he was a patient, until he was repatriated to England on 21 November 1854.[33]

Captain Higginson continues:

One figure stands out in the softened light that falls on the memory of those far-off days, nor can I close the record of them without reference to her, to whose resolute indifference to routine and precedent we owed the organization of the great hospital at Balaclava. The memoirs of Miss Nightingale, so recently published, not only disclose the defects in our hospital system which aroused so much indignation in England, but also reveal the sweeping changes which the patient and intelligent persistence of this quiet English lady prevailed to effect in the whole of our military medical service. I look back with pride to the day when I was first presented to her, and established those respectful friendly relations which, up to a late period of her life, she permitted me to maintain.[34]

Lieutenant Wolseley, of the 90th Regiment, later a field marshal, landed in the Crimea just after the Battle of Inkerman had taken place. He comments as follows:

Our second winter in the Crimea was a great contrast to the first; all our men were well housed in wooden huts; cooking was done under cover, and there was a sufficiency of firewood and of food. The men were well looked after, and we had a very good time of it. We had sports and amusements for them in fine weather, and discipline became somewhat 'tightened-up' from the lax state into which it had sunk from overwork, bad and insufficient food, and also as a rebound from the strictness with which all military duties had been enforced prior to the war. But the boys that came out with each draft from home were worse than ever. One was ashamed to command them. There were plenty of grown men to be had, but the Government had not the wisdom to make the pay of the rank and file in the Crimea good enough to tempt well-grown men to enlist for service there. When will our rulers awake to the necessity of paying the British soldier at the market rate of wages, as is done in the American army, which, as far as its members go, is, I think, the finest army in the world?

I never had any pity for myself or for my brother officers, for once or twice a week we could afford to buy in Balaclava enough wholesome food to keep us alive for days. Besides, we all recognized the advantages of our position. Rewards, promotion and the praise of friends awaited our safe return home. But such were not in store for the most commendable of patriots, the Non-Commissioned Officer and the private soldier. An ugly silver medal was to be his only reward; yet he fought like a hero and suffered with the steadfastness of a martyr. I wish I could put into suitable words my admiration of his character. His devotion to duty, his determination to maintain at all costs the credit of his regiment, is far beyond any praise that I can express in words.[35]

It had taken the British Army a year to overcome the problems caused by want of proper organization and systems to handle army logistics, and to put in place an efficient system for handling and treating soldiers who had been wounded or were suffering from disease. These problems arose from the economies imposed by the Treasury, which made it impossible to maintain a military organization in peacetime, which could be expanded in wartime to enable an efficient expeditionary force to take the field. This was due to the uncaring ignorance and incompetence of the government, members of Parliament, and its civil servants, who did not understand or deliberately ignored these needs.

Notes

1. Drummond, Maj Hugh, *Letters from the Crimea*, Norris & Son, 1857, pp. 82–3.
2. Russell, Sir William, *The British Expedition to the Crimea*, Routledge, 1858, p. 197.
3. *Ibid.*, p. 219.
4. *Ibid.*, p. 219.
5. Captain Alfred Tipping, Grenadier Guards, 'Letters from the East during the Campaign of 1854', MS, 20 September 1854.
6. Bonham-Carter, Victor (ed.), *Surgeon in the Crimea. The Experiences of Dr George Lawson, 1854–1855*, Military Book Society, 1968, pp. 9–10.
7. Fortescue, Sir John, *A History of the British Army*, vol. 13, Macmillan, 1930, pp. 147–50.
8. Higginson, Gen Sir George, *Seventy-One Years of a Guardsman's Life*, Smith Elder, 1916, pp. 219–20.
9. Burnaby, Edwyn, Diary, MS.
10. Gabions are cylindrical wicker baskets, filled with earth and stones, used to build fortifications.
11. Drummond, p. 93.
12. *Ibid.*, p. 105.
13. Lieutenant & Captain Thistlethwaite, Scots Fusilier Guards, who died of disease at Scutari in January 1855.
14. Drummond, pp. 113 & 115.
15. *Ibid.*, pp. 121–2.
16. *Ibid.*, pp. 126–8.
17. *Ibid.*, pp. 131, 138, 145–6, 147–8.
18. *Ibid.*, pp. 154–6, 165.
19. *Ibid.*, pp. 173–5, 177–8.
20. *Ibid.*, p. 183.
21. *Ibid.*, pp. 184 & 187.
22. *Ibid.*, pp. 190–2.
23. *Ibid.*, p. 201.
24. *Ibid.*, p. 95.
25. *Ibid.*, pp. 111–12.
26. *Ibid.*, p. 114.
27. *Ibid.*, pp. 116, 119 & 137.
28. Cooke, Brian, *The Grand Crimean Central Railway*, Cavaliers House, 1997, pp. 70–1.

29. Higginson, p. 190.
30. *Ibid.*, p. 212.
31. *Ibid.*, pp. 229–32 & 271.
32. Woodham, Smith, C., *Florence Nightingale*, Constable & Co., 1953.
33. Tipping, p. 119.
34. *Ibid.*, p. 318.
35. Wolseley, Field Marshal Viscount, *The Story of a Soldier's Life*, Constable, 1903, pp. 206 & 221–2.

CHAPTER 12

The Capture of Sevastopol, June 1855 to January 1856

Guards Brigade Movements and Events

1855

8 June	Mamelon and Redan Quarries. The French Army takes the Mamelon and the British Army takes the Redan Quarries.
16 June	The 1st Division, the Guards and Highland Brigades march back to the Heights above Sevastopol.
6 June	Fourth bombardment of Sevastopol.
18 June	Redan and Malakoff. The unsuccessful assaults by the British Army on the Redan and by the French Army on the Malakoff. The Guards Brigade forms the reserve for the attack on the Redan.
28 June	Field Marshal Lord Raglan dies. General Simpson takes over the position of Commander-in-Chief.
15 August	Battle of the Tchernaya. The French and Sardinian armies defeat the Russian Army at the Battle of the Tchernaya.
16 August	Fifth bombardment on Sevastopol.
17 August	Headquarters order issued for soldiers in the forward trenches to maintain a steady fire of musketry during the night on the Redan and on the works in its rear.
31 August	The new Pattern '53 Enfield rifle is issued to the Guards Brigade.
5 September	Sixth and last bombardment on Sevastopol.
6 September	Malakoff and the Redan. The French Army captures the Malakoff. The British Army is unsuccessful in taking the Redan.
8–9 September	The Fall of Sevastopol. The Russians evacuate the south side of Sevastopol, which the British and French Armies then occupy.
20 September	A parade is held for those who landed in the Crimea before 1 October 1854 to receive medals and clasps.

11 November   General Simpson resigns and Lieutenant General Sir William
               Codrington is appointed Commander-in-Chief of the Army in
               the Crimea.

19 December   Captain Goodlake reports that the Balaclava to Sevastopol road,
               which he and his workforce have repaired, is now properly made
               up and can handle traffic.

18 December   Badges of the Battles of the Alma and Inkerman, and of the
               Siege and Capture of Sevastopol, are to be inscribed on the new
               Colours of the three battalions of the Brigade of Guards that
               served in the Crimea.

The Unsuccessful Attack on the Malakov and the Redan.

On 16 June, the 1st Division, with the Guards and Highland Brigades, marched
back to the Sapoune Heights. They were to be the reserve for this attack.
Unfortunately the assault by the British Army on the Redan and by the French
on the Malakov on 18 June signally failed, through mismanagement.

On 15 June 1855, Captain Drummond writes:

To-morrow our Division, Guards, and three regiments of Highlanders march
up to the front again, and encamp, and everybody expects something decisive
to happen to this beastly town very soon. I have no time to write much as
I have a great deal to do, and two changes of camp in three days gives me
plenty of work.

On 30 June he makes a very wise suggestion:

My idea is that we ought, French and English together, to attack and hold the
Malakoff, and never mind the Redan; Why assault it? If we take the Malakoff
the Redan is untenable; whoever has the Malakoff commands the whole
surrounding country and works. This is precisely what happened, as when
the Malakoff was captured and the Russians evacuated the Redan.

On 23 June 1855, he writes, after the attack has failed, that they tried a sort of
half-and-half mismanaged assault:

All the men were killed; and now goodness knows what will be done. We
are making up our minds for another winter here. I lay and pour down with
perspiration and think, Oh, gooseberry fool! Oh, my country! Oh strawberries
and ice-cream! Oh, the Ministry! Oh, the, beasts! Oh, green peas and
Badminton! This is beastly![1]

Captain Drummond suffered from an attack of fever and diarrhoea and was sent
on board his cousin, Captain Jem Drummond's ship, HMS *Tribune* to recover.
He was on board from 26 June to 6 August.

I cannot, of course, say what the feeling of the army is about it all; but judging from the tenor of Scarlett's letter, spirits are at a low ebb. I do not say discouraged, but: downcast. There seems to be a fate against us; indeed it now requires the utmost fortitude to bear up against it all, after so long a trial. Constant hard duty, extreme heat, clouds of dust, bad water, myriads of flies, no shade, plenty of fever, diarrhoea, and cholera, then this disastrous affair of the 18th, and the sickness and death of so many generals; all these things have a depressing effect on the officers and men's spirits. What they hate most of all is this everlasting trench work. It is the most beastly duty; and there seems no prospect of a speedy termination.[2]

Lord Raglan's Death

When Lord Raglan died, Captain Goodlake wrote on 30 June:

The officers miss him, not for what he could do here, but for what he could have done for the Army at home. The men do not miss him as they feel that he did not care about them. General Simpson then took over as Commander-in-Chief.

In August he writes that he has nearly finished his hutting assignment. He is uncertain about his future and may have to go back to his Battalion, as the new Commander-in-Chief, General Simpson, may appoint his own friends.

In June, Captain Drummond comments about Lord Raglan's death and on the Army's morale:

Lord Raglan gradually sunk, became weaker and weaker, until he died in Burghersh's arms [ADC], at twenty minutes to nine, on Thursday evening. There were no symptoms of cholera, no spasms, no pain; but the dear old man was too old, and had not vitality enough to resist or recover from the attack of diarrhoea. He was in very low spirits after that 18th affair terrible anniversary! Poor man! He was a noble, good man, and good soldier; and kept every thing right in this discordant mess. Who is to succeed him, is now the question? It is a most difficult post; and now he is gone, Lord Raglan's merits will be appreciated; he has had a hard game to play.

We are beginning to be much better off, both in men and food, but last autumn and winter's awful lesson has sadly weakened the confidence of the army in the people of England.[3]

However, on 11 November 1855, General Simpson, who had never been happy as Commander-in-Chief, resigned. He was replaced by Lieutenant General Codrington, a Coldstreamer, who remained in this position until the end of the campaign.

Tactics and Operations

On 4 September 1855, Captain Goodlake correctly guessed that 'the Russians will make a bolt out of the south side of Sevastopol Harbour the moment we take the Malakoff. They did this by building a bridge of boats across the harbour and then evacuating their Army to the north side of the harbour.'[4]

After his criticism of the British Army's failure to take the Redan on 18 June, it is surprising that he made no reference to the British Army's second failure to take the Redan on 8 September. This is almost certainly because the French captured the Malakoff on 8 September and the Russians evacuated the Redan that night, which the Allies then occupied.

That summer, on 12 August, Captain Goodlake writes that 'the poor fellows in the trenches beg to be shot through the legs and arms, so sick are they of burning sun all day. They are graped, shelled, canistered, round-shotted and pelted with bullets all night, 24 hours on duty and 48 hours off.'

On 31 August 1855, the Guards Brigade handed in all its Minie rifles and was issued with the new Pattern '53 Enfield Rifle.

On 4 September, Captain Goodlake mentions the arrival of Alexis Soyer, the Chef of the Reform Club, in the Crimea. He went out at his own expense but with the Government's approval, with his own invention, an efficient portable stove, to show how rations could be cooked. He was inventive and forward looking. Battalions did not have centralized cooking and soldiers were given their rations to cook. Unfortunately there was no tradition of field cooking in the British Army as there was in the French Army.[5]

Between June 1855 and January 1856, there was a major improvement in the condition of the British Army. In June 1855, Captain Drummond writes as follows:

> The army is now 21,000 Infantry, effective less than when we landed. Well may the 'Times' boast and glorify itself. We are not a military nation, as this unfortunate army can testify. We have just half the men we should have for such undertaking and are rapidly becoming an army of boys and recruits. The French get splendid corps of men up fine old regiments; and we, poor little miserable devils.[6]

However by January 1856, Captain Goodlake could boast that the British Army was now in a most luxurious state:

> The French Army was in a bad state and not much better off than we were last winter. The transports of the three armies were lamentable. The English Army was the best fed, the French Army was miserably fed.

Road Building

William Doyne, a qualified engineer and the Superintendent of the Army Works Corps, was in charge of both railway maintenance and road building in the

Crimea, and especially the construction of a new all-weather road from Balaklava to British Headquarters on the Heights. This had to be finished before the onset of the winter weather. The road building operation in the Crimea is described as follows:

> Doyne had an enormous force of troops at his disposal, released by the end of the fighting before Sevastopol. By the 6 October he had 6000 men, and two weeks later he was managing 8600 troops, 1000 Croat labourers as well as 1000 of his own men. They had laid the staggering quantity of 60,000 tons of road metal, when the six and a half miles of road between Balaclava and the British Headquarters was opened on the 10 November, seven weeks after construction started in earnest.[7]

It was also mentioned that Captain Henry Clifford VC, Rifle Brigade, was superintending 2,000 troops in the construction of the road. Captain Goodlake was performing a similar function with his 4,000 men. Both of them would have been carrying out William Doyne's instructions for constructing the new road.

Brevet Major Hugh Drummond's Death

On 13 August 1855, Brevet Major Hugh Drummond was killed by a fragment of a shell in the trenches. Lieutenant Colonel Scarlett wrote to his father on 14 August:

> A shell exploded over his head and a piece entered his brain. He never opened his eyes or shewed any sign of consciousness after. This took place about half-past three pm close to the Quarries. He was gently carried up to camp, and he drew his last breath about half-past nine. He could have suffered no pain; my hand was locked in his when his last sigh expired, so quietly, that, for a moment, we could hardly tell he was dead.
>
> Before the 8th of June, he requested me, should any accident happen to him, to send, said he, 'My sword to my Father, my watch to my Mother, and one of my rings to Fred [his brother].' With regard to the rest of his kit, he requested that it might not be sold, but those among his friends might take what they liked.

Very prophetically, Hugh Drummond had written the following in June: 'I wish Sebastopol was taken, and the army were out of this accursed country; for there will be many more good fellows leave their bones here.'[8]

Brevet Major Drummond had had his horse shot under him at the Alma, was severely wounded at Inkerman and later on had to go on board ship to recover from an illness. It is questionable whether he had recovered fully to return to duty, and whether he should have been sent home, regardless of his wish to remain with the Battalion. By his death, the Army lost a highly dedicated officer, who might have risen to high rank in the Army.

Notes

1. Drummond, Maj H.F., *Letters from the Crimea*, Norris & Son, 1855, pp. 205, 209 & 231.
2. *Ibid.*, p. 215.
3. *Ibid.*, pp. 201 & 214.
4. Springman, Michael, *Sharpshooter in the Crimea*, Pen & Sword, 2005, p. 160.
5. *Ibid.*, pp. 157 & 160.
6. Drummond, pp. 223–4.
7. Cooke, Brian, *The Grand Crimean Central Railway*, Cavaliers House, 1997, p. 123.
8. Drummond, pp. 254 & 217–18.

CHAPTER 13

The Armistice, Peace and the Army's Return Home, January to May 1856

Guards Brigade Movements and Events

1856

16 January	Russia accepts the Austrian Government's suggested terms for peace.
30 March	Peace of Paris signed, ending the war.
2 April	An armistice is declared. Peace terms are communicated to the several armies engaged in the war.
17 April	Review of British and French Armies by the Russian General Staff.
3 June	3 Grenadiers embark at Kamiesch Bay in HMS *St Jean d'Acre*.
4 June	1 Coldstream embark at Kamiesch Bay in HMS *Agamemnon*.
6 June	Lord Rokeby, Commander of the 1st Division, leaves the Crimea accompanied by Captain Goodlake.
11 June	1 Scots Fusilier Guards embarks at Kasatch in the *Princess Royal*.
28 June	1 Coldstream disembark at Spithead and travel by train to Aldershot Camp.
1 July	3 Grenadiers disembark at Portsmouth and travel by train to Aldershot Camp.
4 July	1 Scots Fusilier Guards disembark at Portsmouth and travel by train to Aldershot Camp.

Foreign Service

2 years and 126 days (856 days)[1]	
Malta	48 days
Scutari	45 days
Bulgaria	75 days
Crimea	627 days
At sea	61 days

8 July	Windsor Castle Parade. The Guards Brigade parades before HM Queen Victoria. A representative body of officers and men hear Her Majesty's address.
9 July	Hyde Park Parade the Guards Brigade makes its public entry into London to join the other four Guards battalions to march past Her Majesty and to give the Royal Salute.

1857

26 June	Victoria Cross Investiture in Hyde Park for officers and men awarded the Victoria Cross. Her Majesty Queen Victoria awards this medal to all the recipients, including all officers, non-commissioned officers and private soldiers of the Guards Brigade.

Peace

Sir John Fortescue explains that the British, having overcome their initial state of unpreparedness, were not able to use their revitalized army, as the peace process had advanced too far, owing to the French Government's desire for an end to the war.

Latterly a better class of recruit had come in, and the ranks were filled not with boys but with men. Nearly 70,000 recruits were enlisted between January 1854 and March 1856, of which nearly half were volunteers from the militia. But the numbers were far short of the establishment voted by Parliament in March 1856 actually 40,000 men short and thereupon the Government decided to raise a foreign legion of Swiss, Germans and Italians.

Lastly, 20,000 Turkish troops were taken into British pay, so that Codrington had under his command in the spring of 1856 not far short of 90,000 men, while a reserve force of 18,000 more had been collected at Aldershot. The infantry were also armed with a new rifle, the Pattern '53, called the Enfield rifle. This weapon was an improvement on the Minie, the Pattern '51. After nineteen months of campaigning, the British at last had a really formidable force in the field.

Unfortunately they were too late. The Austrian mediation presently produced a Congress of the Great Powers in Paris. On 29 February 1856, an armistice brought even the semblance of hostilities to an end, and on 30 March a definite peace treaty was signed. Under a special article the Black Sea was neutralized; 'its waters and ports were formally interdicted to the flag of war'; the maintenance of naval arsenals on its shores was forbidden, and ships of war were denied entrance into or passage through the Dardanelles.

Within three years, Austria and France being at war, Russia violated the treaty and, by blockading the Circassian coast, overcame the resistance of the tribes which had long impeded her progress eastward in central Asia. In 1871, France and Germany this time being at war, she again repudiated the article altogether, so that all the benefits of the Crimean War to England were finally cancelled.

Evacuation

Captain Higginson gives his account of his feelings on leaving the Crimea:

At length, early in June, came the order for embarkation of the Brigade of Guards. As the general decided not to leave till after all three battalions were safe on board ship, he and I remained behind till the last boatload had left the shore. I then returned to the hut which my servant and I had constructed many months before, which I was now to occupy for the last time. I strolled down to the deserted camp of the Grenadiers and found my way into the mess hut, in the construction of which so much real artistic skill had been displayed. The mess-table and furniture remained just as the officers had left it in the early morning. Plates and dishes, coffee-pots, spoons, and tablecloths seemed still to await expectant guests and there was something pathetic in the consciousness which fell upon me that within a few hours all would fall a prey to a marauding Cossack or the straggling homeless wanderer attracted to the now deserted camp of the enemy.[2]

Captain Wolseley describes his last moments on leaving the Crimea:

I was one of the last of our Army to leave the Crimea. As I stepped on board the steamer that was to take me home, I scarcely knew the little village that I was leaving.

The crowds of British officers and soldiers that used to throng its narrow muddy streets were all gone dispersed in many directions, some to India, others to Mediterranean garrisons, to North America or to home stations; in fact I may say to every quarter of the globe where our flag flies.

As we steamed out of the deep and land-locked little harbour, so lately crowded with shipping, now without even a boat upon it, there came back to mind the thoughts, hopes, and aspirations of some twenty months before, when, with my battalion, I first steamed into it.

Thus ended our expedition to the Crimea, which was so full of eventful memories. I feel proud indeed of the manly courage of my race as I think of the gallant men I served with there, and I can never forget the uncomplaining manner in which our Rank and File endured want and misery in every form.[3]

Entrance into London

Lieutenant Colonel Higginson describes the Guards Brigade's entry to London and the parade in Hyde Park:

In the following week we made our entry into London amid a scene of enthusiasm only equalled by that displayed at the time of our departure. Detrained at Vauxhall Station, the Brigade marched over Vauxhall Bridge

159

headed by Lord Rokeby, I as brigade major following in front of General Craufurd, who still retained his command. Passing up Birdcage Walk to the tune of 'Home, Sweet Home!' we entered the southern gate of Buckingham Palace, and, forming column of companies, marched past the Queen and Prince Albert who, with their, children, stood at the centre window.

But we had not seen the last of our gracious Sovereign, for, after proceeding up Constitution Hill through a crowd ever increasing in numbers and enthusiasm, we arrived at Hyde Park and found the royal carriages already at the saluting-point opposite Grosvenor Gate, facing which the four other battalions of the Brigade stood in line of columns, intervals being left between the regiments for the reception of their newly arrived comrades. Forming up opposite the intervals, our three battalions advanced and, by a movement now obsolete, countermarched by sub-divisions round the centre, and thus the seven battalions stood in line. An inspection of the line by the Queen, followed by a march past and a general advance in line completed the ceremony. A few kindly words of welcome from Prince Albert, and the three battalions, which had endeavoured during an absence of two years and a half to uphold the dignity of the Brigade of Guards, returned to their ordinary duties as Household troops. My duties as Brigade Major ceased from that moment, and, although I was a lieutenant colonel in the Army, I returned to duty as a subaltern, and within three days was in command of the Buckingham Palace Guard as a Lieutenant![4]

Peace

On 16 January the Russians accepted the Austrian Government's Peace Proposals and on 30 March 1856 the Treaty of Paris was signed, which ended the War. From 2 April 1856, there was an armistice in the Crimea. In the final outcome, however, the war had achieved its objectives:

In any case, in 1856 Russia had been decisively beaten and its military power revealed as a sham. In the short run, the threat to India had been neutralized, and in the long term the Royal Navy still controlled the Mediterranean. In that these limited objectives had been met, for Britain at least, the outcome of the Crimean War was more satisfactory than anyone in the country could have dared to hope at its outset.[5]

Despite the disorganized state of our Army, it was clear that we only won because of the amazing bravery of our soldiers, fighting against superior odds, and because we had made fewer mistakes in the campaign than the Russians. The Press and the British public held the government responsible for the unnecessary deaths of brave men from disease and from the ineffective organization of the Army's logistical, medical and hospital services.

Charities had appealed successfully for funds to supply the Army with food and clothing to make up for the failure of the Commissariat and the Treasury to provide these necessaries. The Prime Minister, Lord Aberdeen, and the Secretary of State for War, the Duke of Newcastle, had been driven from office in 1855. Florence Nightingale, the much-revered heroine of Scutari, throughout her long life, reminded the public of the debt that the country owed to the soldiers of the Crimean War.

The Bentinck Medal

The following article explains the issue of the Bentinck Medal to the Guards Brigade. It appeared in the Household Brigade Magazine, winter 1951, and its author was Ernest J. Martin, Honorary Secretary of the Military Historical Society.

The Bentinck Medal is practically unknown to collectors and the following details concerning it may therefore be of some interest. The donor of the Medal was Major General Sir Henry J. Bentinck. KCB, a Coldstreamer. On the outbreak of the Crimean War he was appointed to command the Guards Brigade with the rank of Brigadier General, being later promoted to command of the 1st Division. Feeling that the men of the Guards Brigade had been inadequately rewarded as far as Medals were concerned, General Bentinck had dies prepared with devices suitable for the three Regiments of Guards and Medals were duly struck from those for presentation.

The first to be ready were those for the Grenadier Guards and the Medals were duly named and presented to the men selected to receive them. On hearing this, the Coldstream Guards protested that as General Bentinck was himself a Coldstreamer, he ought to have issued the Coldstream [medals] first. General Bentinck then replied that as he was giving the Medals he would do as he wished. It is then stated that the Coldstream Guards refused to accept the Medals and that General Bentinck destroyed the Coldstream die and proceeded with the issue to the Scots Guards. This accounts for the fact that no Medals exist bearing the badge of the Coldstream Guards.

The obverse of the Medal issued to the Grenadiers bore the Regimental cipher of Queen Victoria, and the words, 'Grenadier Guards', while those for the Scots Guards bore their Regimental badge with the words, 'Scots Fusilier Guards'. On the reverse was the inscription, 'From Major-General Bentinck to -------- in recognition of the recipient's distinguished conduct during the campaign in the Crimea, 1854–55'. The Medal was suspended from a dark red ribbon and it is possible that this was the reason for a similar ribbon being adopted for the VC on its institution in 1856.

Twelve Bentinck Medals only were awarded and of these four are today in the possession of the Grenadier Guards, three are owned by the Scots Guards, two by Lt Colonel Count A.W.D. Bentinck, the great nephew of the original donor, and two by the Maharajah of Patiala. This leaves but a single specimen unaccounted for.

Casualties

The cost in casualties was high, however, as the table in Appendix E for the Guards Brigade shows. Of the 6,525 NCOs and Rank & File who served in the Crimean War, 276 (4.2 per cent) were killed in action, 134 (2.1 per cent) died of wounds and 1,856 (28.4 per cent) from disease, totalling 2,266 (34.7 per cent). If the total figure of 449 of those invalided and discharged is added to those who died, total losses reach 2,715 (41.6 per cent).

[**Author's Note:** No figures exist for those invalided and discharged by the Scots Fusilier Guards.]

Out of the 255 officers, who served in the war, 19 died in action, 2 from wounds and 7 from disease, making a total of 28 (11.0 per cent). The total loss in officers, including the 7 invalided, was 35 (13.7 per cent). The figure of officers who died in action or from wounds was 21 (8.2 per cent) as against 410 (6.3 per cent) for the NCOs and privates.

In the case of admissions to hospital, figures only exist for the Coldstream Guards. The staggering figure of 2,785 NCOs and privates (135.2 per cent of the total force) were admitted to hospital. The same figure for the officers was 17 (18.7 per cent).

The Coldstream figures for wounded were 243 NCOs and privates (11.8 per cent) and 7 officers (7.6 per cent).

The Regimental System

The one strength the British possessed was the regimental system, whereby each regiment had a pride in its name and a determination that their behaviour on the field of battle would at least equal their successes and honours won in the Peninsular and Waterloo campaigns, and would thus add to their glory. Gradually throughout the campaign, the various regiments adapted to the environment and by the end of the war the conditions in the camps, feeding, clothing, hygiene and medical services were all superior to those in the French Army. By the second winter Florence Nightingale was very impressed by the standards of hygiene in the camps of the Guards and the Highlanders.

Despite the chaotic state of the Army at the beginning of the war, the regimental system did not let the country down. Let Lieutenant Colonel Ross-of-Bladensburg's words provide the epitaph for the brave men who served throughout the horrors of this campaign:

The successes gained were not due to the skill of the Government, which directed the struggle. On the contrary, our statesmanship had little or no claim upon our regard on this occasion. For the military achievements, under disastrous conditions, were justly a cause of pride to our country, and were worthy of the best traditions of a glorious past. These achievements were solely brought about by that indomitable bravery, discipline and power of endurance that have ever characterized our soldiers, as well as by the admirable system, which made British regimental officers and men second to none that existed, at that time, in any other European army. To the rank and file, and to those who led them in the field, is all the merit to be ascribed, and not to any other body of Englishmen.[6]

Notes

1. Ross-of-Bladensburg, Lt Col, *The Coldstream Guards in the Crimea*, Innes, 1896, p. 285.
2. Higginson, Gen Sir George, *Seventy-One Years of a Guardsman's Life*, Smith Elder, 1916, p. 319.
3. Wolseley, Field Marshal Viscount, *The Story of a Soldier's Life*, vol. 1, Constable, 1903, pp. 220–1.
4. Higginson, p. 319.
5. Royle, Trevor, *The Crimea: The Great Crimean War, 1854–1856*, Little Brown, 1999, p. 501.
6. Ross-of-Bladensburg., pp. 295–6.

CHAPTER 14

The Government and the Army

When the standing Army was established in 1660, the Monarch had the right to appoint the Commander-in-Chief, although since 1688, the House of Commons had to approve the amount of money that the Army was allowed every year. Queen Victoria was the last Sovereign to have this power, which after her death reverted to the Secretary of State for War. After this happened, there was no one to check or question the executive about the Army, except the House of Commons.

On 18 December 1857, the Queen wrote to Lord Panmure, the War Minister, informing him that the reduction of the Army to a low peace establishment, in order to meet the demands for the reduction of taxation raised in the House of Commons, would leave the country in an unsafe condition. There are many other instances where the Queen took this matter up with the government ministers involved.[1]

This did not stop the Aberdeen Government in making a disastrous decision to send a totally unprepared Army to war in the Crimea. The problem was, as Lord Wolseley said, that in the Government that sent our men to the Crimea there was no soldier – as all its members were political gentlemen.[2]

The Cabinet and the Military Budget

When Lord Aberdeen resigned as Prime Minister in February 1855, taking the Duke of Newcastle, the War Minister, with him, there was one person missing who had been principally responsible for the disaster: W.E. Gladstone, the Chancellor of the Exchequer. The Treasury had been largely responsible for closing down the logistics side of the Army, the Wagon Train, and had encouraged the House of Commons to believe that in peacetime the Army did not need to maintain a corps of staff officers. Until the camp at Chobham took place in 1853, at the instigation of the Prince Consort, no manoeuvres had taken place. The generals therefore had no experience of handling large numbers of troops.

General Higginson condemned the Government:

A grave and inexcusable fault lies with the British people in ignoring, as they do in time of peace, the existence of a standing army, reducing it to the lowest possible state and yet engaging in a continental war on a gigantic scale. In this long period of peace, its observance of the closest economy in naval and military budgets, resulted in an unpardonable neglect of all preparation for a sudden campaign overseas. At Chobham, it was clear that the duties of a commissariat were not understood and the means of transport so limited that civilian aid would be needed to transfer the camp ten miles. The French superiority in equipment over the British was clear, as well as their greater efficiency.[3]

General Sir Frederick Stephenson, who served with the Scots Fusilier Guards during the war, was sure that the late government had a heavy account to answer for:

Owing to their utter want of forethought and their gross and utter ignorance that they have shown in conducting this war, they have been to this army a far greater enemy than the Russians. They have killed more men by hundreds than the enemy have. They have, in short, done what I deem it impossible for anyone to do, annihilated the finest little army that ever faced an enemy.

Field Marshal Lord Wolseley wrote:

I know that our Generals and our staff were not what they might have been under a different military system. But I agree in the report of the 'Select Committee' which, having investigated this matter, put the saddle on the right horse, and condemned the Cabinet of 1854 as the real author of our misery. The crass military ignorance of that body was only equalled by their baseness in trying to shift the blame of our winter misery from their own shoulders to those of Sir Richard Airey, the ablest officer, in my opinion, who then served the Queen.

Captain Drummond complained about the country's conduct on 11 June 1855: 'A roguish popular government, which dreads being called to account for £. s. d; any reckless expense for a popular idea, but not a farthing for military necessity.'[4]

Sir John Fortescue commented on the Commons Military Committee:

On the 23rd of January 1855 Parliament met, and the motion for a committee of the Commons to inquire into the condition of the Army and the conduct of the war by the various departments was carried by a large majority. Thereupon the government resigned.

After examining many witnesses and asking tens of thousands of questions, the Committee finally came to the conclusion that the expedition 'planned and undertaken without sufficient information, was conducted without sufficient care and forethought.' It also found that 'the conduct on the part of the administration was the first and chief cause of the calamities that befell the Army.'

The Military Committee which sat to examine the administration during the war, found that the problems the Army faced were due to the want of land-transport. They also found that the want of land-transport was due to the want of forage and that this was due to the neglect of the forage and that this was due to the neglect of the Treasury.[5]

They ended by saying:

In truth the entire episode was far from flattering to us as a nation. Ministers are not infallible, and indulgence should be extended to their mistakes. But the Crimean War was brought about less through active and consistent decision than through helplessness, improvidence and irresolution, and these failings which are not so easily forgiven. As to the absurdity of the plan of campaign, the utter ignorance on the part of ministers of the nature and conduct of war, their panic fear of the Press and their consequent disloyalty to their generals, there is no need to say more. Their conduct was most discreditable to them alike as administrators and as the leaders to whom the public at large naturally look for guidance. But a strong minister could, without alienating the Press, still have kept the supreme direction of public opinion in his own hands and inclined it towards calmness and sobriety. A nation, not less surely than a team of horses, instantly detects a weak hand upon the reins and becomes restless and ungovernable.[6]

The Plan of Campaign
In General Higginson's opinion:

The British plan of campaign was faulty and its objectives changed as events changed. The Army was first sent out to protect Constantinople against invasion by the Russians. Then when that threat evaporated, the next objective was to support the Turkish troops in their defence of Silistria. When the Russian troops investing that city were defeated, the English and French governments, not daring to bring troops home, as this would upset public opinion, decided to besiege Sevastopol.

This policy was adopted against the advice of Lord Raglan and Marshal Saint-Arnaud, that the operation was hazardous in the extreme.

To disembark a force of 50,000 men upon an almost unknown shore, with no base of operations, no depots, no sources of supply except the fleet, which could be driven out to sea by adverse weather, violated all the accepted rules of war. Furthermore, to begin the campaign in September in the hope that the city would be captured before the onset of winter was a gamble. If it was unsuccessful the Army would have to besiege the city and operate during winter, when its logistics and medical facilities were not ready to meet this challenge.

The written orders from the Secretary of State for War, the Duke of Newcastle, instructed Lord Raglan that his first duty was to defend Constantinople. He was also informed by the Duke that the war aims of the Government were to check and repel the unjust aggression of Russia and that there was no prospect of a safe and honourable peace until Sevastopol was taken and the Russian fleet destroyed.

Lord Raglan was told by the Duke to find out as much as he could about Russian troop strengths in the Crimea and about the defences of Sevastopol. The maps available were unreliable and there was no clear idea of Russian troop strengths.[7]

[**Author's Note:** After the war was over, the War Office set up a new department called the Map Department, whose remit was to collect up-to-date maps of the world. Later on this department became the Intelligence Department.]

In the opinion of Lieutenant Colonel Ross-of-Bladensburg, the Coldstream Guards historian:

The government suddenly decided on a change of policy to make Russia submit, as Russia had ignored both our diplomatic and our naval demonstrations. The country was losing its patience and wanted action. As the Army was not required to help the Turks, since the Russians had raised the siege of Silistria, some other task had to be found for it to perform. The government then accepted the first plausible scheme put forward, without considering the risks involved. It decided to take Sevastopol by a *coup de main*, although they were in ignorance of the strength, defences, armament and capacity of the fortress and had little idea of its layout.

The highly optimistic opinion of the government assumed that the problem could be resolved in a few months and that the Army would not have to winter in the Crimea. The government knew that both the transport system for supplies and the medical services were defective and that we had no reserves of troops to replace casualties and to reinforce the Army. It also had been informed by our diplomats that winter in the Crimea came in November, leaving only six weeks of good weather to carry out this task.

Furthermore, if this operation could not be successfully completed within the six weeks, it would be necessary to besiege this fortress. To complete this operation successfully, sufficient troops would be required to construct and defend a trench system, and also to contain the enemy's field army. This would take time and no estimate had been made of the number of troops required to carry this out. However, the decision was taken to go ahead, despite the fact that our fleet had control of the Black Sea and that the Russian fleet was blockaded in Sevastopol.

On 29 June 1854 Lord Raglan received a despatch from the Duke of Newcastle instructing him to prepare an expedition to take Sevastopol. Lord Raglan had little option than to comply, which he did against his better judgment.

Hence the descent on Sevastopol was in the nature of an afterthought; a crude design, hastily proposed and rashly adopted, without reflection or calculation and concerted without reference to the Commanders at the seat of war, who nevertheless were forced to accept it and were held responsible for its execution.[8]

Matching Army Size to the Task

General Higginson further commented:

This war was entered into without any reserve being left at home and thus the army out here has been called on to perform duties in the autumn and winter which should have been entrusted to three times its number. The men were worked to death. We are losing all our old soldiers and officers whose experience, zeal and courage are not to be surpassed. We now scarcely have any old soldiers left.

Major Drummond had very strong opinions on the way the Government had let down the Army:

You know I am no croaker, but if England does not take care we shall have to lament a dreadful disaster before long; no men can last much longer as they are up here. There are limits to human endurance, or rather powers; and our men are now, as they always have been, trebly and four times overworked, which at this time of the year will, as it is fast doing, kill them all.

What an admirable [French] government, and what resources! Look how their army is found with everything, and ours with nothing. All their men are in good sheep-skin coats, before we had one. If I were not an Englishman, the English army is the last service I would enter.[9]

Medical and Logistics

General Higginson comments:

Then again, if the Army Medical Service, the Commissariat and the Land Transport Service, which never existed at all, had been kept on a sufficiently decent footing to admit to a rapid expansion when war really broke out, we should not have lost half the men we did.[10]

The Military Surgeons were subject to Military Law but were not commissioned officers. Their advice could therefore be ignored by senior officers. In 1898, the Royal Army Medical Corps was formed and Army doctors and surgeons then held commissioned rank.

The War Department
General Higginson wrote:

It should be borne in mind that, at the outbreak of war, the War Office and the Colonial Office were administered by a single Secretary of State – The Duke of Newcastle. It was decided to separate them; but this was not effected till July, 1855, some months after 25,000 troops had been sent out. The Duke, therefore, cannot be considered to have received a fair start, and this appears in the following extract from the *Report of the Sebastopol Committee*:- 'On accepting the Secretary-ship for War, he found himself in this disadvantageous position; he had no separate office for his Department, no document prescribing his new duties, no precedent for his guidance and his under-secretaries were new to the work … He was imperfectly acquainted with the best mode of exercising authority over the subordinate departments, and these departments were not officially informed of their relative position, or of their new duties towards the new Minister for War. His interference was sought for in matters of detail, wherein his time should not have been occupied, and he was left unacquainted with transactions of which he should have received official cognisance. In these circumstances it is indeed amazing that the confusion was not even more disastrous than we know it to have been![11]

The Secretary of State for War
Captain, later Field Marshal, Lord Wolseley's views on the war were as follows:

What about that Government of ours which sent an army to the Crimea without any means of carrying either food or wounded men! Was there ever a greater public crime than that of sending our little army to the Crimea, where so many died of want and of the diseases which want always engenders?[12]

Yet this is still what we see; a man who is not a soldier, and who is entirely ignorant of war, is selected solely for political reasons to be the Secretary of State for War. It is an infamous, a foolish system, and sooner or later it must land us in serious, if not in some disastrous, national calamity.[13]

The Government in office had given our small army a task far beyond its power to accomplish. In olden times, when a British general failed in the field our practice was to remove him, and now we hear that in future he is to be tried by court martial. But since the days when we first adopted the system of responsible Ministers, we have never yet hanged, nor even tried, the Minister whose folly or stupidity led him to declare war when our Army was not fit to take the field. Most certainly the military force maintained by England when her Ministers declared war with Russia in 1854 could in no sense be justly called an army at all. It was not a 'going military machine'.

Our soldiers were magnificent fighting material; no better have ever pulled a trigger in any war. But since 1815 the interests of what was styled 'economy' were more attended to than the military efficiency of our troops, which were kept in isolated garrisons at home and abroad. They were most carefully drilled for theatrical effect, but not taught the practice of war. It had been deemed by Ministers, who ranked economy before efficiency, a useless expense to maintain in peace even the skeleton of a transport service.[14]

Very few Secretaries of State in my time ever seriously prepared for the possibility of our being engaged in any big war. Mr. Cardwell[15] was indeed the first – may I not add, the last – who during peace ever attempted to do this. Sooner than incur the initial expense of doing so, they have seemingly preferred to allow England to remain hopelessly unprepared 'even for the effective defence of these shores, on the chance that no big war might occur in their time'. Besides, why thus add to their budget, when the chances are fairly even that their political opponents might be in office whenever war may be so forced upon us?

During peace we never have the military stores required for the mobilization of the military forces we depend upon for the defence of these Islands. In fact, the great military problems which such an Empire as ours involve are never duly considered, much less provided for. When war is thrust upon us, as it was recently in South Africa, the nation suddenly discovers that we do not possess the amount of guns, ammunition, saddles, harness, wagons, etc., etc., required to place our army in the field. We can't make them quickly enough ourselves, and owing to the hostile action of foreign Governments we are not allowed to purchase them abroad, as we recently found to our cost.

When anything goes wrong at the opening of a campaign, and things must, under present arrangements, always go wrong with us in any serious war – the cunning politician tries to turn the wrath of a deceived people upon the military authorities, and those who are exclusively to blame are too often allowed to sneak off unhurt in the turmoil of execration they have raised against the soldiers, who, though in office, are never in power.

And so it will always be, until poor deluded John Bull insists upon a certificate being annually laid before Parliament by the non-political Commander-in-Chief that the whole of the military forces of the Empire can be completely and effectively equipped for war in a fortnight; or should he be unable conscientiously to sign such a certificate, he should be obliged to specify all our military deficiencies. Who is it that objects to this necessary precaution against disaster? Not, certainly, the Commander-in-Chief; nor any other soldier at the War Office. If this were made law the people would insist upon our mobilization arrangements being complete at all times, and that the arms and stores, required to place in the field all our military forces, were in our magazines and ready for issue. But there would never then be any such deficiencies, for England would insist upon having them made good as soon as they were thus reported to Parliament. Alas, alas, poor England! Some day or other she will have to pay heavily and seriously for her folly in this respect.[16]

Viscount Wolseley had this to say about Lord Raglan:

Raglan was forced into a campaign which he knew to be unsound if not insane; he saw the scourge: of cholera descend upon his army, he trembled in early autumn for its existence during the winter; but no words and no warnings could move the incompetent government at home. But it is chiefly as a public servant that his character deserves to be held up as an example to the British Army. No commander was ever worse treated but maltreatment only evoked from him the greater loyalty and the higher standard of duty.

Thereby he saved not only his staff from abominable injustice but ministers from the consequences of their own panic. If Raglan had lost his head it is difficult to see where the trouble would have ended. There might well have been confusion and disaster both in Downing Street and in the Crimea. His constancy, his courage and his uprightness alone for a time held the tottering fabric erect, until he had shamed ministers into sharing something of his own undaunted spirit. He realised that he must take great risks, but at the critical moment could never prevail with his colleagues of France to share them.

In the French Army, St Arnaud was unfit, even had he not been mortally stricken, to command an army; Canrobert was timid and irresolute; Pelissier, though a strong and cordial co-operator, lost his head and upset plans at the last moment.

Then, as if these were not troubles enough there were infamous slanders published by anonymous writers in London, which were countenanced rather than repelled by Raglan's craven and disloyal masters in the Cabinet. There was, in fact, a conspiracy of the irresponsible and the responsible, to shift the burden of their shortcomings upon the army, and to sacrifice, if not Raglan himself, then those who had most faithfully served both him and them. This was unutterably mean in itself, but it was even worse when the conspirators invited, even strove to exact Raglan's participation in their meanness.

There are few more shameful pages in the history of the Cabinet's dealings with the army. And amid all this skulking and shuffling of scared politicians Raglan stood unmoved, too great a man to be infected with their panic, too great a gentleman even to pour scorn upon their trepidation, resolute only to do his duty to the army and to his country. His exquisite tact and courtesy have veiled the greatest of his qualities, his moral strength and his moral courage. It is an amazing tribute to him that he kept his army together at all during the winter, and that, though reduced to a shadow by cold, sickness and starvation, it remained a body of disciplined men, facing all hardships with exemplary patience and doing all the duty that its strength permitted.

We can picture the stream of officers resorting to him one after another with tales of misery and despair; but it is not so easy to picture the calm, much-enduring old chief who by his own mysterious power endued them at least with his own courage and his own endurance. As to his conduct of the campaign at large, the absurdity of the whole enterprise entrusted to him and the division of command make criticism practically impossible. As to details I cannot but think that, though a Commander-in-Chief has other things to look to besides outposts, the army would not have been surprised at Inkerman had Lord Seaton or Sir Harry Smith, pupils of Moore and Craufurd, stood in his place.[17]

Conclusion

The modern reader cannot but notice the painful parallels with the present situation now, in 2008. At present the Treasury has unlimited power to restrict the military budget, whilst disregarding the tasks the military have been set by the Prime Minister and the Cabinet. Even if they did consider the military's objectives they are not competent to, nor do they have the skills and experience to make a valid judgement on the men and materiel the military need to achieve these objectives.

Furthermore other members of the Cabinet have their own departmental interests to consider and so will be interested in restricting or reducing the military budget.

It would provide a powerful counterpoise to opponents of Defence in the Cabinet and in the Treasury, if the Defence Committees of the Commons and the Lords were strengthened by giving them powers to force witnesses to testify, as the US Armed Services Committees of both the Senate and the House have. They would also need additional funding to appoint advisers such as retired Chiefs of Staff, who could help them interview the incumbent Chiefs of Staff, and Treasury and Ministry of Defence civil servants, on military plans and preparedness.

Although the majority of casualties in the Crimean War, especially those due to disease, were principally caused by Treasury restrictions on expenditure, the Treasury did not accept responsibility for these deaths.

If these committees insisted on obtaining from the Services, as Lord Wolseley had suggested, an annual certificate of military preparedness, the Government would be forced to keep our forces in a state of military preparedness. They would be prevented from sending troops on military operations without the necessary equipment and appropriate numbers to ensure that our forces suffered the minimum casualties.

The presence of the Chiefs of Staff at cabinet meetings would also help to ensure that the appropriate matters relating to the military would be considered before a decision was made to commit our troops.

Unfortunately politicians tend to forget the past and do not learn from past mistakes. The British Army is a volunteer army. Its soldiers, who are prepared to die for their country, expect to be paid a fair wage, to be well housed and to receive proper medical care if they are wounded, and especially if they are disabled. In the field of battle, they expect to be properly clothed and fed, to have the appropriate equipment suitable for the tasks they have to carry out, as well as a large enough force to carry out those tasks.

If any of these conditions are not met, if the state of a soldier's quarter is so bad that it threatens the health of his wife and family, or if one of his wounded comrades does not receive the treatment he needs promptly and efficiently, then the morale of an active service unit will be adversely affected. If these matters become items of news in the press, it will become *harder* to recruit new soldiers and battle-experienced soldiers will leave the Army, as they do not trust the Government or their generals to look after their interests. Unless there is sufficient time allowed between foreign operations, and for the necessary training, the married and more experienced soldiers may decide to leave the Army. To recruit and retain the soldiers it needs in its volunteer army, the Government must ensure that these conditions are met and that the military contract between the Government and the Army is not broken.

Notes

1. Benson, A.C. and Esher, Viscount (eds), *Letters of Queen Victoria, 1837–1861*, vol. 3, John Murray, 1908, pp. 256–7.
2. Wolseley, Field Marshal Viscount, *The Story of a Soldier's Life*, Constable, 1903, p. 141.
3. Higginson, General Sir George, *Seventy-One Years of A Guardsman's Life*, Smith Elder, 1916, p. 140.
4. *Ibid.*, p. 201.
5. Fortescue, Sir John, *A History of the British Army*, vol. 13, Macmillan, 1930, pp. 162, 166, 168.
6. *Ibid.*, p. 228.
7. Higginson, pp. 75, 114, 127.
8. Ross-of-Bladensburg, Lieutenant Colonel, *The Coldstream Guards in the Crimea*, Innes, 1896, pp. 52–6.
9. Drummond, pp. 92 & 115.
10. Higginson, p. 140.
11. *Ibid.*, p. 225, note.
12. Wolesley, pp. 91–2.

13. *Ibid.*, p. 92.
14. *Ibid.*, pp. 97–8.
15. Edward Cardwell, Secretary of State for War 1868–74. He reformed the structure of the Army creating linked battalions, one at home and one abroad, abolished the purchase of commissions, introduced short service and created a reserve. Created Viscount Cardwell in 1874.
16. Wolesley, pp. 221–4.
17. Fortescue, pp. 205–6.

Battalion Officers of the Brigade of Guards who Served in the Crimean War

Name in Bold Type: Present at the Battle of Inkerman.

Date of Arrival in Bold Type: Sailed with the Battalion from Portsmouth.

Medals: A-Alma, B-Balaklava, I-Inkerman, S-Siege of Sevastopol.

*Received Medals on 16 May 1855 from Her Majesty The Queen on Horse Guards.

Abbreviations: KIA- Killed in Action; DOW – Died of Wounds; W – Wounded; SW – Severely Wounded; POW – Prisoner of War; FBU – Force Broken Up.

Brevet Rank: Dates of appointment are shown in italics. R – Retired; D – Died: K – Killed; H – Half-Pay; E – Exchanged into another Regiment.

Grenadier Guards Officers
3rd Battalion

Name	*Arrival*	*Leave Crimea*	*Medals*	*Wounds/Death*	*Ensign. Lieut.*	*Lieut. Capt.*	*Capt. Lt-Col*	*Major.*	*Col.*	*Maj-Gen.*	*Retired*
Alexander, C., Capt/Adjt	20.12.54	6.6.56	S	Home – BU	11.5.49	14.7.54	31.8.60	22.9.75	10.7.77		1877H
Anstruther, Sir R., Lieut Bt.	**14.9.54**	9.8.54		Invalided – disease	21.1.53	18.6.55	23.7.61				1862R
Bathurst, F., Lieut	**14.9.54**	16.5.55	ABIS	Retd – Deaf	16.5.51	22.12.54	18.1.61				1869R
Birch Reynardson E.B., Col	**14.9.54**	22.5.55	ABIS	Retired	12.6.30	12.10.32	5.4.44				1855R
Bradford, R., Lt Col[1]	**14.9.54**	10.11.54	ABIS	W – Inkerman Home – Invalided	30.9.40	19.12.45	14.7.54				1860R
Bruce, M., Lt Col	12.4.55	30.5.55	S	Med cert.	15.12.40	30.12.45	14.7.54	3.10.62	16.5.65	22.9.75	
*Burnaby, E.S., Bt Maj[2]	**3.11.54**	24.7.55	IS	To Genoa	3.11.46	27.5.53	– – 57	2.1.55	1.10.77	29.4.80	
(Special Service)	? 6.6.56			Home – FBU	29.4.80–			22.9.75			
*Burgoyne, Sir J, Lieut Bt.	**14.9.54**	?	A	W – Alma Invalided – Home	16.8.50		17.10.54	30.11.60			1861R

Name	Arrival Crimea	Leave	Medals	Wounds/Death	Ensign. Lieut.	Lieut. Capt.	Capt. Lt-Col	Major.	Col.	Maj-Gen.	Retired
Burrard, S. Capt	15.8.55	6.6.56	S	Home – FBU	3.4.46	2.5.61	13.2.59				1871R
Cadogan, Hon G., Lt Col	14.9.54	6.6.56	ABIS	Home – FBU	22.2.33	9.1.38	6.8.47				1857H
*Cameron, W.G., Lieut³ (*Assistant Engineer*) (*Sharpshooter*)	14.9.54	13.1.55	AS	Med cert Sharpsh'ng	12.2.47	15.7.53	24. 4.55				1857E
	???	6.6.56									
Carrick, Earl of, Lieut	1.5.55	6.6.56	S	Home – FBU	16.12.53	7.3.56					1862R
Christie, W., Capt	14.9.54	3.55	ABIS	At Scutari	14.4.48	20.6 54					1855R
	– 5. 55	4.6.55		Private Aff'rs							
Clayton, F. Capt	20.12.54	30.7.55	S	Med cert	8.7.53	13.7.55	26.5.62				1871R
Coulson, J.B B., Lieut	31.12.54	6.6.56	S	Home – FBU	28.10.53	9.10.55					1859E
Cox, A., Lt Col.	14.9.54		A	DOD	27.7.32	8.8.37	12.8.47				1854D
Davies, F. Byam, Lieut	14.9.54		AS	DOW – 10.11.54		21.9.52					1854D
*De Horsey, W., Capt	14.9.54	13.1.55	A S	Med cert. Invalided-Home		22.11.44	22.3.50	13.3.57			1877H
Digby, A., Capt	1.5.55	6.6.56	S	Home – FBU		28.3.54	7.12.58				1859R
Ferguson, G.A., Capt	19.2.55	6.6.56	S	Home – FBU	15.12.53	30.11.55	16.7.62				1867R
Ferguson Davie, J.D.F., Capt	29.8.55	6.6.56	S	Home – FBU	18.4.51	6.11.54					1855R
*Fergusson, Sir J. Bt., Lieut	14. 9.54	4.5.55	ABIS	W – Inkerman Elected MP	18.4.51	6.11.54					1855R
Forbes, Hon W., Lieut	20.12.54	6.6.56	S	Home – FBU	17.12.52	18.3.55	17.5.61				1862R
Gascoigne, C., Lieut	29.8.55	4.6.56		Home – FBU	27.10.54	10.4.57	16.5.65				1866R
*Hamilton, F.W., Col⁴	14.9.54	13.10.55	ABIS	W – Inkerman Promoted – Home	12.7.31	1.12.36	3.4.46–58		20.6.54		
Hamilton, R.W., Lieut	14.9.54	21.11.55	ABIS	Private affairs	27.5.53	18.6.55	23.7.61				1869R
*Higginson, G.W., *Maj (Brigade Major, Guards Brigade)*	14.9.54	4.6.56	ABIS	Home – FBU	12.2.45	12.7.50	10.4.57	12.2.54	77		1885R
Hogge, N, Capt	12.4.55	6.6.56	S	Home – FBU	6.8.47	24.2.54	7.12.58				1872R
*Hood, Hon. G., Col	14.9.54		A	KIA – 18.10.54	30.4.27	31.12.30	31.12.41		20.6.54		1854K

*Name	Arrival	Leave Crimea	Medals	Wounds/ Death	Ensign. Lieut.	Lieut. Capt.	Capt. Lt-Col	Major.	Col.	Maj-Gen.	Retired
Kinlock, A., Capt	**14.9.54**	5.1.55	ABIS	Retired.	27.8.46	31.9.52	30.12.45				1855R
Lewis, C., Lt Col	13.8.55	6.6.56	S	Home – FBU	17.7.35	20.2.46			11.1.58		1855R
Lindsay, Hon. C.H., Lt Col	23.9.54	15.2.55	BIS	To Scutari Retired	20.2.46		14.7.54				
Lloyd Wynne, E., Lieut	29.7.55	6.6.56	S	Home – FBU	27.6.54	13.3.57	3.10.62				1870R
Malet, H.C.E., Lieut	3.5.55	?	S	???	24.2.54	26.9.56					1861R
Montresor, A., Lt Col	20.12.54	28.9.55	S	Med cert.	18.5.41	18.5.46	6.11.54				
	15.8.55	6.6.56		Home							
Morant, W., Capt	15.8.55	6.6.56	S	Home – FBU	19.5.46	6.7.52					
Murray, J., Capt	20.12.54	16.3.56	S	Private affairs ???	15.3.50	14.7.54	21.9.50				1863R
		6.6.56		Home – FBU							
Neville, Hon. A., Capt	**14.9.54**		ABI	KIA – 5.11.54	3.9.42	2.10.46					1854K
Newman, Sir R., Bt., Capt	**14.9.54**		ABI	KIA – 5.11.54		29.10.52					1854K
Pakenham, E., Lt Col	**14.9.54**	6.1.55	ABI	KIA – 5.11.54	12.1.38	14.7.43	24.1.54				1854K
***Percy, Hon H.H., VC,** Col (*Special Service*)	**14.9.54**		ABIS	SW – Inkerman.	1.7.37	29.12.40					1877D
	17.5.55	28.7.55		To Genoa.							
Phillimore, W., Capt	– 12.55	6.6.56		Home – FBU	19.7.50	14.7.54	7.3.51	19.6.60			1855R
Ponsonby, Hon A., Capt	20.12.54	5.3.55	S	Private affairs	15.8.50	28.9.54					1855R
Ponsonby, H.F, Lt Col	22.11.54	???	S	Home – FBU	16.2.44	18.7.48	31.8.55	27.12.64	3.8.60		
Reeve, J., Lt Col	**14.9.54**	6.1.55	ABIS	Med cert	1.5.40	14.2.45	20.6.54				1855R
Rowley, E.A., Capt	**14.9.54**		A	KIA – 16.10.54	4.7.45	17.9.50					1854K
***Russell, Sir C., Bt., VC,** Bt Maj	**14.9.54**	1.11.55	ABIS	Private affairs	13.9.53		23.4.58				
(*DAQMG 1st Div*)	13.3.56	6.6.56		Home – FBU							
***Saxe Weimar, HSH Prince Edward of,** Col	**14.9.54**	6.55	ABIS	Private affairs	8.6.41	19.5.46	18.5.55	20.6.54	5.10.55		1866R
Stanley, Hon J., Lieut	3.6.55	6.7.55	S	Med cert	17.3.54	7.11.56					
Stormont, Viscount, Lieut	29.8.55	6.6.56	S	Home – FBU		21.7.54					1856R

*Name	Arrival	Leave Crimea	Medals	Wounds/Death	Ensign./Lieut.	Lieut./Capt.	Capt./Lt-Col	Major.	Col.	Maj-Gen.	Retired
Sturt, N., Capt (*ADC to Brig Gen Craufurd*) Home – 2nd Bn	**14.9.54** 4.10.54 18.11.55	 6.11.54 5.6.56	ABIS	SW – Inkerman Home-FBU	14.2.51	6.11.54	28.12.60	15.9.77	7.8.80		1880H
*****Tipping, A.,** Capt	**14.9.54**	13.1.55	ABIS	SW – Inkerman Invalided Home		13.4.49	11.6.58	12.12.54			1860R
*****Turner, C.,** Capt	**14.9.54**	21.9.55	ABIS	Retired	9.7.52	5.1.55	15.1.51				1855R
*****Verschoyle, H.,** Capt	**14.9.54**	26.9.55	ABIS	Private affairs	19.4.51	22.12.54					1870D
Wynne, E.W.L., Lieut	29.7.55	???	S	???	27.6.54	13.3.57	14.3.63	1.10.77	10.10.79		1879H
Wynyard, E.G., Lt Col	1.5.55	6.6 56	S	Home-FBU	9.1.38	25.10.42	20.6.54	31.8.60			???
Quartermasters, Paymasters and Surgeons											
Atkinson, J., QM/PM	19.2.55	12.55	S	Med cert – to 2nd Bn QM	28.2 51						
*****Blenkins , E., Asst Surg.	**14.9.54** 29.12.54	9.8.54 6.6.56	S	Med cert - Varna[5] Surg Home – FBU Surg Maj	5.10.54						1862R
Hamilton, F.G., Asst Surg	1.3.55	6.6.56	S	Home – FBU	24.1.58	???					
Huthwaite, F.C., Surg Maj	**14.9.54**	6.6.56	A	DOD – 30.9.54							1854D
Lawrence, H.J.J., Asst Surg	7.11.54	6.6.56	S	Home – FBU							
Lilley, J., QM	**14.9.54**	1.55	AS	To join 1st Bn							
Nicoll, C., Asst Surg	22.11.54	15.2.55	S	Med cert[6] Surg Surg Maj	29.12.54	???					1860R
Read, H., Asst Surg	7.11.54	6.6.56	S	Home – FBU	26.6.60						
*****Wardrop, J.J.,** Asst Surg	**14.9.54** 1.3.55	7.11.54 25.11.55	ABIS	Invalided Home Surg 2.3.55 Promotion Surg Maj 21.5.61							

Name	Arrival	Leave Crimea	Medals	Wounds/Death	Ensign. Lieut.	Lieut. Capt.	Capt. Lt-Col	Major. Col.	Col.	Maj-Gen.	Retired
Officers who came out after Sevastopol had fallen, and did not receive the Crimean Medal											
Buck, W.L., Lieut (Stuckley)	26.12.55	6.6.56		Home – FBU							
Clive, E., Lieut	26.12.55	6.6.56		Home – FBU							
Collins, E., QM	26.12.54	6.6.56		Home – FBU							
Cooper, E., Capt	13.10.55	16.3.56		Private affairs							
	???	6.6.56		Home – FBU							
Crichton Stuart, F., Lt-Col.	17.11.55	27.3.56		Private affairs							
	???	6.6.56		Home – FBU							
Dormer, Hon J., Capt	17.11.55	6.6.56		Home – FBU							
Egerton, Hon A.F., Capt	6.11.55	6.6.56		Home – FBU							
Fitzroy, Lord F., Lt Col	17.11.55	6.6.56		Home – FBU							
Foley, Hon A., Col	8.10.55	6.6.56		Home – FBU							
Goulburn, E., Col	17.11.5	19.1.56		Private affairs							
	???	6.6.56		Home – FBU							
Hatton, La Touche, Viscount, Lt Col	13.10.55	6.6.56		Home – FBU							
Hood, Viscount, Lieut	6.3.56	6.6.56		Home – FBU							
Randolph, C., Capt	6.11.55	6.6.56		Home – FBU							
Sefton, Earl of, Lieut	17.11.55	6.6.56		Home – FBU							

Sources

List Prepared from 'Returns Relating to Officers in the Army (Crimea)'. Prepared by G.A. Wetherall, Adjutant-General and ordered by the House of Commons to be printed, 17 March 1857.

Medal Roll 3rd Battalion Grenadier Guards, prepared by David Paine.

Hamilton, Lt Gen Sir George, The Origins & History of the First or Grenadier Guards, John Murray, 1874, p. 160, 'Officers present at Southampton, 22 February 1854.'

1st Battalion Coldstream Guards Officers

Name	Arrival Crimea	Leave Crimea	Medals	Wounds/Death	Ensign./Lieut.	Lieut./Capt.	Capt./Lt-Col	Major.	Col.	Maj-Gen.	Retired
Adair, A.W., Lieut	1.5.55		S		17.1.55	18.5.59					1860E
Amherst, Hon W.A., Capt (Viscount Holmesdale)	18.10.54 / -5.55	24.12.54 / 4.6.56	BIS*	SW – Inkerman / Home – FBU	3.3.54	4.3.55					1862R
Armytage, H., Maj	14.9.54 / -2.56	12.10.55 / 4.6.56	ABIS	Private affairs / Home – FBU	30.7.47	13.12.53	26.10.58	12.12.54			1870R
Baring, C., Maj[7]	14.9.54 / -6.55	-12.54 / -10.55	AS*	Alma – arm amputated. / Med cert.	2.7.47	29.4.53	21.12.55	12.12.54	2.9.68	23.8.78	1890D
Bouverie, H.M., Capt	14.9.54		BI	KIA – Inkerman	13.7.47	27.5.53					1854D
Boyle, Hon. R.E., Lt Col	14.9.54			DOD – Varna							1854D
Burdett, C.S, Lt Col (Ex 60 Foot)	9.12.54	4.6.56	S	Home – FBU	25.6.41	29.10.47	22.8.54				1859R
Burton, F.A.P., Capt	11.12.54	8.4.55	S	Home – 2nd Bn	8.5.46	27.6.51					1855R
Carleton, D.W, Lt Col (Lord Dorchester)	18.10.54 / -3.56	3.10 55	BIS	Med cert	11.6.41	13.7.47	14.7.54	9.11.62	22.6.56		1868E
Caulfield, J.A., Capt (Viscount Charlemont)	-2.55	4.9.55	S	Home – 2nd Bn	???	???					1897D
Cocks, C.L., Lt Col (Ex 54th Foot)	2.5.55 / -2.55	20.6.55 / -3.56	S	Leave / Leave	24.1.40	7.8.46	20.6.54				1858R
Cowell, J.C.M., Lt Col	14.9.54		BIS	KIA – Inkerman	25.9.40	11.6.47	20.6.54				1854D
Crawley, P.S., Maj (Ex 74th Foot)	14.9.54 / -3.56	26.11.55 / 4.6.56	A B I S	Private affairs	23.6.48	14.7.54	?	12.12.54			1867R
Crombie, T., Col[8]	14.9.54	???	???	Home – FBU	12.8.24	18.4.26	8.5.32	16.11.41	20.10.48		1855H

Name	Arrival	Leave Crimea	Medals	Wounds/ Death	Ensign. Lieut.	Lieut. Capt.	Capt. Lt-Col	Major.	Col.	Maj-Gen.	Retired
Cumming, H.W., Lt Col (Ex 49th Foot)	14.9.54	???	???	???	6.3.38	30.12.42	27.5.53				1854R
Daniell, H., Lt Col	2.5.55	9.10.55		S Med cert	13.8.29	27.3.35	29.10.47	9.11.46			1856R
Dawkins, W.G., Lt Col	?		A-B – S	Home – 2nd Bn	6.9.44	25.4.58	6.11.54				1865H
Dawson, Hon T.V., Lt Col	14.9.54		ABIS	KIA – Inkerman	11.8.37	30.5.43	22.8.51				1854D
Disbrowe, E.A., Capt (Ex 85th Foot)	28.6.54		ABIS	KIA – Inkerman	12.3.52	18.2.53					1854D
Drummond, G.D., Lt Col	2.5.55	4.6.56	AB – S	Home – FBU	10.6.26	3.8.30	29.4.44	20.6.54			1856D
Drummond, Hon H.R., Capt	14.9.54		A	DOD – 1.10.55	???	???	???				1855D
Dunkellin, Lord, Lt Col	14.9.54 22.10.54 9.12.54 8.10.55	22.10.54 8.12.54 8.10.55 4.6.56	A S*	POW To 2nd Bn Home – FBU	27.3.46	27.4.49	3.11.54				1860R
Dunlop, Sir James Bt., Lt Col	14.9.54	26.11.54	ABIS	Private affairs	22.11.54	27.4.49	14.7.54	2.4.55			1858D
Eliot, Hon G.C.C., Capt (Adjutant)	14.9.54		ABIS	KIA – Inkerman	11.6.47	31.10.51					1854D
Fitzroy, Lord A.C.L., Lt Col	18.10.54 14.6.55	7.11.54 14.9.55	BI-S*	SW – Inkerman Med cert	17.5.39	24.8.41	30.7.47				1855H
Fremantle, A.J.L., Capt	???	– 8.54		Invalided – Varna	29.4.53	6.11.54					1918D ???
Goodlake, G.L., **VC**, Capt (DAQMG 1st Div)	14.9.54	4.6.56	ABIS	Home – FBU	27.6.51	27.8.54	29.11.59	14.6.56	30.8.69	11.8.79	1890D
Greville, C., Capt	26.9.54		BIS	KIA – Inkerman	10.6.53	???					1854D
Halkett, J., Lt Col (Ex 29th Foot)	18.10.54	7.11.54	BIS	SW – Inkerman	23.4.41	1.7.47	20.6.54				1870D

Name	Arrival Crimea	Leave Crimea	Medals	Wounds/Death	Ensign./Lieut.	Lieut./Capt.	Capt./Lt-Col	Major./Col.	Col.	Maj-Gen.	Retired
Heneage, M.W., Lt Col	18.10.54 – 5.55	24.12.54 15.3.56	BIS	Home – 2nd Bn	13.12.53	23.12.54	21.12.60				1866R
Ives, G.M, Lieut	11.12.54	6.8.55	S	Med cert	2.8.54						1855R
Jolliffe, Hylton, Capt	14.9.54	– 10.54	AS	DOD 4.10.54	15.12.48	9.5.51					1854D
Lambton, A.C.B., Capt	11.12.54	15.3.56	S	Med cert	4.8.54	15.2.56					1886H
Lane-Fox, Hon C.P.L., Capt	6.3.55	30.8.55	S	Home 2nd Bn	19.12.50	8.4.53					1856R
Lane, H.J.B., Capt	2.5.55	4.6.56	S	Med cert	16.1.55	26.10.58					1867R
MacKinnon, L.D., Capt	**14.9.54**		BIS	DOW – Inkerman	30.5.43	25.2.48					1854D
Markham,W.T., Capt (Ex 62nd Foot)	**14.9.54**	1.7.55	S	Home – 2nd Bn	???	???					1886D
Newton, W.S., Lt Col	18.10.54	8.4.55	BIS*	Home – 2nd Bn	5.12.34	31.12.39	25.2.48	18.11.56	28.11.54		1861H
Paulet, Lord Frederick, Col, (Comd Bn, Nov 54)	14.9.54	26.5.55	ABIS	Home – 2nd Bn	11.6.26	21.9.30	8.5.46	20.2.55	20.6.54	13.12.60	1871D
Perceval, S., Col	8.4.55	4.6.56	S	Home – FBU	13.1.57	15.10.41	23.6.48	26.10.58	28.11.54		???
Ramsden, F.H., Capt (Ex Rifle Bde)	**14.9.54**		ABIS	KIA – Inkerman	11.7.51	28.7.54					1854D
Rose, G.E., Lieut (into Rifle Bde)	11.12.54	4.6.56	S	Home – FBU	24.8.54						1857E
Stepney, A. St G.H., Col	– 1.55	???	S	Home – FBU	16.5.34	10.11.37	15.7.54	3.4.48	26.10.58		1866R
Strong, C.W., Lt Col	**14.9.54** ???	1.1.55 6.5.55	ABIS	Med cert Home – 2nd Bn	6.5.42	1.9.48	6.11.54				1869D
Tierney, M.E., Lt Col	**14.9.54**	13.11.54		Retired Regt	10.3.37	27.1.43	27.4.49				1854R
Tower, H., Lt Col (Ex 48th Foot)	**14.9.54**	26.11.55	ABIS	Private affairs	21.11.51	4.9.54	9.3.60				1870D
Trevelyan, W., Lt Col	28.6.54			DOD. 21. 9.54	18.11.17	25.9.25	19.9.26	28.12.32	10.8.41		1854D

Name	Arrival Crimea	Leave	Medals	Wounds/Death	Ensign. Lieut.	Lieut. Capt.	Capt. Lt-Col	Major. Col.	Maj-Gen.	Retired
Upton, Hon G., GCB MP, Lt Col	14.9.54	15.11.54	ABIS*	Sev. wounded Inkerman	24.4.23	29.10.25	2.12.26	16.6.37 11.11.51	26.10.58	1890D
Viscount Templetown (Comd Bn Feb 54)	5.1.55	–3.55		Home – Regt Lt Col						1859R
Whitshed, Sir St V.B.H. Capt	23.11.54	15.3.56	S	Home – 2nd Bn	1.8.54	2.10.55				1859R
Wigram G.J., Capt	11.12.54	15.3.56	S	Home – 2nd Bn	3.8.54	14.2.56				1885H
Wilson, C.T., Capt (Ex 59th Foot)	14.9.54 ???	22.11.54 8.4.55	ABIS*	Med Cer / Home – 2nd Bn	30.12.42	1.5.46	???			1855R
Wood, W M, Lt. Col. (Ex 60th Foot)	18.10.54	5.5.55	BIS	Home – 2nd Bn	22.7.36	24.5.41	13.12.53	28.11.54		1866H
Officers who landed in the Crimea after the Fall of Sevastopol										
Cecil, Lord E., Capt	8.10.55	4.6.56		Home – FBU	13.1.51	20.12.54				1863R
Edwardes, Hon W, Capt	8.10.55	4.6.56		Home – FBU	24.11.54	5.2.58				1870R
Feilding, Hon W.H.A., Capt	8.10.55	4.6.56		Home – FBU	26.7.53	15.12.54				1904D
Forbes, Sir W., Capt	10.2.56	4.6.56		Home – FBU	???	???				1857R
Hall, Sir J.H.H., Capt	27.10.54	20.6.55		???	2.8.54	15.2.56				1882H
Legge, Hon E, Capt	9.3.56	4.6.56		Home – FBU	12.2.55	29.11.59	???			1875R
Mainwaring, Sir S.T., Capt	9.3.56	4.6.56		Home – FBU	???	???				1858R
Newdegate, F., Capt	8.10.55	4.6.56		Home – FBU	???	???				1859R
Reeve, W., Lt Col (Ex 66th Foot)	8.10.55	4.6.56		Home – FBU	29.12.46	21.8.51	30.11.55			1866R
Seymour, Lord W.F.E. Capt	9.3.56	4.6.56		Home – FBU	18.1.55	13.5.59				1884R

Officers who served in the Crimea with Other Regiments

Name	Arrival	Leave Crimea	Medals	Wounds/ Death	Ensign. Lieut.	Lieut. Capt.	Capt. Lt-Col	Major. Col.	Maj-Gen. Retired
Blackett, C.E., Capt	14.9.54	15.3.56	ABS	Home – 2nd Bn	10.47	4.2.54			1875R
Egerton, P.L.B., Capt	14.9.54	13.4.55	AS		11.8.54	23.3.55			1885E
Fitzroy, G.R., Capt	14.9.54	???	AIS*	SW – Inkerman					???
Fremantle, F.W., Lt Col	–11.54	–6.55	S	SW – Redan	14.11.51	22.12.54	24.11.57		1855E
Gordon, R.H., Capt *(ADC to Gen Sir J. Simpson)*	14.9.54	8.4.55	AIS	Private affairs	???	???	???		
Joliffe, Hedworth, Capt.									1855R
(Ex 4th Light Dragoons)	14.9.54	???	ABIS		8.12.48	9.5.51			1899D

Quartermasters, Paymasters and Surgeons

Name	Arrival	Leave Crimea	Medals	Wounds/ Death	Ensign. Lieut.	Lieut. Capt.	Capt. Lt-Col	Major. Col.	Maj-Gen. Retired
Bowen, F. (Asst Surg)	20.5.55	4.6.56		Home – FBU	???				
Cay, C.W. (Asst Surg)	30.11.54	20.11.55	S	Home – 2nd Bn	12.6.46				
Falconer, A. (QM)	**14.9.54**	4.6.56	ABIS	Home – FBU	1.7.53				
Rogers, T.L. (Asst Surg)	12.6.55	4.6.56	S	Home – FBU					
Skelton, J. (Bn Surg)	**14.9.54**	1.11.54	AS*	Sick Leave	20.3.53				1857D
	–10.55	4.6.56		Home – FBU					
Trotter, W. (Asst Surg)	**14.9.54**	15.3.56	S	Home – 2nd Bn	26.5.54				
Wildbore, F. (Asst Surg)	**14.9.54**	1.2.54	???	???					
	–12.54	–10.55		Sick Leave					
	–7.55	–8.55		Sick Leave					
	–8.55	6.6.56		Home – FBU					
Wyatt, J. (Asst Surg)	**14.9.54**	21.12.54	ABIS	Sick Leave	17.6.51				
	???	10.7.55							
(Bn Surg)	10.8.55	4.6.56		Home – FBU	9.4.57				

1st Battalion Scots Fusilier Guards Officers

Name	Arrival	Leave Crimea	Medals	Wounds/Death	Ensign./Lieut.	Lieut./Capt.	Capt./Lt-Col	Major./Col.	Col.	Maj-Gen.	Retired
Annesley, Hon A., Lieut. *(Earl of Annesley)*	14.9.54	10.54	A	SW – Alma							1871R
Astley, Sir J. Bt., Bt Maj	14.9.54 / 2.5.55	9.54 / 11.6.56	A S	Home – 2nd Bn / SW – Alma	29.7.53	7.8.55					1859R
Beresford, E.M., Lieut	8.9.55	11.6.56	S	Home – FBU	3.11.54	29.4.56					1880R
Berkeley, C., Lt Col	14.9.54 / 17.8.55	9.54 / 11.6.56	AS	Wounds – Alma / Home – FBU							1857R
Blane, S.J., Capt *(Asst Engineer – i/c Croatian Labourers)*	14.9.54 / ???	??? / 11.6.56	ABIS	W – Inkerman / Home – FBU	28.6.50	9.10.54		19.1.56			1856R
Buckley, D., Capt	14.9.54	7.9.55	ABIS	KIA – Trenches 7.9.55							1855D
Bulwer, W., Capt	14.9.54	9.54	A	SW – Alma							1910D
Campbell, A., Lieut *(Lord Blytheswood)*	–12.54	???		W – Trenches							1865R
Chewton, Viscount, Capt	15.5.56	11.6.56	S	Home – 2nd Bn / DOW – Alma	17.3.54	4.8.55					1854D
Coke, W.C.W., Lt Col	14.9.54 / –12.54	8.10.54 / ???	A / S	W – Trenches	7.4.48	25.3.53	14.6.48	2.11.53			1868R
Dalrymple, J., Lt Col	14.9.54 / 8.3.56	1.10.54 / 11.6.56	AIS	W – Alma / Home – FBU	10.11.37	31.12.44	25.3.53		8.11.54		1864R
*Dawson-Damer, **Hon L.**, Capt *(Earl of Portarlington)*	14.9.54	–2.55	ABIS	Med cert							1856R
De Bathe, Sir H.P., Col	22.11.54	???	S		1.11.39	14.2.45	17.2.54		28.11.54		1868R
*Drummond, **H.**, Maj/Adjt	14.9.54	13.8.55	ABIS	KIA – Trenches 13.08.55							1855D
Farquharson, J., Lieut	22.11.54	15. 2.56	S	SW – Siege / Home – 2nd Bn	25.3.53	26.12.54	10.8.59				1864R

Name	Arrival	Leave Crimea	Medals	Wounds/Death	Ensign. Lieut.	Lieut. Capt.	Capt. Lt-Col	Major.	Col.	Maj-Gen.	Retired
Fordyce-Buchan, G.W., Lt Col	22.11.54	26.8.55	ABIS	Med cert							1871D
Forestier-Walker, E.W., Lt Col	23.9.54 29.10.55	–11.54 11.6.56	BIS	W – Inkerman Home – FBU	8.3.27	18.10.31	6.12.44	20.6.54	20.6.54		1859R
Fraser, Hon. A. Bt Major	14.9.54 –10.55	–12.54 11.6.56	ABIS	Sick Leave/2nd Bn Home – FBU							1859R
Gipps, R., Capt	14.9.54	–11.54	ABIS	W – Inkerman Home	10.4.49	20.6.54	2.2.58	6.6.56			1881R
Gordon, Capt	14.9.54	11.11.55	ABIS	Home – 2nd Bn	13.2.52	20.12.54					1912D
Gregory, A., Capt	17.1.55	24.4.55	S	Retired							1856R
Hamilton, Sir C., Col	14.9.54	???	A								1855R
Hay, Hon C., Lieut *(Assumed name of Drummond)*	2.5.55	11.6.56	S	Home – FBU	14.4.54	15.6.56					1865R
Haygarth, F., Lt Col	14.9.54	9.54	A	W – Alma	21.5.41	30.9.47	14.7.54				1911D
Hepburn, H., Lt Col	14.9.54	9.54	AS	W – Alma	19.2.41	2.10.46	20.6.54				1877R
Holder, C., Lt Col	2.5.55 30.12.54 –2.56	11.6.56 22.9.55 8.3.56	ABIS	Home – FBU Private affairs Home – FBU							1859R
Hunter-Blair, J.H., Lt Col	18.10.54	???	ABIS	DOW – 6.11.54							1854D
Jocelyn, Hon J.S., Capt	14.9.54 –4.55	–2.55 1.7.55	ABIS	To Scutari Private affairs	14.4.43	31.3.48	6.11.54				1860R
Knollys, W.W., Lieut *(Asst Engineer)*	14.9.54 –10.54	–9.54 11.6.56	ABIS	Medical Cert. Home – FBU							1858R
Knox, G. W., Lieut	17.11.54	11.6.56	S	Home – FBU	10.1.55	25.9.57					1885R
Lambton, F.W., Lt Col	–11.54	11.6.56	S	Home – FBU	28.10.53	22.6.55	4.11.59				1873R
*Lindsay, R., VC, Capt/Adjt *(Baron Wantage)*	14.9.54 –12.54 –8.55 29.2.56	–11.54 –3.55 1.1.56 11.6.56	ABIS	Wounds Home – FBU							1859R

Name	Arrival	Leave Crimea	Medals	Wounds/Death	Ensign./Lieut.	Lieut./Capt.	Capt./Lt-Col	Major./Col.	Maj-Gen.	Retired
Meyrick, A., Lt Col	–11.54	11.6.56	S	Home – FBU	8.9.46	22.2.50	22.6.55			1873R
Moncrieff, G., Col	14.9.54	10.7.54	S	Promoted – Home						1858R
Moncrieff, G.H., Lieut	2.5.55	11.6.56	S	Home – FBU	4.8.54	15.1.56				1886R
Moorsom, R., Lt Col	17.1.55	11.6.56	S	Home – FBU						1858R
Murray, Lord T., Lt Col	18.10.54	28.1.55	BIS	Med cert						1857R
Ridley, W.J., Lt Col	14.9.54	11.1.55	ABIS	Leave	19.6.35	24.5.39	24.11.48	15.12.54	28.11.54	1863R
Seymour, F., Lt Col	14.9.54	–11.54	ABIS	W – Inkerman	16.6.37	4.9.40	28.6.50	14.6.58	28.11.54	1863R
Shuckburgh, G.H., Capt	14.9.54	–11.54	ABIS	W – Trenches						1857R
Stracey, E., Lt Col	14.9.54	11.10.54	ABIS	Invalided						1855R
Stephenson, F.C.A., Lt Col	14.9.54	7.8.55	ABIS	Med cert						
(Bde Maj Guards Bde)	31.12.55	11.6.56		Home – FBU			20.6.54			1874R
Thistlethwaite, A., Lieut	14.9.54	11.54	A	DOD – 12.10.54	25.7.37	13.1.43				1854D
Tottenham, C., Lieut.	11.54	1.6.56	S	Home – FBU	13.1.54	8.9.55				1866R

Officers who landed in the Crimea after the Fall of Sevastopol

Name	Arrival	Leave Crimea	Medals	Wounds/Death	Ensign./Lieut.	Lieut./Capt.	Capt./Lt-Col	Major./Col.	Maj-Gen.	Retired
Aitchison, W., Capt	27.12.55	11.6.56		Home – FBU	24.3.45	2.10.46	24.5.50			1870R
Brownlow, Hon. E., Lieut	8.9.55	11.6.56		Home – FBU						1858R
Charteris, Hon. R., Lt Col	7.11.55	11.6.56		Home – FBU	2.10.40	7.10.42	14.7.47	14.7.54		1862R
Mostyn, Hon R., Capt	17.12.55	11.6.56		Home – FBU	23.3.49	17.2.54				1864R
Paynter, J., Lieut.	7.10.55	11.6.56		Home – FBU	26.12.54	25.9.57				1863R
Sharp, H., Lieut	7.10.55	11.6.56		Home – FBU	22.12.54	16.6.67				1865R
Stewart, R., Lieut	8.9.55	11.6.56		Home – FBU						1857R
Trefusis, Hon W., Lieut	8.3.56	11.6.56		Home – FBU	9.2.55	2.2.58				1885R
Vane-Tempest, Lord A.	2.11.54	??? – – –								1859R
Wheatley, W., Capt	27.12.55	11.6.56		Home – FBU						1859R

Name	Arrival Crimea	Leave Crimea	Medals	Wounds/ Death	Ensign. Lieut.	Lieut. Capt.	Capt. Lt-Col	Major.	Col.	Maj-Gen.	Retired
Officers who served in the Crimea with Other Regiments											
Beaumont, G., Lieut[9]	8.3.56	11.6.56	ABIS	Home – FBU							1866R
Cooper, R.A., Capt[10]			ABS		21.9.54	17.11.57					1863R
Mure, W., Lt Col[11]			AB		11.7.51	29.12.54	16.12.59				1860R
Rous, W.J., Capt[12]			S		25.8.54	23.10.55					1871R
Quartermasters, Paymasters and Surgeons											
*Allen, G. (QM)	14.9.54	11.6.56	ABIS	Home – FBU							1884D
Baker, F. (Asst Surg)	14.9.54	– 9.54	AS	Sick Leave							1871R
	8.3.56	11.6.56		Home – FBU							
*Bostock, J. (Bn Surg)	14.9.54	16.4.55	ABIS	Home – 2nd Bn							1895D
Elkington, A. (Asst Surg)	14.9.54	???	BIS	W – Inkerman							1911D
	17.11.54	11.6.56		Home – FBU							
Perry, G. (Asst Surg)	16.6.55	???	S								1912D
*Robinson, F (Bn Surg)	14.9.54	– 10.54	ABIS	Med cert.							1901D
	– 11.54	11.6.56		Home – FBU							
Turner, H. (Asst Surg)	23.11.54	23.1.55	S	Med cert							1869R
	31.1.55	6.7.55		Home – FBU							

Sources

Maurice, Maj Gen Sir F., *The History of the Scots Guards from the Creation of the Regiment to The Eve of the Great War*, Chatto & Windus, 1934: Page 217, Officers present at Inkerman on 5 Nov 1854. Page 257, Officers present on 11 Apr 1854. Page 290, Officers returning from the Crimea, May and June 1856. Pages 521–2, Officers who served in the Crimea, 1854–6, Appendix R.

Hart's Army List 1860

Notes

1. Joined Battalion from Staff 29.8.54.
2. Sick at Varna – rejoined Battalion on 3 Nov 1854. Missed battles of Alma and Balaklava.
3. In charge of the ten Grenadiers operating as Sharpshooters. Severely wounded and returned as Assistant Engineer.
4. Promoted Mounted Officer 3rd Battalion – arrived Varna 22 July 1854. Retired as Lt Gen.
5. Asst Surgeon Blenkins was left in Varna with the sick and from there was invalided home. He then returned to the Battalion in the Crimea, returning home when the force broke up.
6. Sent to Scutari to examine sick and then invalided home.
7. Lt Gen, 1881.
8. Served in Bulgaria.
9. Served in the Eastern Campaign of 1854 with the 21st Fusiliers, including the Battles of Alma, Balaklava and Inkerman and the Siege of Sevastopol.
10. Served with the 79th Regiment in the Eastern Campaign of 1854–5, including the Battles of Alma and Balaklava, and the Siege and Fall of Sevastopol.
11. Served with the 79th Regiment in the Eastern Campaign, including the Battles of Alma and Inkerman.
12. Served in the 90th Light Infantry at the Siege and Fall of Sevastopol, and was wounded in the attack on the Redan on 8 Sept 1855.

Appendix B

Officers of the Brigade of Guards on the Staff in the Crimean War

Battalion officers who fought in the principal battles and who subsequently became staff officers are included in their Battalion list.

Name in Bold Type: Present at the Battle of Inkerman.

Date of Arrival in Bold Type: Sailed with the Battalion from Portsmouth.

Medals: A-Alma, B-Balaklava, I-Inkerman, S-Siege of Sevastopol.

* Received Medals on 16 May 1855 from Her Majesty The Queen on Horse Guards.

Abbreviations: KIA – Killed in Action; DOW – Died of Wounds; W – Wounded; SW – Severely Wounded; POW – Prisoner of War; FBU – Force Broken Up.

Brevet Rank: Dates of Appointment are shown in italics. R – Retired; D – Died; H – Half-Pay; E – Transferred into another Regiment.

Name	Arrival	Leave Crimea	Medals	Wounds/Death	Retired
Grenadier Guards Officers					
Generals					
Craufurd, J.B., Col	29.10.55	4.6.56		Home – FBU	???
(Comd Guards Bde)					
Ridley, C.W., Col	1.12.54	24.5.56	S	Home – FBU	1867D
(Brig Gen, 2 Bde, 1st Div)					
Staff Officers					
***Balgonie, Viscount**	14.9.54	9.10.55	AIS	Home woth Brig Gen	1857D
(ADC to Sir H. Bentinck)					
Barnard, W., Capt	???	6.6.56	???	Home – FBU	???
(ADC to Gen Barnard)					
***Brownrigg, S.,** Lt Col	14.9.54	23.10.54	ABIS	Private affairs	
(AAG 1st Div)	???	6.6.56		Home – FBU	???
***Cadogan Hon G.,** Lt Col	14.9.54	24.11.54	ABIS	Med cert	1857H
	21.12.54	13.1.55	Med cert		
(Attached Sardinian Army)	6.5.55	20.5.56	Turin & Home		
Cunynghame Sir A., Col	14.9.54	13.5.55	???	Att Turkish Army	???
(AQMG 1st Div)					

Appendix B

Name	Arrival	Leave Crimea	Medals	Wounds/Death	Retired
Ellison, C.G. Bt., Lt Col *(Bde Maj Guards Bde)*	17.10.54	26.10.55	???	Private affairs	???
Gordon, Hon.A., Lt Col *(AAG 1st Div & AQMG HQ)*	14.9.54	1.7.55	???	Private affairs	1856H
Hay, Lord A. Lt. Col. *(AAG 1st Div)*	20.12.54	6.6.56	S	Home – FBU	1863H
Lane Fox, A., Maj[1] *(DAQMG 2nd Div)*	14.9.54	15.10.54	?	Med cert	???
Maitland, C.L.B., Lt Col *(DAAG 4th Div)*	4.9.54	11.11.54	ABIS	SW – Inkerman	???
Malet, H.C.E.,Capt. *(ADC to Brig Gen Craufurd)*	3.5.55	3.6.56	S	Home – FBU	1870R
Mitchell, A., Capt. *(ADC to Brig Gen Ridley)*	20.12.54 5.8.55 29.2.56	12.7.55 17.11.55 24.5.56	S	Med cert Private Affairs Home – FBU	1856R
Pearson, R.L.O. Major *(ADC to Sir G. Brown)*	15.9.54	30.6.55	???	UK – Gen Brown	???
Ponsonby, Hon. A. Capt	22.11.54	1.1.55	S	Medical cert	1855R
Ponsonby, A.E.V., Capt *(ADC to Sir G. Brown & Sir W. Codrington)*	19.4.55	12.7.56	S	Home – FBU	1863E
Poulett, Hon A., Capt *(Extra ADC to Lord W. Paulet)*	17.5.55 ???	5.1.56 6.6.56	S	To Malta. Med cert Home – FBU	1865R
Thesiger, F.A., Maj *(DAQMG HQ)*	31.5.55	6.6.56	S	Home – FBU	1858E

193

Name	Arrival	Leave Crimea	Medals	Wounds/Death	Retired
Coldstream Guards Officers *Generals*					
Codrington, Sir W.J.[2] Lt Gen *(C-in-C) Lt Gen*	**14.9.54**	25.6.56	ABIS	Home – FBU	???
Bentinck, Sir H., Maj Gen *(Comd Gds Bde; Comd 4th Div)*	**14.9.54** 3.6.55	2.12.54 9.10.55	ABIS	W – Inkerman Private affairs	1878D
Staff Officers					
Airey, Sir R., Lt Gen *(QMG, Ex 22nd Foot)*	28.3.56	6.10.55 15.6.56	ABIS	Private Affairs Home – FBU	1867R
Baring, C., Maj *(Staff – Bde & Div)*	14.9.54	22.9.54	A*	W – Alma Arm amputated Med cert	1872R
Bingham, Lord, Maj *(Extra ADC to Earl of Lucan – Ex 21st & 89th Foot)*	14.6.55 **14.9.54** 3.10.55	10.10.55 17.2.55 4.6.56	ABI*	Home + Gen Home – FBU	1860R
Boyle, Hon W.G., Capt *(ADC to Gen De Lacy Evans – Ex 21st & 89th Foot)*	14.9.54	3.11.54	ABIS	Eng + Gen	???
Byng, Hon H.W. Lt Col Earl of Strafford *(ADC ???)*	10.11.55	4.6.56		Home – FBU	1899D
Burghesh, Lord, Lt Col (later Earl of Westmorland) *(ADC to Lord Raglan)*	**14.9.54**	3.7.55	ABI	Home 2nd Bn	???
Campbell, Hon H.W., Capt *(ADC to Gen Sir W. Codrington)*	**14.9.54** 1.10.55 1.12.55 8.5.56	1.10.55 25.10.55 8.5.56 26.6.56	S	Med cert Med cert Home + C-in-C	

Name	Arrival	Leave Crimea	Medals	Wounds/Death	Retired
Clarke-Jervoise, H. Capt (*ADC to Maj Gen Airey – DAQMG 1st Div – Ex 42nd Foot*)	**14.9.54**	2.6.56	AIS	Home – FBU	1873R
Connolly, J.A., **VC**, Maj (*DAAG Cavalry Div – ADC to Gen Bentinck Ex 49th Regt*)	14.9.54 / 29.8.55	2.11.54 / 22.12.55	AS	SW – Inkerman / Private affairs	1870R
Cust, H., Capt. (*ADC to Gen Bentinck*)	**14.9.54**	???	A	KIA – Alma	1854D
Feilding, Hon P.R.B.,[3] Lt Col (*Bde Maj, Alma – (DAQMG 1st Div)*)	**14.9.54** / – 8.55	7.11.54 / 4.6.56	ABIS*	SW – Alma	1904D
Goodlake, G.L., **VC**,[4] Capt (*DAQMG 1st Div*)	**14.9.54**	4.6.56	ABIS	Home – FBU	1890D
Hardinge, Hon A., Lt Col (*AQMG HQ*)	**14.9.54**	26.6.56	ABIS	Home – FBU	1892D
Le Couteur, J.H. Maj (*Musketry Instructor Turkish Contingent*)	11.12.54	4.6.56	S	Home – FBU	1868R
Maxse, H.F.B. Capt (*ADC Lord Cardigan – Ex 21st Foot*)	14.9.54	28.11.54	ABS*	W – Balaklava	1858H
Somerset, P.G.H., Capt (*ADC to Lord Raglan – Ex 33rd Foot*)	14.9.54	3.7.55	ABIS	Home – 2nd Bn	1855H
Steele, T.M., Col (*Military Secretary to Lord Raglan*)	14.9.54	27.11.55	ABIS	Home – 2nd Bn	1890D
Thellusson, A.G.B., Capt (*ADC to Col Drummond*)	2.5.55	6.6.56	S	Home – FBU	1855R
Wellesley, Hon W.H., Capt Viscount Dangan (*ADC to Lord Rokeby*)	12.7.55	24.5.56	S	Home – FBU	1863R

Scots Guards Fusiliers Officers

Generals

Name	Arrival	Leave Crimea	Medals	Wounds/Death	Retired
Cambridge, Duke of, Gen[5] (*GOC 1 Div*)	14.9.54	11.54	ABIS	Sick to UK	1861R
Rokeby, Baron, Lt Gen (*GOC 1st Div*)	2.2.55	6.6.56	S	Home – FBU	1883R

Staff Officers

Name	Arrival	Leave Crimea	Medals	Wounds/Death	Retired
*****Baring, F.**, Bt Maj (*DAAG 1st Div*)	14.9.54	11.6.56	ABIS	W – Inkerman / Home – FBU	1868R
*****Ennismore, Viscount** Capt	14.9.54	30.9.54	A	W – Alma	1856R
(*ADC to Lt Gen Windham*)	1.10.55	9.2.56		Private affairs	
*****Gordon, G.G.**, Capt (*ADC to Sir J. Simpson*)	14.9.54	5.9.55	ABIS	Home – 2nd Bn	1877R
Greville, A.C., Capt (*ADC to Sir H. Bentinck*)	14.9.54	10.11.54	ABIS	Home – 2nd Bn	1856R
	3.6.55	9.10.55		Home – 2nd Bn	1856R
Kingscote, N., Capt (*ADC to Lord Raglan*)	14.9.54	3.7.55	ABIS	Home – 2nd Bn	
Neville, E., Bt Maj (*ADC to Sir R England*)	14.9.54	1.8.54	ABIS	Home – 2nd Bn	1866R
	6.3.56	11.6.56		Home – FBU	
*****Scarlett, Hon W.F.**, Lt-Col	14.9.54	22.11.54	ABIS	Private Affairs	1877R
(*ADC to Lt Gen Hon W. Scarlett*)	– 3.56	11.6.56		Home – FBU	
Seymour, C.F., Lt Col (*AAG 4th Div*)	14.9.54	5.11.54	ABIS	KIA – Inkerman	1854D
Stephenson, F.C.A., Lt Col (*Bde Maj Guards Bde*)	14.9.54	7.8.55	ABIS	Med cert	1874R
	31.12.55	11.6.56		Home – FBU	

Name	Arrival	Leave Crimea	Medals	Wounds/Death	Retired
Tyrwhitt, C., Lt Col *(Extra ADC to HRH The Duke of Cambridge)*	14.9.54	3.11.54	ABI	Home with HRH	1854R
Wetherall, E.R., Col *(AQMG HQ)*	14.9.54	26.6.56	ABIS	Joined Turkish Contingent	1856R

Sources

List Prepared from 'Returns Relating to Officers in the Army (Crimea)', prepared by G.A. Wetherall, Adjutant-General, and ordered by the House of Commons to be printed, 17 March 1857.

Medal Roll 3rd Battalion Grenadier Guards, prepared by David Paine.

Hamilton, Lt Gen Sir George, *The Origins & History of the First or Grenadier Guards*, John Murray, 1874:

Page 160 Officers present at Southampton, 22 Feb 1854.

    Page 180 Officers landing in the Crimea & present at the Alma, 14 Sept 1854.

    Page 217 Officers present at Inkerman, 5 Nov 1854.

    Page 257 Officers present on 11 Apr. 1854.

    Page 290 Officers returning from the Crimea, May & June 1856.

Pages 521–2 Officers who served in the Crimea, 1854–6, by date of arrival, Appendix R.

Maurice, Maj Gen Sir F., *The History of the Scots Guards from the Creation of the Regiment to the Eve of the Great War*, Chatto & Windus, 1934:

Pages 78–9, Appendix 1, Officers of the Scots Fusiliers Guards, 1854–5.

Pages 283–371, Nominal Roll of Officers, 1642–1934.

Hart's Army List 1854, 1855, 1860.

Notes

1. Major Lane Fox later changed his name to Pitt-Rivers.
2. Codrington, Lt Gen, 6 June 1856.
3. Feilding served as Brigade Major, Brigade of Guards at the Battle of the Alma and on the staff of the 1st Division for the Battles of Balaklava and Inkerman, and for the Siege of Sevastopol.
4. Present at the Battles of Alma, Balaklava, Inkerman and Tchernaya, and the Siege and Fall of Sevastopol. He volunteered for the Sharpshooters of the Brigade of Guards, commanded them for forty-two days and was engaged at the repulse of the sortie of 26 Oct 1854; he served on the Quartermaster. General's staff from Feb 1855. See Hart's Army List 1860, p. 165.
5. Lt Gen, 19 June 1854; Gen 15 July 1856.

197

The Commanders of the 1st Division, the Guards Brigade and the Three Battalions

There were many changes in the command of the 1st Division, the Guards Brigade and its three battalions the 3rd Grenadiers, the 1st Coldstream and the 1st Scots Fusilier Guards during the Crimean War, owing to death, disease, promotion or for other reasons.

The 1st Division was formed by General Order, issued in May 1854, when the Division was in the Turkish Dominions. When it landed in the Crimea, it was commanded by HRH Major General the Duke of Cambridge, with Brigadier General Bentinck commanding the Guards Brigade. Colonel Thomas Wood commanded 1st Grenadiers, Colonel C. Hay the 1st Coldstream and Colonel G. Dixon the 1st Scots Fusilier Guards.

The Brevet of the 20th June 1854 resulted in a number of changes. The Duke of Cambridge became a Lieutenant General, and both Bentinck and Sir Colin Campbell were promoted to the rank of Major General. Colonel Wood was promoted to Regimental Lieutenant Colonel of the Grenadier Guards and was repatriated, and Colonel Grosvenor Hood then became the Grenadier's Commanding Officer. Colonel C. Hay became a Major General and went home. He was replaced as Commanding Officer of the 1st Coldstream by Colonel C. Upton. Colonel Dixon also became a Major General and was repatriated, and command of the 1st Scots Fusilier Guards went temporarily to Colonel Sir C. Hamilton, until Colonel E.W.F. Walker arrived on 23 September to take over command, after the Battle of the Alma.

On 14 October 1854, Sir Colin Campbell, now a Major General by the last Brevet, moved to Balaklava, to take command of the troops there. The Highland Brigade, less the 93rd Highlanders, remained with the 1st Division and was commanded by Colonel Duncan Cameron. After the Battle of Balaklava on 26 June 1854, the complete Highland Brigade remained at Balaklava, under Sir Colin, while the remainder of the 1st Division, including the Guards Brigade, returned to the Heights.

On 18 October 1854, Colonel Hood, Commanding Officer of the 3rd Grenadiers, was killed in the trenches. Colonel Reynardson took over temporarily as Commanding Officer until the arrival of Colonel Ridley on 1 December.

The Battle of Inkerman resulted in a number of changes. Major General Bentinck had been wounded halfway through the action and was replaced as Brigade Commander by Colonel Upton. After the battle, the Duke of Cambridge went sick and was replaced temporarily by Colonel Upton. He had been wounded but remained in command of the Division until 15 November, when he retired to the hospital at Balaklava. Colonel Reynardson then replaced Colonel Upton as temporary Brigade Commander and Colonel F.W. Hamilton took over command of the Grenadiers.[1]

The Commander of the 1st Coldstream at Inkerman should have been Colonel Upton but he had been on night duty on 4/5 November, Colonel Lord F. Paulet, the next senior officer, was ill, so Colonel Dawson commanded and was killed at the Sandbag Battery. On his death, as Colonel Upton was now temporary Brigade Commander, Lieutenant Colonel Newton took over temporarily as the 1st Coldstream's Commanding Officer, until Lord F. Paulet returned to the Crimea on 16 January 1855.

The Scots Fusilier Guards' Commanding Officer, Colonel E.F.W. Walker was also wounded at Inkerman. Colonel C.F. Seymour took over temporarily until Colonel Walker returned to the Crimea on 29 October 1855 and reassumed command of the Battalion.

On 22 November 1854, the 1st Division and the Guards Brigade moved to the Sapoune Heights and the Division came under the temporary command of Brigadier General Lockyer, 97th Foot, until he returned to the front on 15 January 1855, to command 2 Brigade in the 2nd Division.

Colonel Upton retired to hospital on 15 November and from then until 23 November, when Brigadier Lockyer became Divisional Commander, this position appears to have been vacant. It also appears that the appointment of Divisional Commander was unfilled from when Brigadier Lockyer left on 15 January 1855 to 2 February when Major General Lord Rokeby took over as temporary Divisional Commander and as Brigade Commander.

It could be that Lord Raglan was keeping these positions open, as both the Duke and Major General Bentinck could still have been on the staff of the Army and thus had a right to return to take up their positions.[2] In Bentinck's case this would have ended when he was promoted to Local Lieutenant General on 22 January 1855.[3] For the Duke, Colonel Browning's transfer from the 1st Division to the Light Division as Assistant Adjutant General on 5 March 1855 would have confirmed that he (the Duke) was not returning to the Crimea.

Colonel C.W. Ridley arrived in the Crimea on 1 December 1854 to command the Grenadiers. However he took over temporarily as Guards Brigade Commander from Colonel Reynardson, as he was the senior of the two. Colonel Reynardson then took over as temporary commander of the Grenadiers.

Colonel Upton, on his return from hospital, reassumed temporary command of the Guards Brigade on 15 January 1855. Meanwhile, Colonel Ridley took over command of the Grenadiers from Colonel Reynardson, who went home to retire from the Regiment on 22 May 1855.[4] On 16 January, Colonel Lord F. Paulet returned to take over command the 1st Coldstream from Lieutenant Colonel Newton.

When Major General Lord Rokeby first arrived in the Crimea on 2 February 1855, he took over as Brigade Commander and acting Divisional Commander.[5] Colonel Upton then reassumed command of 1st Coldstream from Colonel Lord F. Paulet. However on 22 February 1855, Colonel Upton returned home to take up the position of Regimental Lieutenant Colonel Commanding the Coldstream Guards.[6] Colonel Lord F. Paulet also returned home on this date to take command of the 2nd Coldstream, so Colonel G. Drummond became Commanding Officer of the 1st Coldstream.

Although the commanders of the three battalions remained the same from February to July 1855, there were a number of changes at divisional level. After the losses the Guards Brigade had incurred at Inkerman, their strength had been reduced to 312 men able to do duty.[7] They were therefore excused trench duty and sent to Balaklava on 22 February 1855 to rest and recuperate.

This period the Brigade spent in Balaklava becomes very difficult to fathom. A General Order of 1 March gives Sir Colin temporary command of the Guards Brigade. It appears, however, that the 1st Division was broken up, as Colonel Brownrigg, the Assistant Adjutant-General of the Division was transferred to the Light Division on 5 March 1855. However, according to Hamilton,[8] the troops in and around Balaklava were placed under the command of Sir Colin Campbell, but as the Guards formed an independent brigade under Lord Rokeby, the services of an AAG to 1st Division were dispensed with and Colonel Brownrigg joined the Light Division.

By 1 April 1855, Sir Colin Campbell definitely had temporary command of the Guards Brigade. This is confirmed by Hamilton who states that during March 1855, Sir Colin, not wishing to be taken by surprise as the Army confessed to being on 5 November selected an alarm post on the opposite heights that were most exposed to an attack, for the Guards Brigade to occupy during the night hours. This continued for the whole of April.[9]

On 16 June, the Guards Brigade under Lord Rokeby, and the Highland Brigade, both part of the 1st Division, under the command of Major General Sir Colin Campbell, were once more sent to the front.[10]

On 30 July, Lord Rokeby was promoted to Local Lieutenant General. He had refused the offer of the command of the 4th Division, so instead it had been decided to create a new division, the Highland Division, to be commanded by Sir Colin Campbell. On 16 August, Lord Rokeby took over command of the reformed 1st Division, which consisted of the Guards Brigade and a newly formed 2 Brigade. On 11 August, Colonel G. Drummond became temporary commander of the Guards Brigade when Lord Rokeby went on leave the following day. Colonel F. Daniell took over as temporary Commanding Officer of the 1st Coldstream.

Colonel Ridley had been promoted to Brigadier General to take over command of 2 Brigade of the 1st Division. This Brigade was not formed until early September, so when Lord Rokeby went on leave from 12 August to 1 September, Brigadier

Ridley, as the most senior officer in the Division, became temporary commander of the First Division, resuming command of the newly formed 2 Brigade on 1 September, when Lord Rokeby returned from leave.

On the same day, 13 August, that Brigadier General Ridley became temporary divisional commander, Colonel F. Lewis arrived in the Crimea and took over from him temporary command of the 3rd Grenadiers. This situation lasted until 8 October 1855, when Colonel Hon. A. Foley landed in the Crimea to take over command of the Grenadiers.

In August 1855, Colonel F. Seymour, Scots Fusilier Guards, was severely wounded and was sent home. Lieutenant Colonel Berkeley, who had been wounded at the Battle of the Alma and repatriated, had returned to the Crimea on 17 August 1855. He then took over as temporary Commander of 1st Scots Fusilier Guards until Colonel Walker returned. On this same date, Colonel F. Daniell went home and temporary command of 1st Coldstream went to Colonel Spencer Percival.

On 29 October 1855, Brigadier General J. Craufurd, Grenadier Guards, landed in the Crimea and took over command of the Guards Brigade from Colonel G. Drummond, who then resumed command of the 1st Coldstream. On this same day, Colonel Walker returned, his wounds having recovered, to take back command of the 1st Scots Fusilier Guards.

The Grenadiers, together with Brigadier General Craufurd embarked to return home on 3 June 1856, and the Coldstream left the next day. The assumption therefore is that the 1st Division was broken up when Lord Rokeby left the Crimea on 6 June; the Guards Brigade became an independent brigade. Colonel Walker was promoted to Acting Brigade Commander on 7 June and the Scots Fusilier Guards left the Crimea on 11 June 1856.

Over a period of twenty-one months, there had been ten changes of command of the 1st Division, involving six people, and in the Guards Brigade, nine changes, involving eight people. The figures for the three battalions were as follows: Grenadiers, eight changes, six people; Coldstream, nine changes, seven people; Scots Fusiliers, six changes, five people.

Notes

1. Hamilton, Lt Gen Sir George, *The Origins & History of the First or Grenadier Guards*, vol. 3, John Murray, 1874, p. 244.
2. Hamilton, p. 252.
3. *Ibid.*, p. 252.
4. Ross of Bladensburg, Lt Col, *The Coldstream Guards in the Crimea*, Innes, 1897, pp. 221–2.
5. *Ibid.*, pp. 224–5 & 232.
6. *Ibid.*, pp. 221–2.
7. Hamilton, p. 254.
8. *Ibid.*, p. 255.
9. *Ibid.*, p. 256.
10. *Ibid.*, p. 262.

1st Division Command Diary

Date	1st Div	Gds Bde	3GG	1CG	1SFG	Remarks
21.2.54	Maj Gen Duke of Cambridge	Brig Bentinck	Col Wood	Col C. Hay	Col G. Dixon	Bentinck – Local Brig
Landing						
14.9.54	"	"	"	"	"	
Brevet						
20.6.54	Lt Gen Duke of Cambridge	Maj Gen Bentinck				Duke of Cambridge – Lt Gen
						Bentinck, Maj Gen
						Campbell, Maj Gen
						Lord Rokeby, Maj Gen in UK.
						Hay, Maj Gen to UK.
						Dixon – Maj Gen to UK.
						Wood to Lt Col Regt, UK.
			Col G. Hood			Col Hood to comd 3GG.
				Col G. Upton		Col G. Upton to 1.CG
					Col Sir C. Hamilton	Hamilton temp for Col Walker.
Alma						
20.9.54	"	"	"	"	"	
23.9.54	"	"	"	"	Col E.W.F. Walker	Arrives Crimea as CO 1SFG
14.10.54						Sir Colin Campbell moves to Balaklava to command.
18.10.54	"	"	KIA *Col. Reynardson*	"	"	Col Hood killed in trenches. Col. Reynardson to 3GG
1.11.54	The Duke of Cambridge	Maj Gen Bentinck	*Col. Reynardson*	Col Upton	Col E.W.F Walker	Col Sir C.Hamilton to UK

Date	1st Div	Gds Bde	3GG	1CG	1SFG	Remarks
Inkerman						
5.11.54	Duke of Cambridge Sick	Maj Gen.Bentinck Col. G. Upton	Col. Reynardson	Col. Dawson KIA[1]	Col E.W.F. Walker	Maj Gen Bentinck wounded. Cols Upton & Walker wounded. Col Dawson KIA Col Upton – Gds Bde Comd.
7.11.54	Col Upton	Col Reynardson[2]	Col F.W. Hamilton	Lt Col Newton	Col C.F Seymour	Lt Col Newton to 1 CG. Col Seymour to 1 SFG Duke of Cambridge to UK. Col Upton comd 1st Div. Reynardson to Gds Bde. Col F.W. Hamilton to 3GG.
15.11.54	No GOC	"	"	"	"	Col Upton to Balaklava, wounded. No GOC 1st Div.
	Col Upton	Col Reynardson	Col F.W. Hamilton	Lt Col Newton	Col C.F Seymour	
Sapoune Heights						
22.11.54		"	"	"	"	Guards Brigade to Heights.
23.11.54	Brig Gen Lockyer	"	"	"	"	Lockyer – Brig Gen, 19.11.54.
1.12.54	Brig Gen Lockyer	Col C.W. Ridley	Col Reynardson	Lt Col Newton	Col C.F Seymour	Ridley arrives to replace Hood. Becomes Acting Bde Comd. Reynardson to 3GG as Actg CO.
15.1.55	?	Col. G Upton[3]	Col.C.W.Ridley	"	"	Lockyer returns to Command 2 Brigade. Upton returns as acting Bde Comd. Ridley to 3GG. No Div GOC.
16.1.55	?	"	"	Col Lord. F Paulet	"	Paulet returns to 1CG.

203

Date	1st Div	Gds Bde	3GG	1CG	1SFG	Remarks
22.1.55	?					Bentinck Local Lt Gen. Campbell Local Lt Gen. Rokeby to Crimea – 1st Div & Comd Gds Bde.
2.2.55	*Maj Gen Lord Rokeby*[4]	Lord Rokeby	*Col. C.W. Ridley*	*Col Lord F. Paulet*	*Col C.F. Seymour*	Col G. Upton to 1CG
20.2.55	*Maj Gen Lord Rokeby*	Maj Gen Lord Rokeby	"	Col G. Upton Col G. Drummond	"	Upton – Regt Lt Col, UK. Paulet Home to 2CG. Drummond to 1CG.
To Balaklava[5]						
22.2.55		Maj Gen Lord Rokeby	Col Ridley	Col G. Drummond	*Col C.F. Seymour*	*Independent Brigade?*
1.3.55	*Sir Colin Campbell*					Sir C. Campbell Div Comd.
5.3.55		"	"	"	"	1st Div broken up.
22.5.55	"		"	"	"	Col Birch Reynardson home.[6]
Back to the Front Line[7]						
16.6.55	*Sir Colin Campbell*	Maj Gen Lord Rokeby	Col Ridley	Col G. Drummond	*Col C.F. Seymour*	Guards & Highland Brigades to front.
28.6.55	"	"	"	"	"	Raglan dies Simpson C.in.C
30.7.55	Sir C. Campbell	Lt Gen Lord Rokeby	Brig C.W. Ridley	*Col F. Daniell*	*Col C.F. Seymour*	Lord Rokeby – Local Lt Gen. Col C.F. Ridley – Local Brig.
3.8.55	Lord Rokeby					Lord Rokeby – Lt Gen, 1st Div. Col Drummond To Gds Bde.
11.8.55	"	*Col G. Drummond*	"	"	"	Highland Division formed. Sir W. Codrington to Lt Gen.

Date	1st Div	Gds Bde	3GG	1CG	1SFG	Remarks
13.8.55	Brig C.W. Ridley	Col G. Drummond	"	"	"	Lord Rokeby on leave – 13 Aug to 1 Sept. Ridley acting Div Comd as 1st Div reformed.
15.8.55	"	"	Col C. Lewis	"	"	Col Lewis arrives to succeed Ridley at 3GG Formation of 2 Bde postponed TFO.
26.8.55	Brig Ridley	Col G. Drummond	Col. C. Lewis	Col. F. Daniell	Col. C.F. Seymour	Formation of 2 Bde, 1st Div.
1.9.55	Lord Rokeby	"	"	"	"	Lord Rokeby returns. Brig.Ridley to 2 Bde.
8.10.55	"	"	Col Hon A. Foley	"	"	Col. Foley arrives to comd 3GG.
9.10.55	"	"	"	Col S. Percival	"	Col. Daniell leaves Crimea.[8] Col Percival – CO 1CG
13.10.55	"				Lt Col.Berkeley	Col Seymour severely wounded – home. Lt Col Berkeley temp CO[9]
29.10.55	Lord Rokeby	Brig J. Craufurd[10]	Col Hon A. Foley	Col G. Drummond	Col E.W.F. Walker	Col F.W. Hamilton home. Brig. Craufurd arrives Crimea appointed Local Brig 25.9.55. Col. Drummond – 1CG. Col Walker returns to 1SFG.
9.11.55	"	"	"	"	"	Simpson resigns. Codrington C-in-C. Windham–Chief of Staff.
3.6.56	"	HOME	HOME	"	"	Repatriation to UK.
4.6.56	"			HOME	"	"
6.6.56	HOME				"	Lord Rokeby home. Div broken up.
7.6.56		Col E.W.F.Walker			Col. E.W.F. Walker	Temp Bde Comd.
11.6.56					HOME	Repatriation to UK

References

Hamilton, Lt Gen Sir F.W., *The Origins & History of the First or Grenadier Guards*, vol. 3, John Murray, London, 1874.

Ross-of-Bladensburg, Lt Col, *The Coldstream Guards in the Crimea*, Innes, London, 1897.

Maurice, Maj Gen Sir F., *The History of the Scots Guards from the Creation of the Regiment to the Eve of the Great War*, vol 2, Chatto & Windus, London, 1934.

Weatherall, G.A., *Returns Relating to Officers in the Army (Crimea)*, House of Commons, 1857.

General Orders of the Army of the East.

Notes

1. Coldstream Guards at Inkerman. Col Upton was on night duty 4/5 November. Col.Lord F.Paulet, the next senior officer, was ill. The next senior, Col Newton, was Field Officer of the Day. Therefore Col Dawson commanded and he was killed at the Sandbag Battery. When Maj Gen Bentinck was wounded, Col.Upton became Brigade Commander. He was also wounded but remained in command of the Brigade until 15 Nov 1854 and was then repatriated. Lt Col Newton became Commanding Officer 1CG until Lord F. Paulet returned to the Crimea on 16 Jan 1855 Ross-of-Bladensburg, Lt Col, *The Coldstream Guards in the Crimea*, Innes, 1897, pp. 151–2.

2. Brigade Commander. After Inkerman, Brig Bentinck, Col Upton and Col E.F.Walker were wounded and unable to command. Col E. Birch Reynardson, the next senior officer, assumed command of the Guards Brigade on 11 Nov 1854 and Col Hamilton became CO 3GG. These officers retained their posts until Col Ridley arrived to succeed Col Hood on 1 Dec 1854. Hamilton, Lt Gen Sir F.W., *The Origins & History of the First or Grenadier Guards*, vol. 3, John Murray, 1874, p. 244.

3. Col Upton. Returns and resumes command of the Brigade. Col Ridley resumes command of 3GG. Hamilton, p. 252.

4. Lord Rokeby. Arrives in the Crimea on 2 Feb 1855, assumes command of 1st Div and the Guards Brigade. On 22 Feb 1855, the Brigade, now only with 312 men able to do duty, were relieved of trench duties, left the Sapoune Heights and marched to Balaklava to rest and recuperate. The Brigade remained there until 16 June 1855, when the Guards Brigade and the Highland Brigade returned to the front. See Ross-of-Bladensburg, pp. 221–2, 224–5 & 232.

5. Balaklava. The services of Col Browning were not needed as AAG 1st Div. He was transferred to the Light Div wef 5.3.55. The Guards Brigade returned to the 1st Div, presumably on 16 June 1855. 1st Div was suspended over this period and Div was broken up in March, when it was at Balaklava, as Campbell was GOC defences there, and was reunited under Campbell in April. The Guards Brigade acted as an independent brigade when it moved to Balaklava. See Hamilton, p. 225.

6. Col Reynardson home. Weatherall, G.A., *Returns Relating to Officers in the Army (Crimea)*, House of Commons, 1857.

7. 1st Div.Reformed. On 16 June 1855, the Highland Brigade and the Guards Brigade, with Sir C. Campbell commanding, marched to the front. Just under two months later, the Highland Division was formed.

8. Colonel Daniell. See Wetherall.

9. Col C.F. Seymour. Severely wounded in August 1855. See Wetherall.

10. See Hamilton, p. 227.

Appendix D

Victoria Crosses and Distinguished Conduct Medals Awarded to All Ranks in Each Battalion

Victoria Cross Citations

3 Grenadier Guards

Colonel Hon H.H.M. Percy VC. At a moment when the Guards were at some distance from the Sandbag Battery at the Battle of Inkerman, Colonel Percy charged singly into the Battery followed by the Guards. The embrasures of the Battery, and also the Parapet, were held by the Russians who kept up a most severe fire of musketry. At the Battle of Inkerman Colonel Percy found himself with men of various regiments, who had charged too far, and were nearly surrounded by the Russians, and without ammunition. Colonel Percy, by his knowledge of ground, though wounded, extricated these men and, passing under a heavy fire from the Russians then in the Sandbag Battery, brought them safe to where ammunition was to be obtained, thereby saving some 50 men, and enabling them to renew the combat. He received the approval of His Royal Highness the Duke of Cambridge, for this action, on the spot. Colonel Percy was engaged with, and put *hors de combat*, a Russian Soldier. *London Gazette*, 24 February 1857.

Major Sir C. Russell VC. Offered to dislodge a party of Russians from the Sandbag Battery, if any one would follow him:- Sergeant Norman, Private A. Palmer and Bailey (who was killed) volunteered the first. The attack succeeded. *London Gazette*, 24 February 1857.

Sergeant A. Ablett VC. On the 2nd September 1855, seeing a shell fall in the centre of a number of Ammunition Cases and Powder, he instantly seized and threw it outside the trench, it burst as it touched the ground. *London Gazette*, 24 February 1857.

Private A. Palmer VC. Present when the charge was made in defence of the Colours, and also charged singly upon the enemy, as witnessed by Sir C. Russell, said to have saved Sir C. Russell's life. *London Gazette*, 24 February 1857.

1 Coldstream Guards

Brevet Major J.A. Conolly VC. In an attack by the Russians against a position held by the 2nd Division, 26th October 1854, Major Conolly, then a Lieutenant in the 49th Regiment, while in command of a company of that Regiment, on outlying picquet, made himself most conspicuous by the gallantry of his behaviour. He came particularly under the observation of the late Field Marshal Lord Raglan, while in personal encounter with several Russians, in defence of his post. He ultimately fell, dangerously wounded. Lieutenant Conolly was highly praised in General Orders, and promoted to the Coldstream Guards, as a reward for his exemplary behaviour on this occasion. *London Gazette*, 5 May 1857.

Major Gerald Goodlake VC. For distinguished gallantry, whilst in command of the sharpshooters, furnished by the Coldstream Guards on the 28th October 1854, on the occasion of 'the powerful sortie on the 2nd Division', when he held the Windmill Ravine, below the Picquet House, against a much larger force of the enemy. The party of sharpshooters then under his command killed thirty-eight (one an officer) and took three prisoners of the enemy (of the latter, one an officer) Major Goodlake being the sole officer in command. Also for distinguished gallantry on the occasion of the surprise of a picquet of the enemy, in November, at the bottom of Windmill Ravine, by the sharpshooters, under his sole leading and command, when the knapsacks and rifles of the enemy's party fell into his hands. *London Gazette*, 24 February 1857.[1]

Private Stanlock VC. For having volunteered, when employed as one of the sharpshooters in October 1854, for reconnoitring purposes, to crawl within six yards of a Russian sentry, and so enabled the officer in command to effect a surprise; Private Stanlock having been warned beforehand of the imminent risk he would run in the adventure. By preventing the sentry from giving the alarm, he enabled the others to pounce on the picquet and bear their knapsacks and arms back to camp. *London Gazette*, 24 February 1857.[2]

Private Strong VC. For having, when on duty in the trenches in the month of September, 1855, removed a live shell from the place where it had fallen. *London Gazette*, 24 February 1857.

1 Scots Fusilier Guards

Brevet Major R.J. Lloyd-Lindsay VC. When the formation of the line of the Regiment was disordered at Alma, Captain Lindsay stood firm with the Colours and by his example and energy greatly tended to restore order. At Inkerman, in a most trying moment, he with a few men charged a party of Russians, driving them back and running one through the body himself. *London Gazette*, 24 February 1857.

Lieutenant J.S. Knox VC (Rifle Brigade). When serving as a Sergeant in the Scots Fusilier Guards, Lieutenant Knox was conspicuous for his exertions in re-forming the ranks of the Guards at the Battle of the Alma, subsequently, when in the Rifle Brigade he volunteered for the ladder party in the attack on the Redan on 18th June (in the words of Captain Blackett, under whose command he was) behaved admirably, remaining on the field until twice wounded. *London Gazette*, 24 February 1857.)

Drill-Sergeant I. Craig, VC (Adjutant, Military Train). For having volunteered and personally collected other volunteers to go out under heavy fire of grape and small arms on the night of 6th September 1855, when in the right advanced sap in front of the Redan to look for Captain Buckley, Scots Fusilier Guards, who was supposed to be wounded. Sergeant Craig brought in, with the assistance of a drummer boy, the body of that officer, whom he found dead – in performance of which act he was wounded. *London Gazette*, 24 February 1857.

Sergeant James McKechnie VC. When the formation of the Regiment was disordered at Alma, for behaving gallantly and rallying the men round the Colours. *London Gazette*, 24 February 1857.

Private William Reynolds VC. When the formation of the line was disordered at Alma, for having behaved in a conspicuous manner in rallying the men around the Colours. *London Gazette*, 24 February 1857.

Distinguished Conduct Medals Awarded[3]
This medal was instituted by Royal Warrant on 13th September 1862. It replaced the Meritorious Service Medal for Distinguished Conduct in the Field or Silver Medal. It was awarded to Non-Commissioned Officers and Private Soldiers for gallantry on the field of battle.

Grenadier Guards
Sergeant Major William Thomas
Colour Sergeant Benjamin Norman
Corporal Benjamin Owen   Inkerman
Corporal Thomas Horseman   Inkerman
Corporal James Lee   Inkerman
Corporal George Evans
Private Alfred Ablett VC
Private Isaac Church   Inkerman

Private Joseph Selby
Private John Morse
Private James Bancroft   Inkerman
Private Thomas Fox
Private William Ovison
Private Charles Gilham
Private Matthew Higgins
Drummer William Swingler
Drummer Thomas Keep
Total: 17 (Inkerman 5)

Coldstream Guards

Sergeant Shephard Carter
Sergeant John Packwood
Sergeant John Tucker
Corporal William Finch
Corporal Charles Maidment
Corporal Frederick Smith   Inkerman
Corporal William Smith
Private Josiah Carter   Inkerman
Private Charles Dogrel
Private James Smith
Private Joseph Smith
Private William Stanlock VC
Private Charles Troke   Inkerman
Private William John Trotter
Private John Tucker
Private Samuel Vicary
Private William Wilden
Total: 17 (Inkerman 3)
Queries Wm Wildich CG

Scots Fusilier Guards

Sergeant Major Edward Edwards
Sergeant Major George Sharp   Inkerman
Sergeant Donald McBeath
Corporal Edward Dawes   Inkerman
Corporal James Dey   Inkerman
Corporal Emanuel Bullock   Inkerman
Corporal George Thomson
Private Alexander Ferguson
Private William Findlayson   Inkerman
Private John Forrest   Inkerman

Private John G. Holmes
Private Alexander Hannah   Inkerman
Private Frederick Minster   Inkerman
Private Hugh Morrison
Private Everett Ranby   Inkerman
Private Charles Reed   Inkerman
Private James Wyatt   Inkerman
Total: 17 (Inkerman 11)

Notes

1. Springman, Michael, *Sharpshooter in the Crimea*, Pen & Sword Books, 2005, pp. 53–7.
2. *Ibid.*, p. 57.
3. Abbott, P.E., *Recipients of the Distinguished Conduct Medal 1855–1909*, J.B. Howard, 1987, pp. 10–32.

APPENDIX E

Guards Brigade Effective Strengths and Casualties, Crimean War, 1854–1856

Battalion	Officers				NCOs and R&F				Total			
Effective Strength	GG	CG	SFG	Total	GG	CG	SFG	Total	GG	CG	SFG	Total
Embarked, Feb 1854	35	35	29	99	949	919	935	2,803	984	954	964	2,902
Reinforcements	50	56	50	156	1,424	1,141	1,157	3,722	1,474	1,197	1,207	3,878
Total	85	91	79	255	2,373	2,060	2,092	6,525	2,458	2,151	2,171	6,780
Permanent Losses												
Killed in Action	5	9	5	19	111	81	84	276	116	90	89	295
Died of Wounds	1	1	–	2	33	54	47	134	34	55	47	136
Died of Disease	3	3	1	7	756	564	536	1,856	759	567	537	1,863
Invalided & Discharged	–		7	7	338	111	–	449	338	111	7	456
Transferred to Other Regiments	–	–	–	–	30	–	–	30	30	–	–	30
Total	9	13	13	35	1,268	810	667	2,745	1,277	823	680	2,780
Returned Home, 1856												
Battalion[1]	23	–	39		1,095	–	1,104	–	1,190		1,143	
On Command[2]	53				19							
	76				1,114							

Admissions to Hospital (Regimental & General)

Figures exist only for the Coldstream Guards and are:

	Officers	NCOs & Men	Total
Disease	17	2,785	2,802
Wounds	7	243	250
Accidents	–	73	73
Total	24	3,101	3,125

Sources

Hamilton, Lt Gen Sir F.W. The Origins & *History of the First or Grenadier Guards,* vol. 3, John Murray, 1874, tables on pp. 292 & 294.

Ross-of-Bladensburg, Lt Col, *The Coldstream Guards in the Crimea,* Innes, 1897, Appendix E, pp. 306–7.

Maurice, Maj Gen Sir F., *The History of the Scots Guards,* vol. 2, Chatto & Windus, 1934, p. 86 & tables on pp. 53 & 112.

Notes

1. RHQ Coldstream Guards has no figures for the number of officers and other ranks of 1st Coldstream, who landed in England after the war.
2. On Command figure is made up of officers not serving with the Battalion, those on the Staff, and those officers on leave.

APPENDIX F

Bibliography

Grenadier Guards – Crimean War Sources

Published Books

Burgoyne, Sir George, *Some Bedfordshire Diaries*, 1860, privately printed. Sir George was wounded at Alma and sent home. List of officers serving in the Regiment in the Crimea.

Burnaby, Edwyn Sherard, *An Account of the Right Flank Company of the 3rd Battalion Grenadier Guards, defending the right of the British position, and subsequently the colours of the Battalion, when surrounded by the enemy at the battle of Inkerman, 5th November 1854*, Staunton & Son, London, 1857.

Bush, R.J. (ed.), *Letters written from Turkey & Crimea, 1854 to Lord Braybrooke*: Father, published 1876. Neville, Hon Henry A., Captain, Grenadier Guards (killed at Inkerman). Neville, Hon Grey, 5th Dragoon Guards (died of wounds received at Balaklava).

Clark, Major Frank, *Through Hell to Immortality: A story of the Crimean War and of The First Suffolk Soldier to win the Victoria Cross – Sergeant Ablett VC, Grenadier Guards*, Leiston Press, Suffolk.

Hamilton, Lieutenent General Sir F.W., *The Origins & History of the First or Grenadier Guards*, 3 vols, John Murray, London, 1874.

Hanning, Colonel Henry, *The British Grenadiers*, Pen & Sword Books, 2006.

Higginson, General Sir George, *Seventy One Years of a Guardsman's Life*, John Murray, 1916.

Percy, Algernon, *A Bearskin's Crimea: Colonel Henry Percy & His Brother Officers*, Leo Cooper, 2005.

Whitworth, R.W., *The Grenadier Guards*.

Diaries, Letters and Articles

Albert, HRH Prince, Letters, Royal Archives, Windsor Castle.

Bishop, Private Thomas, Mrs V.A. Spinks, Location unknown.

Blenkins, Surgeon-Major, Medical History of Grenadier Guards.

Cameron, Lieutenant & Captain William Gordon, NAM 1983-11-13-298 to -321.

Grenadier Gazette 1996, Re-enactment of The Roll Call by the 3rd Battalion by Lady Butler. General Higginson as mounted officer.

Hamilton, Lieutenant General Sir George, Crimean Letters of her Great Uncle – Lady Raglan. Lord Raglan, Cefntilla, Usk, Gwent.

Higginson, General Sir George: Letter to Captain Hatton, Regimental Adjutant, on Little Inkerman, 27 Oct 1854 (RHQ). Letter to Captain Hatton on Inkerman, 4 & 6 Nov 1854 (RHQ).

Hood, Colonel The Hon Grosvenor, Letters/diaries quoted by Kinglake. Location NAM 9406-1 Archives.

Household Brigade Magazine, 'The Diary of an Officer in the Crimean War February 1884.

Neville, Captain the Hon Henry, Grenadier Guards, Crimean Letters, Mrs L.M.Chesterton, location unknown.

Paine, David, Crimean Medal Roll of 3rd Battalion Grenadier Guards.

Reynardson, Colonel E.B., Crimean Diaries, microfilm (20 feet), National Army Museum – 7908–56. Letter on Inkerman to Colonel Woods, of 7 Nov 1854 (RHQ).

RHQ Grenadier Guards: Crimean Orders, 1854–6 (handwritten). Nominal Roll 3rd Battalion Grenadier Guards, forming part of the Army serving in the East during the years 1854 & 1855 (handwritten).

Ridley, Brigadier General, Charles William, NAM 1989-03-47.

Russell, Sir Charles Bt., Crimean War Diary, with account of action at the Sandbag Battery, MS. Was in RHQ but now misplaced. Letter on Inkerman, No. 1 Piquet before Sevastopol, 7 Nov 1854, *Household Brigade Magazine*.

Skelton, J., Surgeon, Letters on the Crimea, *Household Brigade Magazine*, 1831.

Tipping, Captain Alfred, 'Letters from the East during the Campaign of 1854', MS, Mr Egerton Skipwith, 1854–55.

Wood, Colonel, Regimental Lieutenant Colonel's letter to Major E.S. Burnaby on his recommendations for receiving the VC, 8 Nov 1856 and his reply, 11 Nov 1856, with map of Sandbag Battery (RHQ).

Household Brigade Magazine, Obituaries:
Viscount Balgonie
General, Lord Chelmsford
General Cameron
James Haiter (last Grenadier Crimean War veteran to die)
Colonel C.N. Hogge
Sir Campbell Munro
General Lord Henry Percy VC
Major General Sir Charles Ridley
Colonel Stanley
Lieutenant Colonel The Marquis of Tweeddale
Lieutenant Colonel Verschoyle

Artefacts (at RHQ)

3rd Battalion Grenadier Guards – gilt crown from Queen's Colour of the Battalion carried during the Crimean War.
Ablett, Sergeant Alfred – medal board with VC, campaign medals and picture.
Palmer, Private – medal board with VC, campaign medals and picture.
Russell, Captain Sir Charles Bt. – medal board with VC, campaign medals and picture.

Coldstream Guards – Crimean War Sources
Published Books
Coldstream Guards RHQ, *Regimental Records.*

Coldstream Guards RHQ, *A History of the Coldstream Guards,* Leo Cooper, London, 2000.

Coldstream Guards RHQ, *Sergeant William McMillan's Diary,* published by the Coldstream Guards.

Coldstream Guards RHQ, *A Short History of the Regiment's Victoria Cross Holders,* Lance Sergeant L. Pearce.

Mansfield, H.O. *Charles Ashe Windham, A Norfolk Soldier (1810–1970),* Terence Dalton, Lavenham, Suffolk, 1973.

Marker R., *Record of the Coldstream Guards, 1650–1918,* published 1923. British Infantry, Acc. no. 25758.

Ross-of-Bladensburg, Lieutenant Colonel, *A History of the Coldstream Guards from 1815 to 1895,* Innes, London, 1896. (A continuation of Daniel MacKinnon's *Origin & Services of the Coldstream Guards,* 2 vols, Richard Bentley, London, 1835).

——, *The Coldstream Guards in the Crimea,* Innes, London, 1897.

Springman, Michael, *Sharpshooter in the Crimea. The Letters of Captain Gerald Goodlake, V.C.,* Pen & Sword Books, 2005.

Wilson, Captain C.T., Coldstream Guards, *A Regimental Officer, Our Veterans of 1854 In Camp & before the Enemy,* Street, London, 1859.

Windham, Lieutenant General Sir Charles, *Diary & Letters,* edited by Major Hugh Pearse, Keegan Paul, 1897.

Wyatt, Battalion Surgeon John, *A History of the 1st Battalion Coldstream Guards during the Eastern Campaign from February 1854 to June 1856,* London, 1858.

Diaries and MSS
Amherst Wm, Letters 23–24 Oct 1854. Colonel Lord F. Paulet letter on his being wounded, National Army Museum, 7305–75.

Chadburn, Sergeant, Crimean Letters, Mrs Alma Chadburn.

Clarke Jervoise, Henry, 42nd Highlanders, ADC to Lieutenant General Airey, transferred Coldstream Guards. Letters 1854–56, vol. 1, 310 pages; vol. 2, 375 pages (RHQ).

Cocks, Captain and Lieutenant Colonel C.L., Coldstream Guards, Diary, 22 Feb to 15 July 1854, and Letters on the Crimean War; photostat copy; National Army Museum Archives, 1988-06-29. Original at RHQ Coldstream Guards.

Codrington, Major General Sir William, Coldstream Guards, Letters, 1851–5, National Army Museum, Archives, 1968-07-375 to 381 & 1978-08-90.

Goodlake, Captain Gerald VC, Coldstream Guards, Crimean War Letters, Mar 1854 to May 1856; typescript bound volume, RHQ Coldstream Guards.

Heneage, Lieutenant Michael, Coldstream Guards, Crimean War Letters, RHQ Coldstream Guards.

Paulet, Colonel Frederick, Lord, NAM 1973-05-75.

Ricketts, Asst Surgeon, Crimean Diary, *United Services Magazine,* March 1855.

Skelton, Dr Joseph, Surgeon, Coldstream Guards, Crimean Letters, Mrs Diana Drummond, Great-Great-Great Niece.

Tower, Captain H., Coldstream Guards, Crimean Diary, 1854–6; Alma, Balaklava, Inkerman, 218 pages. National Army Museum Archives, Acc. No. 8202–18.

Windham, Major General Charles Ash, NAM. 1968-07-288 & 1968-07-376-18.

Scots Guards – Crimean War Sources
Published Books

Airlie, Mabel, Countess of, *With the Guards We Shall Go*, Hodder & Stoughton, London, 1933.

Bostock, Deputy Surgeon-General J.A., *Letters from India & the Crimea*, Surgeon-Major, Scots Fusilier Guards, Crimea.

Drummond, Major H.F., Adjutant 1st Battalion Scots Fusilier Guards, *Letters from the Crimea*, Norris & Son, 1855.

Maurice, Major General Sir F. Maurice, *The History of the Scots Guards from the Creation of the Regiment to The Eve of the Great War*, 2 vols, Chatto & Windus, London, 1934.

Robinson, Surgeon F., *A Diary of the Crimean War*, Richard Bentley, London, 1856.

Stephenson, Lieutenant Colonel F.C.A, *At Home and on the Battlefield*, Murray, 1915.

Wantage, Lady, *Lord Wantage VC, KCB: A Memoir by his Wife*, Smith Elder & Co. London, 1907.

Diaries Letters

Aitchison, General Sir John, Crimean War Letters, RHQ Scots Guards.

Annesley, Ensign and Lieutenant Hugh, SFG, Letters from the Crimea, National Army Museum Archives, 1976-06-10.

   Diaries – Lady Constance Malleson.

Cambridge, Lieutenant General HRH George William Frederick Charles, Duke of, NAM 1968-07-288 & -292.

Colville, Sir Henry and Rockley, Lord, Letters 1847–52, National Army Museum Archives.

Dolton, Corporal, SFG, Crimean War Diaries, RHQ Scots Guards.

Gordon, Lieutenant Colonel Grant Gordon, Crimean Letters RHQ Scots Guards.

Haygarth, Captain F., SFG, Diaries Crimean War, RHQ Scots Guards.

Hunter-Blair, Colonel J., Letters and Diaries, James Hunter-Blair, Blairquhan Castle, Ayrshire.

Kingscote, Major Robert Nigel Fitzhardinge, NAM 1973-11-170.

Knollys, Sir William, Letters, National Army Museum Archives, 8105–62.

Lindsay, Ensign Robert, Letters and Diaries, Earl of Crawford & Balcarres.

Letters from the Crimea – General R. Gipps, Lord Wantage, Mr Kinglake & others. MS, bound volume, re Alma. RHQ Scots Guards.

Notebook relating to the First Battalion's Crimean Service, National Library of Scotland, Manuscripts Division, MS9319.

Regimental Diary, Scots Guards (including the Crimean War), RHQ Scots Guards.

Wantage, Lord, VC, 'Crimean Diary 1854–56', MSS, RHQ, Scots Guards.

General
Published Books

Abbot, P.E., *Recipients of the Distinguished Conduct Medal 1855–1909*, J.B. Howard, 1987.

Adkin, Mark, *The Waterloo Companion*, Aurum Press, London, 2001.

Anonymous, *Russian Account of the Battle of Inkerman from the German*, John Murray, 1856.

Aubrey-Fletcher, H.L, *A History of the Foot Guards to 1856*, Constable, London, 1927.

Barthorp, M., *Heroes of the Crimea*, Blandford, 1991.

Benson, A.C. and Esher, Viscount (eds), *The Letters of Queen Victoria*, vol. 3, 1854–1861, John Murray, London, 1908.

Bentley, Nicolas, *Russell's Despatches from the Crimea*, London, 1970.

Bonham Carter, Victor (ed.), *Surgeon in the Crimea. The Experiences of George Lawson, 1854–1855*, Military Book Society, London, 1968.

Caldwell, George and Robert Cooper, *Rifle Green in the Crimea*, Bugle Horn Publications, 1994.

Calthorpe, Colonel S., *Letters from Headquarters, by an Officer on the Staff*, John Murray, London, 1856.

Cooke, Brian, *The Grand Crimean Central Railway*, 2nd edition, Cavaliers House, 1997.

Creagh, Sir O'Moore, VC and Humphreys, E.M., *The Victoria Cross 1856–1920*, reprinted by J.B. Hayward & Son, 1985.

Dictionary of National Biography.

Encyclopaedia Britannica, 1911 Edition.

ffrench-Blake, R.L.V, *The Crimean War*, Leo Cooper, London, 1971.

Fortescue, Sir John, *History of the British Army*, vol. 13, Macmillan, London, 1930.

Gordon, Hampden, *The War Office*, Putnam, London, 1935.

Hamley, General Sir Edward, *War in the Crimea*, Seeley, London, 1896.

——, *The Story of the Campaign of Sevastopol*, Blackwood, 1855. Reprinted by the Naval & Military Press, 2003.

Hargrave Mawson, Michael, *Eyewitness in the Crimea: The Crimean War Letters of Lieutenant Colonel George Frederick Dallas*, Greenhill Books, London, 2001.

Harries Jenkins, G., *The Army in Victorian Society*, London, 1977.

Hart, Lieutenant Colonel H.G., *Annual Army Lists, 1853–60*.

Hibbert, C, *The Destruction of Lord Raglan*, Viking, London, 1984.

——, *Wellington: A Personal History*, HarperCollins, London, 1977.

Holmes, Richard, *Redcoat. The British Soldier in the Age of Horse & Musket*, HarperCollins, London, 2001.

Kinglake, A.W, *The Invasion of the Crimea*, vol. 3 (1866), vol. 4 (1868), vol. 5 (1875), vol. 6 (1880), vol. 7 (1882), vol. 8 (1887), Blackwood, Edinburgh & London.

Knollys, J. and Elliott, Major V.J., *The Victoria Cross in the Crimea*, Dean, London, 1877.

Lambert, Andrew and Badsey, Stephen, *The War Correspondents. The Crimean War*, Bramley, 1994.

London Gazette, Victoria Cross Citations, 24 February 1857.

Longford, Elizabeth, *Wellington, Pillar of State*, Weidenfeld & Nicolson, London, 1972.

——, *Wellington, The Years of the Sword*, HarperCollins, London, 1985.

McGuigan, Ron, *Into Battle: The British Order of Battle for the Crimean War 1854–56*, Withycut House, Bowden, 2001.

Massie, Alistair, *The National Army Museum Book of the Crimean War: The Untold Stories*, Sidgwick & Jackson, London, 2004.

Mercer, Patrick, *Give them a Volley & Charge. The Battle of Inkerman, 1854*, Spellmount, Staplehurst, Kent, 1998.

——, *Inkerman 1854: The Soldier's Battle*, Campaign Series, Osprey, 1998.

Pack, Colonel Reynell, *Sebastopol Trenches and Five Months in Them*, Kerry & Endeen, 1878. Reprinted by Pallas Armata, 2001.

Paget, Colonel Sir Julian, *The Story of the Guards*, Osprey, London, 1976.

Parry, Douglas H., *Britain's Roll of Glory*, Cassell, 1895. Renamed 1913, *VC – Its Heroes & Their Valour*.

Pemberton, W. Baring, *Battles of the Crimean War*, B.T. Batsford, London, 1962.

Pillinger, Dennis and Staunton, Anthony, *Victoria Cross Presentations & Locations*, Published by the Authors, 2000.

Reeve, Henry, *The Greville Memoirs, Queen Victoria's Reign*, vol. 5 (1841–46), vol. 6 (1846–52), vol. 7 (1852–55), vol. 8 (1855–60), Longmans Green, London, 1888.

Robins, Major Colin, *Captain Dunscombe's Diary*, Withycut House, Bowdon, 2003.

——, *Romaine's Crimean War*, Army Records Society, Sutton Publishing, 2005.

Rodger, Professor N.A.M., *The Command of the Ocean. A Naval History of Britain 1649–1815*, Penguin Allen Lane, 2004.

Royle, Trevor, *The Crimea: The Great Crimean War, 1854–1856*, Little Brown, London, 1999.

Russell, Sir William Howard, *The British Expedition to the Crimea*, Routledge, London, 1858.

Ryan, George, *The Lives of Our Heroes of the Crimea*, James Field & Co, London, 1855.

Sayer, Captain, *Despatches & Papers Relative to the Campaign in Turkey, Asia Minor & the Crimea*, Harrison, London, 1857. Reprinted by Pallas Armata, 2001.

Seaton, Albert, *The Crimean War: A Russian Chronicle*, London, 1977.

Selby, J., *The Thin Red Line of Balaklava*, Hamish Hamilton, London, 1970.

Small, Hugh, *Florence Nightingale: Avenging Angel*, Constable, London, 1998.

Spiers, Edward M., *The Late Victorian Army, 1868–1902*, Manchester University Press, 1992

Strachan, Hew, *From Waterloo to Balaklava: Tactics, Technology & the British Army 1815–54*, Cambridge University Press, 1985.

——, *Wellington's Legacy: Reform of the British Army 1830–54*, Manchester University Press, 1984.

St Aubyn, Giles, *The Royal George. The Life of Prince George, Duke of Cambridge*, Constable, London, 1963.

Steevens, Lieutenant Colonel Nathaniel, *The Crimean Campaign with The Connaught Rangers, 1854–55–56*, Griffith & Farran, London, 1858. Reprinted by the Naval & Military Press, 2002.

Sweetman, John, *War and Administration: The Significance of the Crimean War for the British Army*, Scottish Academic Press, Edinburgh, 1984.

Todleben, Général F.E.L., *La Défense de Sebastopol*, 1863–70.

Trevelyan, M, *England Under the Stuarts*, Methuen, London, 1904.

Tyrrell, Henry, *History of the War with Russia,* vols. 1–6, London Printing & Publishing Company, 1856.

Warner, Philip, *The Crimean War. An Appraisal,* Wordsworth Editions, Ware, Herts, 2001.

Wedgwood, C.V, *The Great Rebellion: The King's Peace, 1637–1641,* Collins, London, 1955.

Weintraub, Stanley, *Albert: Uncrowned King,* John Murray, London 1997.

Wetherall, G.A, *Returns Relating to Officers in the Army (Crimea.),* The House of Commons, London 1857.

Wilkinson, Philip, *A History of the Victoria Cross,* Constable, 1894.

Wolseley, Field Marshal Viscount, *The Story of a Soldier's Life,* vols 1 & 2, Constable, London, 1903.

Wood, Field Marshal Sir Evelyn, *The Crimea in 1854 & 1894,* Chapman & Hall, London 1895.

——, *From Midshipman to Field Marshal,* Methuen, 1906.

Woodham Smith, C., *The Reason Why,* Constable & Co, 1953.

——, *Florence Nightingale,* Constable & Co, 1950.

Woodward, E.L., *The Age of Reform 1815–70,* Clarendon Press, Oxford, 1938.

Journals

Guards Museum, 'History of the Bearskin Cap' by Captain D.D. Horn, Curator.

Military History Society, 'Victoria Cross Biography on Captain Gerald Goodlake VC' by Canon W.M. Lummis MC.

Royal Statistical Society, 1980, 'The Purchase System in the British Army, 1660–1871' by Anthony Bruce.

Sherwood Foresters' Annual 1934, p. 215, Davis, letter.

Society for Army Historical Research Journal, vol. 12, p. 221, 'The Era of Army Purchase' by Brigadier General H. Biddulph.

'Frederick Turner: An Artillery Officer in Flanders', p. 40, by Jonathan Spain, spring 2006.

Victorian Military Society, Journal of the, issue No. 69, June 1992. 'Crimean Sharpshooters' by Michael Barthrop.

War Correspondent, Journal of the Crimean War Research Society.

Vol. 14 No. 1, April 1996, 'Infantry Shoulder Arms of the Crimean War', Part Five, Great Britain, Minie Rifle Pattern 51 by W.S. Curtis.

Vol. 14 No. 1, April 1996, 'Double Rank in the Guards' by Major Colin Robins.

Periodicals

The Journal of the Household Brigade.

Illustrated London News (July–September 1854)

Punch, vols 25–27, 1853–4.

Colbourne's United Services Magazine.

Index

Notes

1. British military personnel in the Crimea are included in the main alphabetical listing, together with other personalities referred to in the text. Army units are grouped under the heading 'British Army in the Crimea'. French and Russian military personnel are each separately grouped, together with Army units. Grouped entries are also used for locations within specific countries (e.g. Bulgaria, Turkey) and key areas of the Crimean War zone (e.g. The Alma, Balaklava). Other locations in the Crimea are included in the main alphabetical listing.

2. General references to the main Crimean protagonists – Britain, France and Russia – and to the Crimea itself, are not indexed. Neither are those to the Brigade of Guards.

3. The spelling of place names (and of some personnel) vary in the accounts given by serving officers (e.g. Sevastopol/Sebastopol; Balaklava/Balaclava). These have been standardized in the index.

4. Abbreviations used for British Army units and personnel in the Crimea are as follows: Gds Bde (Brigade of Guards); Gren Gds (Grenadier Guards); Cold Gds (Coldstream Guards); SFG (Scots Fusilier Guards); RA(Royal Artillery); RE (Royal Engineers); RF (Royal Fusiliers); RWF (Royal Welch Fusiliers); Div (Division); Regt (Regiment); 1st, 2nd, 3rd etc. (regimental battalions); AWC (Army Works Corps); RN (Royal Navy); C-in-C (Commander-in-Chief); GOC (General Officer Commanding); CO (Commanding Officer); FM (Field Marshal); Gen (General); Lt Gen (Lieutenant General); Maj Gen (Major General); Brig Gen (Brigadier General); Adjt Gen (Adjutant General); Col (Colonel); Lt Col (Lieutenant Colonel) Maj (Major); Capt (Captain); Lt (Lieutenant); RSM (Regimental Sergeant Major); C/Sgt (Colour Sergeant); Sgt (Sergeant); Cpl (Corporal); Pte (Private); att (attached to).

5. Ranks and positions held are those ultimately attained by listed officers during the course of the Crimean War. Ranks subsequently attained are additionally shown only when an officer is described thus in the text – e.g. as a quoted source.

221

Austria, 157-8
Azov, Sea of, 134, 145

Bakshiseai, 69
Balaklava (& battle):
(generally) 12, 35-6, 68, 71, 72-3, 79, 81,
106, 116, 124, 133-7, 140, 144, 146-8,
152, 155
(specific to) Harbour, 136
Balgonie, Capt Viscount, Gren Gds, 45, 137
Baring, Capt F., Cold Gds, 49, 143
Bathhurst, Capt F., Gren Gds, 137, 139
Belbek, River, 35, 68
Bentinck, Lt Col Count A., 161
Bentinck, Sir Henry, GOC 1st Div
(previously Brig Gen, Guards Bde), 17,
19, 33, 41, 44, 48-9, 57, 59, 64, 79, 88,
95-6, 99, 108, 119, 161
Berkeley, Lt Col H.F., SFG, 45, 61-3
Birch Richardson, Col E.B., Gren Gds,
93-6
Black Sea:
(generally) 32, 145, 158, 168
(specific to) Bessarabia, 69
Odessa, 93
Blair, Lt Col J. Hunter, SFG, 63, 95, 113
Bouverie, Capt H.M., Cold Gds, 109
Boyce, Sgt, SFG, 62
Bradford, Lt Col R., Gren Gds, 45, 95, 98
British Army (generally), 4, 5, 7-14
British Army in the Crimea:
1st Division:
Brigade of Guards (generally) 11-12
(specific to) 3rd Gren Gds, 15-20,
22-3, 29-31, 33, 36-8, 41-2, 44-8,
51-5, 57-62, 64-5, 69-70, 79, 84,
86-9, 93-101, 108, 110-11, 118,
123-4, 128-31, 135, 138-9, 143,
146, 151-2, 157, 159, 161, 168
1st Cold Gds, 7, 11, 15-18, 23, 26-
31, 33, 36-7, 41-2, 44-5, 47-9,
55-62, 64-5, 68-74, 79, 84, 86-93,
95, 99, 104-10, 113, 120-1, 129,
131, 133, 136, 139, 143, 151-2,
157, 161-2, 167
1st SFG, 15-16, 18, 23, 33, 36-7,
41-6, 48, 53, 57-8, 60-5, 67, 79,
84, 86-90, 95, 108-9, 112-13,
116-17, 122-3, 129, 131, 134,
151-2, 157, 161-2, 165
Sharpshooters, 36, 80, 133
Highland Brigade (generally) 11, 31,

36, 41, 45, 47-9, 53, 57-8, 61, 65,
70, 151-2, 162
(specific to) 42nd Highlanders, 27,
57
79th Highlanders, 57
93rd Highlanders, 57
Regiments within other divisions:
7th RF, 44-5, 58, 61
20th Regt, 90, 92, 119, 124
23rd RWF, 58
30th Regt, 81, 122
33rd Regt, 58
41st Regt, 84
46th Regt, 91-2
47th Regt, 129
49th Regt, 81
50th Regt, 29
55th Regt, 42, 99
63rd Regt, 143
68th Regt, 92
95th Regt, 42, 45, 47, 119
Royal Artillery, 106
General references:
Army Medical Service, 168 (Royal
Army Medical Corps, 169)
Army Land Transport Corps, 133, 168
Army Works Corps, 154-5; Foot
Guards, 106
Household Brigade, 87
Rifle Brigade, 83
Royal Artillery, 9
Turkish & other foreign troops in
British pay, 158, 166-7
Brown, Lt Gen Sir George, GOC Light
Div, 11, 36, 42, 58-9, 61, 79, 91, 105,
108
Brownrigg, Lt Col S., Gren Gds, 45
Buckley, Capt, SFG, 45, 61-3
Bulganak, River, 35
Bulgaria:
(generally) 73-4, 157
(specific to) Aladyn, 16, 25-6, 29
Balchik Bay, 31, 35
Devna, Lake, 16, 25
Dschaseli, 16
Galata Serai, 16
Gevreclek, 16, 25, 29-30
Varna (& Bay), 16, 20-1, 23, 25-6, 29-32,
35-6, 74, 99
Buller, Brig Gen Sir George GOC 2nd Bde,
45, 62, 79
Bulwer, Capt, SFG, 45, 63